**Georgiana Farnoaga
Anita Reetz
Susan Rivers
Setsuko Toyama**

198 Madison Avenue
New York, NY 10016 USA

Great Clarendon Street, Oxford OX2 6DP UK

Oxford University Press is a department of the University of Oxford.
It furthers the University's objective of excellence in research, scholarship,
and education by publishing worldwide in

Oxford New York

Auckland Cape Town Dar es Salaam Hong Kong Karachi
Kuala Lumpur Madrid Melbourne Mexico City Nairobi
New Delhi Shanghai Taipei Toronto

With offices in

Argentina Austria Brazil Chile Czech Republic France Greece
Guatemala Hungary Italy Japan Poland Portugal Singapore
South Korea Switzerland Thailand Turkey Ukraine Vietnam

OXFORD and OXFORD ENGLISH are registered trademarks of
Oxford University Press

Copyright © 2003 Oxford University Press

All rights reserved. No part of this publication may be reproduced, stored in a retrieval system, or transmitted, in any form or by any means, electronic, mechanical, photocopying, recording, or otherwise, without the prior written permission of Oxford University Press, with the sole exception of photocopying carried out under the conditions described below.

This book is sold subject to the condition that it shall not, by way of trade or otherwise, be lent, resold, hired out, or otherwise circulated without the publisher's prior consent in any form of binding or cover other than that in which it is published and without a similar condition including this condition being imposed on the subsequent purchaser.

Photocopying
The Publisher grants permission for the photocopying of those pages marked "Permission granted to reproduce for instructional use" according to the following conditions. Individual purchasers may make copies for their own use or for use by classes they teach. School purchasers may make copies for use by their staff and students, but this permission does not extend to additional schools or branches.

In no circumstances may any part of this book be photocopied for resale.

Editorial Manager: Nancy Leonhardt
Senior Editor: Paul Phillips
Associate Editors: Nishka Chandrasoma, Sarah Wales McGrath
Assistant Editor: Jessica Gillman
Art Director: Lynn Luchetti
Design Project Manager: Maj-Britt Hagsted
Designer: Ruby Harn
Layout Artist: Julie Macus
Art Editor: Justine Eun
Production Manager: Shanta Persaud
Production Coordinator: Eve Wong

Illustrations: Mena Dolobowsky, Ruth Flanigan, Patrick Girouard,
Lane Gregory, Richard Kolding

Cover Design: Silver Editions
Cover Art: Jim Talbot

ISBN-13: 978 019 436429 4
ISBN-10: 019 436429 1

Printing (last digit): 10 9 8 7 6 5 4 3

Printed in Hong Kong.

Table of Contents

Syllabus 4
Introduction 6
Sample Pages and Lesson Plans 8
    Conversation Time 8
    Word Time 10
    Focus Time 12
    Practice Time 14
    Reading Time 16
    Your Time 18
Unit Lesson Plans 20
    Do You Remember? 20
    Classroom Language 21
    Unit 1 22
    Unit 2 34
    Unit 3 46
    Unit 4 58
    Unit 5 70
    Review 1 82
    Unit 6 88
    Unit 7 100
    Unit 8 112
    Unit 9 124
    Unit 10 136
    Review 2 148
Games and Activities 154
Workbook Instructions and Answer Key 157
Storybook Instructions and Answer Key 180
Worksheet Instructions and Answer Key 183
    Worksheets 188
Test Instructions and Answer Key 208
    Tests 216
Card List 236
Word List 238

Syllabus

Unit	Topic	Conversation Time	Word Time	Focus Time	Practice Time	Reading Time
1	Buildings Prepositions	Asking about a museum's hours, entrance fees, and exhibits over the telephone	school library barbershop bank hotel train station post office sidewalk bridge theater	beside behind across from in front of near above	Was there a library beside the post office? Yes, there was. No, there wasn't.	Ice Cream in America (historical reading)
2	Food Quantities	Ordering food in a restaurant	root beer lemonade roast beef ham chicken soup fruit salad iced tea coffee garlic bread apple pie	a bottle of root beer a can of lemonade a slice of ham a piece of apple pie a bowl of chicken soup a glass of iced tea a cup of coffee a loaf of garlic bread	How much root beer did she have? She had one bottle of root beer. How many bottles of root beer did she have? She had three bottles of root beer. (all pronouns)	Papa Joe's Restaurant Opens (newspaper article)
3	Daily activities alone or with others	Shopping for a pie at a bakery	walk to school go to the dentist do laundry chop vegetables iron a shirt slice fruit take a bus wash my hair stay home buy groceries	by myself by himself by herself by yourself by yourselves by themselves by ourselves	I ironed a shirt by myself. I didn't iron a shirt by myself. (all pronouns)	Bill Forgot! (story)
4	Activities at a movie studio Frequency	Making a telephone call and leaving a message	wear a wig drive a sports car put on makeup fall in love get a sunburn listen to pop music take a nap talk on the phone sign autographs have an accident	always usually often sometimes hardly ever never	Do you ever fall in love? Yes, I always/usually/often/sometimes fall in love. Does he ever fall in love? No, he hardly ever/never falls in love. (all pronouns)	Hi, Emily! (postcard)
5	Activities in town Frequency	Talking about the weather and inquiring after family	feed the birds read a newspaper take medicine go on a date visit a museum take the subway give a speech take a math test bake bread get a haircut	once a day twice a week three times a month four times a year	How often do you read a newspaper? I read a newspaper once a month. How often does she read a newspaper? She reads a newspaper once a month. (all pronouns)	Dear Gabby (advice column)

Review of Units 1–5

Unit	Topic	Conversation Time	Word Time	Focus Time	Practice Time	Reading Time
6	Musical instruments Adverbs	Helping a friend clean up	tuba flute cymbals drums xylophone electric keyboard harp cello recorder trumpet	well badly quietly loudly quickly slowly happily sadly	How did he play the tuba? He played the tuba well. How did they play the tuba? They played the tuba well. (all pronouns)	Sunnyville Students Give Spring Performance (newspaper article)
7	Animals Movement	Making an emergency telephone call	tiger eagle panda bear kangaroo parrot moose camel baboon leopard	run → ran walk → walked fly → flew hop → hopped	What were you doing when the baboon walked by? We were washing the car when the baboon walked by. What was he doing when the baboon walked by? He was washing the car when the baboon walked by. (all pronouns)	Welcome to Sunnyville Zoo's Giant Panda Home (informational sign)
8	Young children's activities Remembering abilities	Encouraging someone to try again	say the alphabet throw a ball blow a bubble count to ten build a sand castle spell a word catch a frog cut out a heart peel an orange speak English	Annie **is** tall. Annie **was** short. Ted **can** play basketball. Ted **could** play basketball.	When I was little, I could peel an orange. When you were little, you couldn't peel an orange. (all pronouns)	Dear Stan (personal letter)
9	Cities around the world Months	Interviewing an airline pilot	Rome Taipei Tokyo London Seoul New York City Paris Honolulu San Francisco Hong Kong	January February March April May June July August September October November December	When did he go to Hong Kong? He went in April. How long was he there? He was there for one week. When did they go to Hong Kong? They went in April. How long were they there? They were there for one week. (all pronouns)	Welcome to New York City, the Big Apple! (tourist brochure)
10	Actions at school Consequences	Discussing yesterday's TV programs	skip lunch forget my homework go to bed late fall off my chair get a good grade lose my favorite pencil make a mistake take off my jacket win a prize turn off the fan	hungry nervous tired embarrassed happy sad disappointed cold hot proud	If I skip lunch, I'll be hungry. If she skips lunch, she'll be hungry. (all pronouns)	The History of TV (timeline)

Review of Units 6–10

Syllabus

Introduction

Course Description

English Time is a six-level communicative course intended for elementary school students studying English for the first time. It was designed specifically for children studying in an English as a Foreign Language (EFL) context who do not generally hear English spoken outside the classroom. The syllabus progresses at a steady pace, offering students opportunities to practice each new language item in a variety of contexts. The aim of the series is to develop students' speaking, listening, reading, and writing skills through activities that reward their curiosity and appeal to their sense of fun. Three recurring characters, Ted, Annie, and Digger the dog, maintain student interest and involvement throughout the course.

The *English Time* series is preceded by a two-level introductory series, *Magic Time*. These two courses can be used separately or as one complete eight-level course. The *Magic Time* syllabus provides a solid foundation of communicative language on which the syllabus of *English Time* is built.

The components of each level of *English Time* are: Student Book, Audio Cassette and CD, Wall Charts, Workbook, Storybook, Storybook Cassette, Teacher's Book, and Picture and Word Card Book.

Components

The Student Books
The Student Books feature beautiful full-color illustrations, and a clear, simple design. The illustrations draw students into the pages to explore and experience the language, enhancing student interest and motivation. *English Time* Levels 5 and 6 contain ten 6-page units and two 6-page reviews. Each unit is built around a theme, such as *Food* or *Musical Instruments,* to provide a real-life context to the language. Each page of a unit practices a single language function in order to keep the focus of the page clear. The short units help students progress rapidly, thus building their confidence and motivation. After every five units, the 6-page review recycles previously learned language in a new, meaningful context.

At the back of the Student Books there are Checklists (one for every five units). These give students an opportunity to check what they know, thus building their confidence and allowing parents to follow their child's progress in English.

The Audio Cassettes and CDs
The Cassettes/CDs contain all Student Book conversations, vocabulary words, grammar patterns, songs, chants, and phonics sounds and words. Additional exercises on each cassette/CD provide further listening practice.

The Wall Charts
The Wall Charts feature large versions of each Conversation Time and Word Time page.

The Workbooks
The Workbooks are an extension of the Student Books, providing additional reading and writing practice for each lesson. The Workbooks help teachers assess students' reading comprehension and general language retention.

The Teacher's Books
The Teacher's Books provide step-by-step lesson plans for introducing, practicing, and reviewing the language presented in the Student Books. The lesson plans also provide tasks for individual, pair, and group work. The Teacher's Books also contain the tapescript and answer keys.

Included in each Teacher's Book are Workbook and Storybook instructions and answer keys; photocopiable Worksheets; individual unit, midterm, and final Tests; and a Games and Activities section. The reproducible Worksheets allow for additional practice of language presented in the Student Books. The Tests allow teachers and parents to assess students' proficiency in the language as well as their progress. The Games and Activities section provides a multitude of fun game ideas to enhance any lesson. Also provided are instructions on how to introduce and check both the Workbook and the Storybook activities.

The Storybooks and Cassettes
The Storybooks present the Student Book language and main characters in compelling, continuing stories. This allows students to experience language in contexts similar to the way it is used in everyday life. Students can easily understand the story as no new grammar points are introduced, and new vocabulary items are defined on the pages.

The Levels 5 and 6 Storybooks are divided into six chapters, with each chapter corresponding to specific Student Book units. A Storybook chapter can thus be read after students have completed the corresponding Student Book units. Alternatively, the entire Storybook can be read after completing the whole Student Book. Reviews and a new word list are also provided. Each Storybook is accompanied by a cassette.

The Picture and Word Card Books
The Picture and Word Card Books provide one picture card and one word card for each vocabulary word in the Student Books. There is also one grammar card for each word in the target patterns presented in the Student Books. The picture and word cards are useful for introducing, practicing, and reviewing language. They can be enlarged to any size, depending on the teacher's

needs. They can be copied onto cardboard or regular paper. Students can personalize the cards by cutting them out and coloring them as they wish.

Course Philosophy

English Time is based on the premise that children learn best when their natural curiosity and sense of fun are engaged, and when new language is introduced in small, manageable amounts. *English Time* introduces all language in a spiraling syllabus that builds on and reinforces previously learned language. Thus, at each new level students maintain and add to the language they know.

The unit topics and situations are both familiar and of universal appeal to children. Students immediately relate to these situations, which results in greater language production and retention.

English Time emphasizes student-centered learning, as it creates opportunities for students to produce language in a manner resembling "real-life" communication. For this purpose, practice and review activities in *English Time* systematically involve pair and group work.

The theory of multiple intelligences suggests that in any language class there are students with different learning styles. By engaging students orally, visually, logically, kinesthetically, and musically, *English Time* activities maximize students' participation during each lesson.

The *English Time* lesson plans do not follow one particular teaching methodology. Instead, a variety of different, successful methodologies are employed to provide exciting, stimulating lessons. Information gap activities, role play, survey, and interviews are employed to create a real need for communication and appeal to as many students as possible. Students hear the target language before they produce it (receptive exposure before production). Listening is emphasized so that students are exposed to correct pronunciation and intonation.

Lesson Planning

Thorough planning and preparation are crucial to the success of any lesson. A well-prepared lesson includes more activites than may seem necessary. This allows teachers to maintain the steady pace of the lesson, abandon activities that are not working, and keep students focused on their learning. A comprehensive lesson plan includes activities to review previously learned language as well as introduce and practice new language in a systematic and enjoyable manner. *English Time* Teacher's Books provide a detailed, step-by-step lesson plan for each Student Book page. Teachers are encouraged to be flexible and adapt these lesson plans to meet their individual needs.

English Time Lesson Plans
1. Warm-Up and Review
Each lesson plan begins with an activity that reviews the language practiced in the previous lesson. This helps students to both recall the language and "switch" to English-speaking mode. In some lessons, a second review activity focuses on language related to the target vocabulary or grammar patterns.

2. Introduce the Target Language
New language is introduced before students open their Student Books so that they focus on the meaningful demonstration of the language. Step-by-step suggestions show how to introduce the target language using Picture and/or Word Cards, real objects (realia), drawings, charts, and/or gestures.

3. Practice the Target Language
Students open their Student Books at this stage. Each Student Book page provides exercises to practice the language. The Teacher's Book provides detailed instructions on how to fully exploit each Student Book page. The tapescript, answer keys, and ideas on how to check exercises are provided where appropriate.

4. Games and Activities
All lessons include games and activities that offer students further practice with the target language. Activities frequently combine previously learned language with the target language, so that students are continually building on what they have learned. Teachers can choose the games and activities that are appropriate to their needs. Optional photocopiable Worksheets at the back of the Teacher's Books provide extra grammar and reading practice.

5. Finish the Lesson
Each lesson plan concludes with a fun activity that reviews the new language, gives the lesson a feeling of closure, and ends the class on a positive note.

Conversation Time Sample Page and Lesson Plan

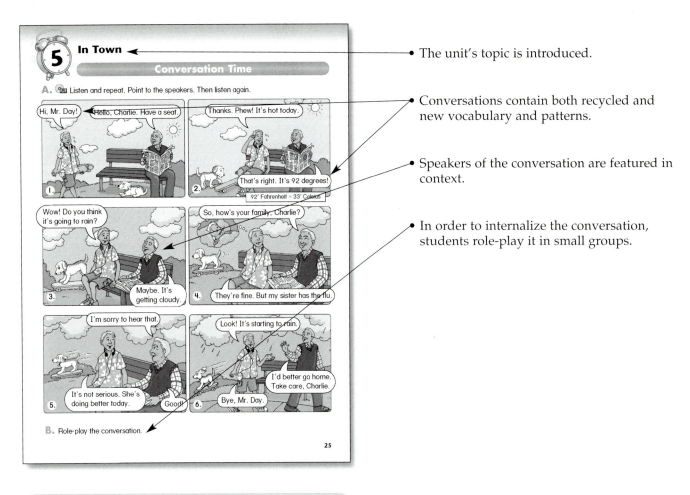

- The unit's topic is introduced.
- Conversations contain both recycled and new vocabulary and patterns.
- Speakers of the conversation are featured in context.
- In order to internalize the conversation, students role-play it in small groups.

Warm-Up and Review

1. Do an activity to review vocabulary, patterns, and topics from the previous unit. An activity is provided in each lesson plan.
2. Check the Your Time Workbook page that students did in class or for homework. Answer keys and detailed instructions on how to check the activities are provided at the back of the Teacher's Book.

Introduce the Conversation

1. Set the scene and clarify the meaning of new words or phrases in the conversation through explanations, drawings, or actions. Students retain language better if they understand the meaning. Detailed examples are provided as necessary.
2. Model the conversation in such a way that students can see it presented in a natural way. To do this, bring students (one student for each speaker in the conversation) to the front of the classroom and have them face each other. Stand behind each student and model his/her line(s) of the conversation, using natural facial expressions and body language. In this way, students know who says which line of the conversation. Each lesson plan contains examples of appropriate body language and facial expressions for each line of the conversation.
3. Divide the class into groups (one group for each speaker in the conversation). Model each line of the conversation again. Group A repeats the first line of the conversation, Group B repeats line two, and so on. Groups then change roles and repeat the conversation until each group has practiced each role.
4. Students open their Student Books for the first time at this point. Ask students questions about the conversation and speakers in order to elicit language and familiarize students further with the scenes. Encourage students to answer using complete sentences whenever possible. Prompt if necessary. Suggested questions are provided in each lesson plan.

Practice the Conversation

A. Listen and repeat. Point to the speakers. Then listen again.

1. Play the first version of the recording. This version is spoken at slightly slower than natural speed and has no sound effects so that students can focus on the pronunciation of the words and the new language. Students listen to the conversation and repeat, pointing to each speaker.

2. Play the second version of the conversation. This version is dramatized, spoken at natural speed, and has sound effects so that students can hear the language as spoken in real life. This time students just listen.

B. Role-play the conversation.

Using their Student Books for reference, students produce the conversation by role-playing it, using body language and facial expressions from Introduce the Conversation. Students continue role-playing the conversation until each student has taken on each role.

Games and Activities

In order to internalize the new conversation, students practice it through various games and activities. Students are not expected to memorize the entire conversation. Rather, they should be able to understand its meaning and produce parts of it in meaningful exchanges. Three games and activities are provided in each lesson plan, engaging students in pair or group exchanges, as well as in individual versus class interaction. One of these activities is always a "Make It Your Own" substitution activity, in which students expand the structures and concepts from the conversation to explore how they can be used in other situations.

Finish the Lesson

1. Finish the lesson with a quick game or activity to further practice the conversation. An activity is provided in each lesson plan.

2. Explain and assign the Conversation Time Workbook page to be done in class or for homework. It is important that students know what to do for each activity so that they can concentrate on the target language. Detailed instructions on how to do the activities are provided at the back of the Teacher's Book.

Word Time Sample Page and Lesson Plan

- Ten new vocabulary words are introduced per unit.

- Students review the target vocabulary, as well as previously learned conversations and patterns, by listening to the recording, then finding and pointing to the speakers.

- All new vocabulary items are featured in context for students to find in the large scene.

Warm-Up and Review

1. Do an activity to review the conversation learned in the previous lesson. An activity is provided in each lesson plan.

2. Check the Conversation Time Workbook page that students did in class or for homework. Answer keys and detailed instructions on how to check the activities are provided at the back of the Teacher's Book.

Introduce the Words

1. Hold up and name each of the unit's Word Time Picture Cards. Students listen. Hold up and name the cards again, and have students repeat. Hold up the cards in random order and have students name them.

2. Attach the unit's Word Time Picture Cards in a row to the board. Stand the unit's Word Time Word Cards on the chalktray under the corresponding picture cards. Point to each picture/word card pair and read the word. Students repeat. Then reposition the word cards so they are no longer directly below the corresponding picture cards. Volunteers come to the board one by one and place a word card under its corresponding picture card, then point to and read the word. Seated students repeat.

Talk About the Picture

1. Students open their Student Books for the first time at this point. They look at the large scene and use complete sentences to identify and discuss anything they can.

2. Talk about what is happening in the large scene in order to recycle language and bring the picture to life. It is *not* important that students understand each word, as this is a receptive exercise focusing on exposure to English and recycling previous language items in a new context. A short reading is suggested in each lesson plan. When reading a word in **bold** type, point to its picture in the scene. When reading an *italicized* word, pantomime it. This conveys the

meanings of words students have not heard before. Alternatively, use a Wall Chart instead of a Student Book to describe the people and actions in the picture.

3. Ask questions about the large scene in order to elicit language and familiarize students further with the picture. Encourage students to answer using words, phrases, or simple sentences. Prompt if necessary. Suggested questions are provided in each lesson plan.

Practice the Words

A. Listen and repeat.

1. Focus students' attention on the vocabulary box at the top of the page. Play the recording. Students listen to the vocabulary items and repeat.

2. Say the words in random order. Students listen and point to the words in the vocabulary box.

B. Point and say the words.

Individually, students point to and name each of the target vocabulary items in the large scene in any order they wish.

OPTIONS:
1. Point to each vocabulary item on the Wall Chart, and have students point to and name the same item in their books.

2. Divide the class into pairs. Either on the Wall Chart or in their Student Books, students in each pair take turns pointing to and naming each of the target vocabulary items.

C. Listen and point.

Focus students' attention on the large scene. Play the recording. Students listen to the sound effects and words. As they hear a vocabulary item named, they find and point to the corresponding item in the large scene. As they hear a conversation, they find and point to the speakers. Play the recording as many times as necessary for students to complete the task.

Games and Activities

In order to internalize the new vocabulary, students practice it through various games and activities. Three games and activities are provided in each lesson plan. The games/activities often combine the new vocabulary with previously learned language.

Option: Personalize the Vocabulary. Students work in groups to use the vocabulary in personalized situations, thus getting involved more fully in the topic and language. An activity is provided in each lesson plan.

Finish the Lesson

1. Finish the lesson with a quick game or activity to further practice the vocabulary. An activity is provided in each lesson plan.

2. Explain and assign the Word Time Workbook page to be done in class or for homework. It is important that students know what to do for each activity so that they can concentrate on the target language. Detailed instructions on how to do the activities are provided at the back of the Teacher's Book.

Focus Time Sample Page and Lesson Plan

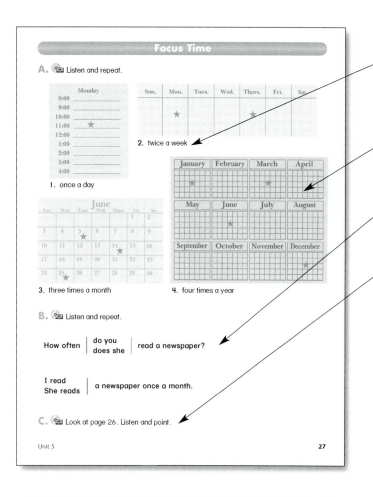

- Four to twelve new words or phrases are introduced per unit. Students will use them in a new grammar pattern.

- Simple art helps to illustrate each new word or phrase.

- New grammar patterns are presented as complete sentences.

- Students practice the target pattern by looking back to the Word Time page, listening to the recording, and finding and pointing to the people and/or actions being talked about.

Warm-Up and Review

1. Do an activity to review the vocabulary learned in the previous lesson. An activity is provided in each lesson plan.
2. Check the Word Time Workbook page that students did in class or for homework. Answer keys and detailed instructions on how to check the activities are provided at the back of the Teacher's Book.

The introduction of the Focus Time Lesson is divided into two parts. In Part 1, students learn new vocabulary that they will use in the new grammar pattern taught in Part 2.

Part 1: Introduce the Words

Introduce each new word or phrase in such a way that students both hear it and understand its meaning. Detailed instructions are provided in each lesson plan.

Practice the Words

Students open their Student Books for the first time at this point.

A. Listen and repeat.

Focus students' attention on the new vocabulary at the top of the page. Play the recording. Students listen and repeat.

Part 2: Introduce the Patterns

Introduce the target patterns in a methodical step-by-step way. Once students are familiar with the patterns, provide an activity that allows students to use the patterns immediately. Detailed instructions are provided in each lesson plan. Explaining grammar rules is not recommended at this level, as students are best able to learn and understand the patterns through meaningful experiences with the language.

Practice the Patterns

B. Listen and repeat.

1. Write the text from the pattern box(es) on the board so all students can see it clearly. Play the recording, pointing to each word. Students listen.

2. Play the recording again. Students look at the pattern box(es) in their books and repeat, pointing to each word.

3. Students work with partners to say the new patterns, while looking at the pattern box(es) in their books. Prompt if necessary, or play the recording again until students can do this with ease.

C. Look at page X. Listen and point.

Focus students' attention on the Word Time scene. Play the recording. Students look at the pictures and listen to the words, pointing to each item, action, or person they hear named. Play the recording as many times as necessary for students to complete the task.

Games and Activities

In order to internalize the new vocabulary and patterns, students practice the language through various games and activities. Three games and activities are provided in each lesson plan. The first activity often focuses on the new vocabulary, and the second and third activities provide students practice of the entire new pattern.

Finish the Lesson

1. Finish the lesson with a quick game or activity to further practice the vocabulary and patterns. An activity is provided in each lesson plan.

2. Explain and assign the Focus Time Workbook page to be done in class or for homework. It is important that students know what to do for each activity so that they can concentrate on the target language. Detailed instructions on how to do the activities are provided at the back of the Teacher's Book.

Sample Pages and Lesson Plans

Practice Time Sample Page and Lesson Plan

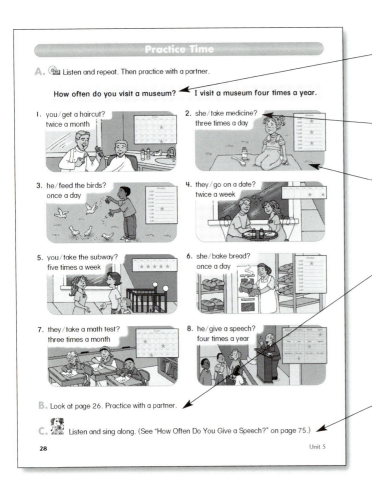

- Students are reminded of the new grammar patterns they learned in the previous Focus Time lesson.

- Eight substitution exercises serve as controlled practice for the target patterns.

- Simple situational art for each substitution exercise helps to provide meaning.

- Students look back to the Word Time page. Then, using the unit's vocabulary and grammar, they make sentences about various scenes on the page. This allows students to use the grammar patterns in a less controlled and more meaningful, natural context.

- A grammar song or chant in each unit provides a fun review of the target grammar patterns.

Warm-Up and Review

1. Do an activity to review the patterns learned in the previous lesson. An activity is provided in each lesson plan.

2. Check the Focus Time Workbook page that students did in class or for homework. Answer keys and detailed instructions on how to check the activities are provided at the back of the Teacher's Book.

Practice the Patterns

Students open their Student Books for the first time at this point.

A. Listen and repeat. Then practice with a partner.

1. Play the recording. Students listen and repeat, pointing to each picture in their books.

2. Students form pairs and take turns saying all the patterns they have just practiced. They then change roles and do the same again.

B. Look at page X. Practice with a partner.

For statement patterns: Students remain in pairs. Focus their attention on the Word Time scene. They take turns pointing to the pictures and making sentences using the target patterns. An example is provided in each lesson plan.

For question and answer patterns: Students remain in pairs. Focus their attention on the Word Time scene. They take turns pointing to the pictures and asking and answering questions, using the target patterns and vocabulary items. An example is provided in each lesson plan.

C. Listen and sing along or chant.

1. The lyrics for each song and chant are provided at the back of the Student Book. Students turn to that unit's song or chant. Have them cover up the text and focus their attention on the pictures. Students talk about what they see. Read the lyrics line by line. Students repeat each line. Play the recording. Students listen and follow along in their books.

Alternatively, write the lyrics on the board. Attach picture cards above the corresponding words to assist reading. Play the recording and point to each word. Students listen. Next, read the lyrics, pointing to each line, and have students repeat. Students listen and follow along in their books.

2. Play the recording again. Students listen and sing along or chant, using their books for reference. Play the recording as many times as necessary for students to become sufficiently familiar with the song or chant.

3. Do an activity with the song or chant that allows students to become more involved. An activity is provided in each lesson plan.

Games and Activities

In order to internalize the target patterns, students practice the language through various games and activities. Three games and activities are provided in each lesson plan.

> **Extra Practice**
> Explain and assign the Practice Time Worksheet. There is one Worksheet per Practice Time page to give students further practice with the target patterns. Worksheets can be done at home or in class. They can also be used to challenge more advanced students while the teacher spends time with students who need more help. For Worksheets and detailed instructions, see Teacher's Book pages 183–207.

Finish the Lesson

1. Finish the lesson with a quick game or activity to further practice the patterns. An activity is provided in each lesson plan.

2. Explain and assign the Practice Time Workbook page to be done in class or for homework. It is important that students know what to do for each activity so that they can concentrate on the target language. Detailed instructions on how to do the activities are provided at the back of the Teacher's Book.

Sample Pages and Lesson Plans

Reading Time Sample Page and Lesson Plan

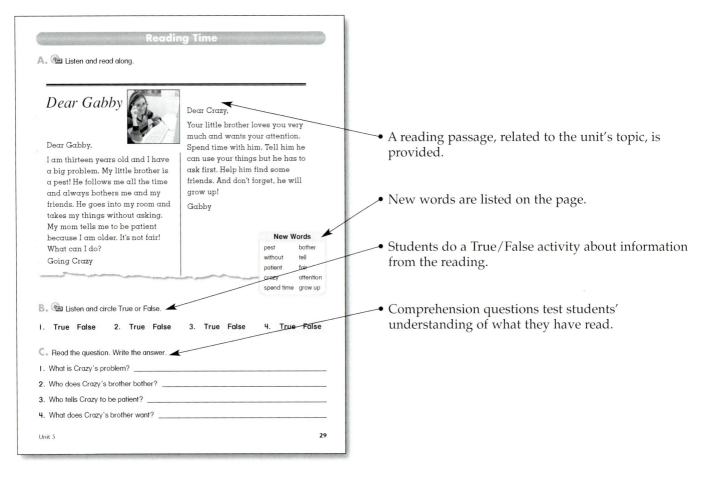

Warm-Up and Review

1. Do an activity to review the patterns practiced in the previous lesson. An activity is provided in each lesson plan.

2. Check the Practice Time Workbook page that students did in class or for homework. Answer keys and detailed instructions on how to check the activities are provided at the back of the Teacher's Book.

Introduce the Reading

1. Students may learn the new vocabulary within the context of the reading, or each new word can be taught before students encounter it in the reading. If you choose to teach the new words before students read the passage, write the new words in a column on the board. Then point to and read each word before explaining its meaning. Detailed explanations of how to present each new word are provided in the lesson plans.

2. If appropriate, ask students questions abut their own experiences with the reading's topic.

3. Students open their Student Books for the first time at this point. They look at the reading and pictures and talk about what they see. Ask students what they think the reading will be about.

Practice the Reading

Students read the passage silently to themselves.

A. Listen and read along.

1. Play the recording. Students listen and read along in their Student Books.

2. Play the recording again, stopping it after each sentence. Students listen and repeat each sentence.

3. Divide the class into pairs. Students in each pair take turns reading the passage aloud to their partner.

B. Listen and circle True or False.

Play the recording. For each number, students listen and circle *True* if the statement is true, and *False* if it is not. An answer key and suggestions on how to check students' answers are provided in each lesson plan.

C. Read the question. Write the answer.
Students read each comprehension question and answer it based on the reading in exercise A. An answer key and suggestions on how to check students' answers are provided in each lesson plan. The wording of students' answers may vary slightly from that given in the answer key. Accept any answers that are grammatically correct and contain the correct information.

Games and Activities

In order to practice reading, students engage in various games and activities. Three games and activities are provided in each lesson plan. Since these games and activities are related to the reading, students may use their Student Books for reference as they work.

Extra Practice
Explain and assign the Reading Time Worksheet. There is one Worksheet per Reading Time page to give students further reading practice. Worksheets can be done at home or in class. They can also be used to challenge more advanced students while the teacher spends time with students who need more help. For Worksheets and detailed instructions, see Teacher's Book pages 183–207.

Finish the Lesson

1. Finish the lesson with a quick game or activity to further practice the reading. An activity is provided in each lesson plan.

2. Explain and assign the Reading Time Workbook page to be done in class or for homework. It is important that students know what to do for each activity so that they can concentrate on the target language. Detailed instructions on how to do the activities are provided at the back of the Teacher's Book.

Your Time Sample Page and Lesson Plan

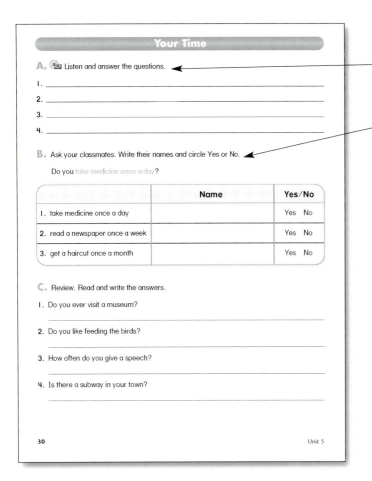

- Students answer questions about themselves that they hear on the recording.

- In order to further personalize the unit's topic and language, students interact with their classmates to find out related personal information.

Warm-Up and Review

1. Do an activity to review the reading practiced in the previous lesson. An activity is provided in each lesson plan.

2. Check the Reading Time Workbook page that students did in class or for homework. Answer keys and detailed instructions on how to check the activities are provided at the back of the Teacher's Book.

Introduce the Lesson

Ask students personalized questions that relate to the unit's language and topic. Suggested questions are provided in each lesson plan.

Practice the Lesson

Students open their Student Books for the first time at this point.

A. Listen and answer the questions.

Play the recording. For each number, students listen to the question and answer it based on their own knowledge and experience. Suggestions on how to check students' answers are provided in each lesson plan.

B. (Personalized interactive activity).

Through a variety of different types of activities—often pairwork—students interact with their classmates to find out personal information relating to the unit's topic and language.

C. (Personalized reading and writing activity).

Through a variety of different types of reading and writing activities, students further personalize the language they previously learned. Suggestions on how to check students' answers are provided in each lesson plan.

Games and Activities

In order to internalize and further personalize the unit's language and topic, students practice the language through various games and activities. Three games and activities are provided in each lesson plan.

Finish the Lesson

1. Finish the lesson with a quick game or activity to further personalize the language. An activity is provided in each lesson plan.

2. Explain and assign the Your Time Workbook page to be done in class or for homework. It is important that students know what to do for each activity so that they can concentrate on the target language. Detailed instructions on how to do the activities are provided at the back of the Teacher's Book.

> **Assessment**
> Give the unit Test in order to check students' comprehension of the new language items. There is one Test per unit. An extensive midterm and final are also provided. For Tests and detailed instructions, see Teacher's Book pages 208–235.

Sample Pages and Lesson Plans

Do You Remember?

Focus: *English Time* Level 4 Review
Function: Introducing oneself; giving personal information
Materials Needed: CD/cassette and player

Work with the Pictures

Students open their Student Books to pages vi and vii.

1. Divide students into groups of three. Groups find and name any items or characters they recognize in the eight scenes.

2. Ask each group how many items they found. Encourage groups to name as many items or characters as they can.

3. When groups have finished, have each group name one item, and write it on the board. Once all the items have been listed, point to and say each word. Students repeat, pointing to those items in their books.

Practice the Language

Listen and repeat.

1. Play the recording. Students listen and repeat each line of dialogue.

1. Annie: *Hi! I'm Annie Day. He's Ted Lee. My dog's name is Digger.*
   Ted: *We're making dinner. We're going to have spaghetti.*
   Digger: *Yum! My favorite!*

2. Annie: *I'm fourteen.*
   Ted: *I'm fourteen, too.*
   Digger: *Smells good.*

3. Annie: *We like playing video games.*
   Ted: *I want to program computers. Annie wants to be an engineer.*

4. Annie: *Monkeys and giraffes are my favorite animals.*
   Ted: *I like dolphins.*
   Digger: *I like dogs.*

5. Annie: *Ted swims really well.*
   Ted: *I love to swim. I'm going to go to the beach in the summer.*

6. Annie: *I like to ski. I went skiing in the winter.*
   Ted: *Annie skis really well.*

7. Annie: *Our friends are here! Is it time to eat?*
   Ted: *Well, we cooked the spaghetti, made the salad, and set the table. Yes, let's eat!*

8. Ted: *Try some.*
   Ivy: *It's delicious!*
   Annie: *Study English with us and have fun!*

2. Ask students what roles are needed to role-play the conversation. List the roles on the board (*Annie, Ted, Digger, Ivy*). Then divide the class into Groups A, B, C, and D. Group A role-plays Annie's lines, Group B role-plays Ted's lines, Group C role-plays Digger's lines, and Group D role-plays Ivy's line. Groups then change roles and role-play the scenes again.

3. Bring four volunteers to the front of the classroom. Play the recording and have these volunteers act out the conversation along with the recording. They then role-play the conversation on their own, without the recording.

4. Divide the class into groups of four and have students in each group role-play the conversation. They then change roles and role-play the conversation again.

Finish the Lesson

1. **How About You?** Divide the class into groups of three. Students in each group take turns looking at Scenes 1–6 and inserting their personal information into the sentences (two students in each group talk to the third student). For example: a student named Joe looks at the first scene and says *Hi! I'm Joe Smith. He's Ed Jones.* The second student, Ed, says *We're studying English.* Students in each group change roles until each student has taken on each role.

2. Explain and assign Workbook pages iii and iv. (For instructions, see Teacher's Book page 157.)

Classroom Language

Focus: Frequently used classroom language
Materials Needed: CD/cassette and player

Warm-Up and Review

1. **Listen and Repeat.** Play the *Do You Remember?* recording. Students listen. Play the recording again, and have students repeat each line.
2. Check Workbook pages iii and iv. (For instructions and answer key, see Teacher's Book page 157.)

Introduce the Language

Tell students that in this lesson they are going to hear language that they can use in different classroom situations. Brainstorm with students different things they might want to say to each other or to their teacher during English class. See if students can then produce language to use in the different situations they have brainstormed. Accept any reasonable answers, and write them on the board.

Practice the Language

Students open their Student Books to page viii.

Listen and repeat.

1. Students look at the six scenes to see if any of the situations they brainstormed are illustrated on the page.
2. Play the recording. Students listen and repeat.

   A: *Please number your papers from one to five. We're going to have a spelling test.*

   A: *Joe, will you turn on the CD player, please? Go to track ten.*
   B: *Okay.*

   A: *What's the homework assignment for tomorrow?*
   B: *Do page three in your workbook.*

   A: *We're going on a field trip on Friday. Please ask your parents to sign your permission form.*
   B: *Where are we going?*
   C: *The History Museum.*

   A: *Annie, please stay after class and finish your homework.*
   B: *Okay, Ms. Apple.*

   A: *Have a good weekend, class! Don't forget, your projects are due on Monday.*
   B: *Bye, Ms. Apple!*

3. Play the recording again. Students listen and point to the speakers. Play the recording as many times as necessary for students to complete the task.

Teacher Tip: Use this classroom language as often as possible so that it becomes natural to students. The recording can be played at the beginning of each lesson until students are completely familiar with the classroom language.

Games and Activities

Role Play. Divide the class into pairs. Students in each pair work with their partners to role-play each classroom language situation. After five to seven minutes, have several pairs of volunteers come to the front of the classroom and role-play the dialogues. Students can use their Student Books for reference, if necessary.

Finish the Lesson

What's Next? Say the first line of one of the classroom language dialogues. Students respond with the second line. Do the same with all the dialogues. Students can use their Student Books for reference, if necessary.

Classroom Language

1 In Old Sunnyville

Conversation Time

Language Focus: Asking about a museum's hours, entrance fees, and exhibits over the telephone

Materials Needed: CD/cassette and player; Wall Chart 1

For general information on Conversation Time, see pages 8–9.

Warm-Up and Review

Review. Students open their Student Books to page viii. Point to each scene and elicit the dialogue. Then divide the class into pairs, and have each pair practice role-playing the six different scenes.

Introduce the Conversation

1. Set the scene and clarify meaning by pretending to push the buttons of a telephone and hold a telephone receiver to your ear. Say *Today's conversation is a telephone call between Ted, who is calling a museum, and a woman who works at the museum.* Then introduce the new words by writing each word on the board. Point to and read each word before explaining its meaning. Students repeat the word.

   daily: Say *The museum is open on Sunday, Monday, Tuesday, Wednesday, Thursday, Friday, and Saturday. It's open daily.*

   except: Have four students stand up. Three of them should be wearing the same color shirt. Then say *They're all wearing (blue) shirts, except for (Ann).*

   holidays: Write the dates of some popular holidays on the board. Point to each date and name the holiday. Say *These dates are holidays.*

   free: Write *free = $0* on the board. Then say *Free means that you don't have to pay.*

2. Bring two students to the front of the classroom. Both students should pretend to be speaking into telephones. Stand behind each student and model his/her lines of the conversation in the following way:

   A: *Good morning, Sunnyville Museum. How can I help you?*
   Speak cheerfully.

   B: *Hi! What are your hours?*
   Speak in a friendly, questioning tone.

   A: *We're open from 9:00 to 6:00.*
   Speak in a friendly tone.

   B: *Are you open on Sundays?*
   Speak in a friendly, questioning tone.

   A: *Yes. We're open daily, except on holidays.*
   Speak in a friendly tone.

   B: *How much does it cost to get in?*
   Speak in a friendly, questioning tone.

   A: *It's three dollars for adults and two dollars for children. Children under five are free.*
   Speak in a friendly tone.

   B: *Does that include the special photo exhibit of old Sunnyville?*
   Speak in a friendly, questioning tone.

   A: *Yes, it does. Tours are at 10:00, 2:00, and 5:00.*
   Speak in a friendly tone.

   B: *Thanks for your help.*
   Speak in a friendly tone.

   A: *You're welcome. Have a nice day.*
   Speak in a friendly tone.

3. Divide the class into Groups A and B. Model the conversation again using facial expressions and body language. Group A repeats the first line of the conversation, Group B repeats line two, and so on. Encourage students to copy your facial expressions and body language. Groups change roles and say the conversation again in the same way.

4. Attach Wall Chart 1 to the board or open a Student Book to page 1. Students then open their Student Books to page 1. Ask the following questions:

> Where is the woman?
> What are the museum's hours?
> Is the museum open daily?
> When is the museum closed?
> How much does the museum cost for adults? How much for children?
> How much does it cost for children under five?
> Does the cost include the photo exhibit?

Practice the Conversation

A. 🔊 **Listen and repeat. Point to the speakers. Then listen again.**

1. Play the recording (first version of the conversation). Students listen and repeat, pointing to each speaker.

   1. Receptionist: *Good morning, Sunnyville Museum. How can I help you?*
   2. Ted: *Hi! What are your hours?*
      Receptionist: *We're open from 9:00 to 6:00.*
   3. Ted: *Are you open on Sundays?*
      Receptionist: *Yes. We're open daily, except on holidays.*
   4. Ted: *How much does it cost to get in?*
      Receptionist: *It's three dollars for adults and two dollars for children. Children under five are free.*
   5. Ted: *Does that include the special photo exhibit of old Sunnyville?*
      Receptionist: *Yes, it does. Tours are at 10:00, 2:00, and 5:00.*
   6. Ted: *Thanks for your help.*
      Receptionist: *You're welcome. Have a nice day.*

2. Play the recording (second version of the conversation). Students listen.

B. Role-play the conversation.

Students choose a partner and, using their Student Books for reference, role-play the conversation. They then change roles and role-play the conversation again.

Games and Activities

Note: For all Conversation Time activities, students may use their Student Books for reference.

1. **Back-to-Back.** Divide the class into pairs. Students sit with their backs to their partners and role-play the conversation without looking at each other. Partners then change roles and repeat the activity.

2. **True/False/I Don't Know.** Say five to six statements about the conversation (see Suggested Statements below). Students say *True* if the statement is true, and *False* if it is false. If a statement is false, choose a volunteer to make it true. If students don't have enough information to determine if the statement is true or false, they say *I don't know*.

   Suggested Statements:
   The Sunnyville Museum is open on Sundays.
   It costs three dollars for a four-year-old child to get in.
   Ted wants to go to the museum on Tuesday.
   There is a tour of the Train Exhibit daily at 10:00.
   The woman on the phone works at the museum daily.
   If Ted's mother and father go to the museum, they will pay six dollars to get in.

3. **Make It Your Own.** Write the following on the board:

   A: *What are your hours?*
   B: <u>*We're open from 9:00 to 6:00.*</u>

   Students read the dialogue on the board. Then divide the class into pairs and write the following on the board:

   1. *Monday through Friday we're open from 9:00 to 5:00. Saturday and Sunday we're open from 10:00 until 3:00.*
   2. *Monday through Friday we're open from 10:00 to 6:00. We're closed on Saturday and Sunday.*
   3. *We're only open on Tuesday and Thursday from 8:00 until 10:00.*

   Students read each new response. Quickly clarify meaning if necessary. Then each pair of students role-plays the dialogue on the board, substituting the new responses into the underlined part of the target conversation.

Finish the Lesson

1. **You Tell Me.** Ask students the following questions about their own school: *When is our school open? What are its hours? Is it open on Saturdays? On Sundays? Is our school open on holidays?* Then ask the following questions about the movies. *Do you like going to the movies? How much does it cost you to get in? How much does it cost your mother or father? Does that include the popcorn?*

2. Explain and assign Workbook page 1. (For instructions, see Teacher's Book page 157.)

Word Time

Language Focus: Public buildings and structures (*school, library, barbershop, bank, hotel, train station, post office, sidewalk, bridge, theater*)

Materials Needed (excluding materials for optional activities):
CD/cassette and player; Wall Chart 2; Unit 1 Word Time Picture Cards, 1 set; Unit 1 Word Time Word Cards, 1 set (see Picture and Word Card Book pages 1 and 2)

For general information on Word Time, see pages 10–11.

Warm-Up and Review

1. **Conversation Review: Listen, Please.** Play the recording of the Unit 1 conversation. Students listen and take notes if necessary to remember the information they hear. Then ask students four to five questions about the conversation (see Suggested Questions below).

   Suggested Questions:
   What are the Sunnyville Museum's hours?
   Is it open on Sundays?
   How much does it cost for an adult to get in?
   How much does it cost for a child to get in?
   When are the tours of the special photo exhibit of old Sunnyville?

2. Check Workbook page 1. (For instructions and answer key, see Teacher's Book page 157.)

Introduce the Words

1. Hold up and name each of the Unit 1 Word Time Picture Cards. Students listen. Hold up and name the cards again, and have students repeat. Hold up the cards in random order and have students name them.

2. Attach the Unit 1 Word Time Picture Cards in a row to the board. Stand the Unit 1 Word Time Word Cards on the chalktray under the corresponding picture cards. Point to each picture/word card pair and read the word. Students repeat. Then reposition the word cards so they are no longer directly below the corresponding picture cards. Volunteers come to the board one by one and place a word card under its corresponding picture card, then point to and read the word. Seated students repeat.

Talk About the Picture

1. Students open their Student Books to page 2. They look at the large scene and use complete sentences to identify anything they can.

2. Attach Wall Chart 2 to the board or open a Student Book to page 2. Read the following "story" while pointing to or touching the pictures (**bold** words) and pantomiming the actions (*italicized* words). If students repeat, do not stop them, but they are not required to do so.

Note: It is not important that students understand each word. This is a receptive exercise focusing on exposure to English.

> This picture shows an old town. What was in the town? We can see a **bridge**. There is a **train station**. We can see a **library**, a **school**, a **bank**, a **post office**, a **barbershop**, a **hotel**, and a **theater**. There is a **sidewalk** in front of the buildings. There are some students going to school.

3. Ask the following questions while pointing to or touching the pictures (**bold** words) and pantomiming the actions or adjectives (*italicized* words).

> (**bridge**) What's this?
> Does the bridge go *over* a river?
> (**post office**) Is this a school?
> Can you mail a letter at the post office?
> (**theater**) What do people do here?
> Can you *read books* at the **library**?
> What do people do at a **barbershop**?
> Can you *in-line skate* on a sidewalk?

Practice the Words

A. Listen and repeat.

1. Play the recording. Students listen and repeat, pointing to each word in the vocabulary box.

   1. *school*   2. *library*
   3. *barbershop*   4. *bank*
   5. *hotel*   6. *train station*
   7. *post office*   8. *sidewalk*
   9. *bridge*   10. *theater*

2. Say the words in random order. Students point to them in the vocabulary box.

B. Point and say the words.

Students point to each of the target vocabulary items in the large scene and name them.

C. Listen and point.

Play the recording. Students listen to the words. For the vocabulary, they point to the named item; for the conversations, they point to the speakers. (References are shown in parentheses.) Play the recording as many times as necessary for students to complete the task.

Bank.   *Sidewalk.*
Post office.   *School.*
Bridge.   *Library.*
Theater.   *Hotel.*
Barbershop.   *Train station.*

Now listen and point to the speakers.

A: *Are you open on Sundays?* (men outside barbershop)
B: *Yes. I'm open from 7:00 to 10:00.*
A: *Good. I need a haircut.*

A: *Dad, can we see the show?* (father and daughter by theater)
B: *Sure. How much does it cost to get in?*
A: *It's one dollar for adults. Children are free.*

A: *Let me help you, Ms. Lark.* (boy and woman outside library)
B: *Thanks. Be careful. They're heavy.*
A: *No problem.*

Games and Activities

1. **Name the Place.** Divide the class into teams of three to four. Describe one of the target vocabulary items (see Suggested Descriptions below). The first team to correctly name the building or structure gets a point. Continue with the remaining target items. The team with the most points at the end wins. Then have students on each team work together to write their own description of each target item. Once all teams have written at least four to five descriptions, have them take turns reading them to the class and have other teams name the described building or structure.

   Suggested Descriptions:
   You take a train there.
   You mail a letter there.
   You walk across the river on it.
   You see a movie there.
   You walk on it.
   You sleep there.
   You get a haircut there.
   You study there.
   You read books there.
   You get money there.

2. **Find the Clue.** Write the following words on the board: *book, money, train, letter, haircut, river, movie, walk, sleep, study*. Point to each word and have students read it. Clarify meaning as necessary. Then divide the class into teams of three to four. Say *library*. The first team to say the related word from the board then uses both the target word and related word in an appropriate sentence. If they do so correctly, they win a point. For example, students say either *Book. You read a book at the library* or *Study. I like to study at the library*. Continue with the remaining target items. The team with the most points at the end wins.

3. **Pantomime.** Divide the class into groups of three to four. A student in each group (S1) begins by pretending to be at one of the target buildings or structures. For example, a student pretends to walk up to a post office, buy some stamps, and put a letter in the mailbox. The other members of the group say *You're at the (post office)*. S1 says either *Yes, I am* or *No, I'm not*, continuing to pantomime until the place is correctly named. Another member of the group then takes a turn pantomiming. Groups continue in the same way for seven to nine minutes.

4. **Option: Personalize the Vocabulary.** Divide the class into groups of two to three. Students in each group work together to draw a map of their town, labeling everything they can. Groups then take turns standing up and telling the class about their maps.

Finish the Lesson

1. **Association.** Hold up a Unit 1 Word Time Picture Card. Students try to be the first to say another word with a logical association to the illustrated building or structure. For example: *barbershop/hair, library/books, bridge/water*. Accept any answers that make sense. The first student to call out an appropriate word wins a point. Do the same with the remaining picture cards. The student with the most points at the end wins.

2. Explain and assign Workbook page 2. (For instructions, see Teacher's Book page 158.)

Focus Time

Language Focus: Prepositions of location (*beside, behind, across from, in front of, near, above*)

Yes/No questions with *was* [*Was there a (library) (beside) the (post office)? Yes, there was./No, there wasn't.*]

Function: Asking about past location

Materials Needed: CD/cassette and player; Wall Chart 2; Unit 1 Word Time Picture Cards, 1 set; Unit 1 Word Time Word Cards, 1 set per 2 students; Unit 1 Focus Time Picture Cards, 1 set; Unit 1 Focus Time Word Cards, 1 set per 2 students; Unit 1 Grammar Cards, 1 set per 2 students (see Picture and Word Card Book pages 1, 2, 3, 4, and 45)

For general information on Focus Time, see pages 12–13.

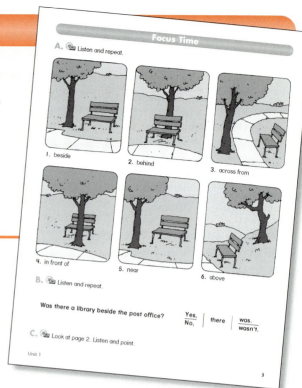

Warm-Up and Review

1. **Vocabulary Review: Buildings and Structures.** Stand the Unit 1 Word Time Picture Cards in pairs along the chalktray. Point to each card and have students name it. Point to one of the cards in the first pair and ask *Where's the (school)?* Point to the other card and answer *It's next to the (library).* Write the question and answer on the board. Point to the sentences and have students read them. Quickly review meaning if necessary. Point to a card in the next pair. Students on the left side of the classroom ask the question, and students on the right side of the classroom answer. Point to the other card in the pair. Groups reverse roles. Continue in the same way with the remaining cards.

2. Check Workbook page 2. (For instructions and answer key, see Teacher's Book page 158.)

This lesson is in two parts.

Part 1: Introduce the Words

1. Stand beside your desk. Point to yourself and then the desk and say *beside*. Students repeat. Write *beside* on the board. Point to it and say *beside*. Students repeat. Do the same with *behind, across from, in front of, near,* and *above,* moving around the desk to demonstrate each word. (Hold your hand above the desk to demonstrate *above*.)

2. **Practice for Fluency.** Students stand up at their desks. Hold up the *in front of* picture card, move in front of your desk, and say *I'm in front of the desk.* Students move in front of their desks and repeat. Do the same with the remaining Unit 1 Focus Time Picture Cards.

Practice the Words

Students open their Student Books to page 3.

A. Listen and repeat.

Play the recording. Students listen and repeat each word.

1. *beside*
2. *behind*
3. *across from*
4. *in front of*
5. *near*
6. *above*

Part 2: Introduce the Patterns

1. **Was there a (library) (beside) the (post office)? Yes, there was./No, there wasn't.** Attach Wall Chart 2 to the board or open a Student Book to page 2. Point to the post office and ask *Was there a library beside the post office?* Students repeat. Write *Was there a library beside the post office?* on the board. Point to and read each word. Students repeat. Then ask the question again, point to the building beside the post office, shake your head, and say *No, there wasn't.* Write *No, there wasn't.* on the board to the right of *Was there a library beside the post office?* Point to and read each word. Students repeat. Do the same with *hotel/above/barbershop, school/beside/library, bank/behind/bridge.*

2. **Practice for Fluency.** Say *sidewalk, in front of, theater*. Students say the target question. Then nod your head *yes* and have students say the target answer. Do the same with four to five different combinations of buildings/structures and prepositions of location.

Practice the Patterns

B. Listen and repeat.

1. Write the text from the pattern boxes on the board. Play the recording, pointing to each word. Students listen.

   A: *Was there a library beside the post office?*
   B: *Yes, there was.*

   A: *Was there a library beside the post office?*
   B: *No, there wasn't.*

2. Play the recording again. Students look at the pattern boxes in their books and repeat, pointing to each word.

3. Students work with partners to say the question and answers, while looking at the pattern boxes in their books.

C. Look at page 2. Listen and point.

Play the recording. Students look at page 2 and listen to the words, pointing to each item they hear named. Play the recording as many times as necessary for students to complete the task.

   A: *Was there a bridge beside the school?*
   B: *No, there wasn't.*

   A: *Was there a theater across from the library?*
   B: *Yes, there was.*

   A: *Was there a train station behind the hotel?*
   B: *Yes, there was.*

Games and Activities

1. **Cat and Mouse.** Place a chair at the front of the classroom. Two volunteers come to the chair. One is the "cat," and the other is the "mouse." The volunteers position themselves with relation to the chair, with the mouse trying not to be too near the cat. Then they change positions. After each change of position, the cat and the mouse stand still so that seated students can describe their former location. For example: *The mouse was (beside) the chair. The cat was (behind) the chair.* Continue in the same way for four to five minutes.

2. **Living Buildings.** Divide the class into groups of four and give each group a set of Unit 1 Word Time Word Cards and Focus Time Word Cards. Two students in each group (S1 and S2) stand up, each holding up a Unit 1 Word Time Word Card. Then another student in each group holds up a Focus Time Word Card. S1 and S2 position themselves in relation to each other so as to illustrate the word on the Focus Time card. Then they sit down. The last student in each group describes the past location of the two "living" buildings, saying *There was a (theater) (across from) the (post office).* Groups continue in the same way with the remaining cards, changing roles each time.

3. **Make the Sentences.** (See Game 17, pages 155–156.) Do the activity using Unit 1 Word Time Word Cards, Focus Time Word Cards, and Grammar Cards.

Finish the Lesson

1. **Where Was It?** Arrange several classroom items on a desk at the front of the classroom. Students look at the items and take notes on the items' locations in relation to each other for about 30 seconds. Then change the arrangement of the items and ask students target questions about the past location of the items.

2. Explain and assign Workbook page 3. (For instructions, see Teacher's Book page 158.)

Practice Time

Language Focus: Prepositions of location; Yes/No questions with *was* [*Was there a (bank) (near) the (school)? (Yes), there (was).*]

Function: Asking about past location

Materials Needed: CD/cassette and player; Unit 1 Word Time Picture Cards, 1 card per student; Unit 1 Focus Time Word Cards, 1 set (see Picture and Word Card Book pages 1 and 4)

For general information on Practice Time, see pages 14–15.

Warm-Up and Review

1. **Pattern Review: The Vanishing Book.** Stand the Unit 1 Focus Time Word Cards on the chalktray. Point to each card and have students read it. Then write *Was there a book in front of the desk? No, there wasn't.* on the board and have students read the sentences. Bring two volunteers (S1 and S2) to the board and give S1 the *above* word card. S1 displays the card to the class. S2 positions a book above a desk, then hides the book behind his/her back. Students on the left side of the classroom ask students on the right side *Was there a book above the desk?* Students on the right answer *Yes, there was.* Next, S1 holds up the *(beside)* word card, while S2 continues to hold the book behind his/her back. Students on the left then ask students on the right *Was there a book (beside) the desk?* Students on the right answer *No, there wasn't.* Bring another two to four pairs of volunteers to the board and continue in the same way for three to four minutes. Seated students change roles with every pair.

2. Check Workbook page 3. (For instructions and answer key, see Teacher's Book page 158.)

Practice the Patterns

Students open their Student Books to page 4.

A. Listen and repeat. Then practice with a partner.

1. Play the recording. Students listen and repeat, pointing to each picture in their books.

   A: *Was there a bank near the school?*
   B: *Yes, there was.*

   1. *Was there a school beside the library?*
      Yes, there was.
   2. *Was there a train station behind the hotel?*
      Yes, there was.
   3. *Was there a sidewalk in front of the bridge?*
      No, there wasn't.

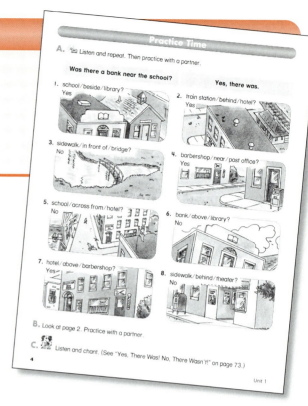

   4. *Was there a barbershop near the post office?*
      Yes, there was.
   5. *Was there a school across from the hotel?*
      No, there wasn't.
   6. *Was there a bank above the library?*
      No, there wasn't.
   7. *Was there a hotel above the barbershop?*
      Yes, there was.
   8. *Was there a sidewalk behind the theater?*
      No, there wasn't.

2. Students practice numbers 1–8 in pairs. (S1 in each pair asks the questions, and S2 answers.) Students then change roles and repeat the activity.

B. Look at page 2. Practice with a partner.

Students remain in pairs and look at page 2. They then take turns asking and answering questions about buildings and structures in the large scene using the target patterns and vocabulary items. For example: S1 (pointing to the barbershop): *Was there a hotel above the barbershop?* S2: *Yes, there was.*

C. Listen and chant.

1. Students turn to the *Yes, There Was! No, There Wasn't!* chant on page 73. They cover up the text, look at the pictures, and talk about what they see. Read the lyrics line by line. Students repeat each line. Play the recording. Students listen and follow along in their books.

Yes, There Was! No, There Wasn't!

Was there a theater beside the school?
  Yes, there was!
    No, there wasn't!
Was there a barbershop beside the school?
  Yes, there was!
    No, there wasn't!

Was there a post office near the bank?
  Yes, there was!
    No, there wasn't!
Was there a train station near the bank?
  Yes, there was!
    No, there wasn't!

Was there a library across from the bridge?
  Yes, there was!
    No, there wasn't!
Was there a hotel across from the bridge?
  Yes, there was!
    No, there wasn't!

2. Play the recording again. Students listen and chant along, using their books for reference. Play the recording as many times as necessary for students to become familiar with the chant.

3. Give each student a Unit 1 Word Time Picture Card. Play the karaoke version. Students chant along, standing up and showing their picture card each time it is named. Students exchange cards and chant again.

Games and Activities

1. **Move Around.** Divide the class into pairs and have each student stand up next to his/her partner. Say *behind*. One student in each pair (S1) stands still as a statue. S2 then moves behind S1 and says *I'm behind (Tom)*. Say *beside*. S2 moves beside S1 and says *I'm beside (Tom)*. Continue in the same way with the remaining target prepositions of location. Then have students switch roles and do the activity again.

2. **Listen Carefully.** Read the following paragraph to students, having them take notes as necessary.

   My grandmother lived in New York when she was five years old. Every morning, she bought donuts from the bakery that was across from her house. Then she went to school. Her school was near the theater. Sometimes after school she saw a movie. But sometimes she didn't see a movie—she studied English at the library that was next to the theater.

   Ask the following questions about the above reading, having students refer to their notes for reference. If necessary, read the paragraph several times.

   Was there a barbershop across from my grandmother's house?
   Was there a theater near my grandmother's school?
   Was there a library above the theater?

3. **Write a Story.** Give students 10–15 minutes to write a story that includes details about the location of their home and school. Once students have finished writing their stories, have volunteers take turns reading their stories to the class.

> **Extra Practice**
> Explain and assign Worksheet 1, An Old Town, page 188. (For instructions and answer key, see page 183.)

Finish the Lesson

1. **Name the Location.** Stand behind your desk. Then sit down and ask *Was I above my desk?* Then stand in front of your desk, sit down, and ask *Was I in front of my desk?* Continue in the same way for three to four minutes.

2. Explain and assign Workbook page 4. (For instructions, see Teacher's Book page 158.)

Reading Time

Language Focus: Reading a historical narrative

Materials Needed (excluding materials for optional activities):
CD/cassette and player

For general information on Reading Time, see pages 16–17.

Warm-Up and Review

1. **Pattern Review: Chant.** Play the Unit 1 chant, *Yes, There Was! No, There Wasn't!* Students listen. Play the chant again and have students chant along.

2. Check Workbook page 4. (For instructions and answer key, see Teacher's Book page 158.)

Introduce the Reading

Note: Students may learn the new vocabulary within the context of the reading, or each new word can be taught before students encounter it in the reading. Follow the steps below to introduce the new vocabulary and/or introduce the reading content.

1. Write the new words in a column on the board. Point to and read each word before explaining its meaning.

   invent: Say the names of several inventors that students know (for example: Thomas Edison, Alexander Graham Bell, Eli Whitney). Say *These people were inventors. They invented many things.*

   history: Name several important dates/events in your country's history. Then say *You study these things in history class.*

   first: Name the first leader of your country and explain that he/she was the first person to be leader.

   churn: Explain that an ice cream churn is a device used to make ice cream by hand.

   factory: Say *A factory is a big building where many people work to make things.* If there are any factories in your area, name them and say *These are factories.*

   cone: Draw an ice cream cone on the board. Point to the cone and say *cone.*

   every: Write *every = all* on the board. Point to and read each word. Students repeat. Then say *All of you are in my English class. Every student is in my English class.*

   a lot of: Explain that a lot of means many. Say *A lot of you like to (play video games).*

   flavor: Name several flavors of ice cream in the students' native language. Then say *These are flavors of ice cream.*

   vanilla: Say *Vanilla is an ice cream flavor. Vanilla ice cream is white.*

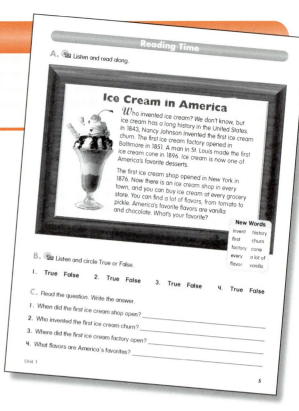

2. Ask students about their own experiences with ice cream (see Suggested Questions below).

   Suggested Questions:
   Do you like ice cream?
   Is ice cream your favorite dessert?
   Can you buy ice cream at a drugstore?
   Is there an ice cream shop near your home?

3. Students open their Student Books to page 5. They look at the reading and pictures and talk about what they see. For example: *Here is some ice cream. It looks delicious.* Ask students what they think the reading will be about.

Practice the Reading

Students read the story silently to themselves.

A. Listen and read along.

1. Play the recording. Students listen and read along in their Student Books.

   Ice Cream in America

   Who invented ice cream? We don't know, but ice cream has a long history in the United States. In 1843, Nancy Johnson invented the first ice cream churn. The first ice cream factory opened in Baltimore in 1851. A man in St. Louis made the first ice cream cone in 1896. Ice cream is now one of America's favorite desserts.

   The first ice cream shop opened in New York in 1876. Now there is an ice cream shop in every town, and you can buy ice cream at every grocery store. You can find a lot of flavors, from tomato to pickle. America's favorite flavors are vanilla and chocolate. What's your favorite?

New Words
invent
history
first
churn
factory
cone
every
a lot of
flavor
vanilla

2. Play the recording again, stopping it after each sentence. Students listen and repeat each sentence.

3. Divide the class into pairs. Students in each pair take turns reading the story aloud to their partner.

B. Listen and circle True or False.

1. Play the recording. For each number, students listen and circle *True* if the statement is true, and *False* if it is not.

   1. *We know who invented ice cream.*
   2. *The first ice cream churn was invented in 1846.*
   3. *The first ice cream shop opened in New York.*
   4. *Americans don't like vanilla ice cream.*

2. Check answers by saying *Number 1. We know who invented ice cream.* Students say *True* if they circled *True*, and *False* if they circled *False*. If the statement is false, choose a volunteer to make it true. Do the same for numbers 2–4.

   Answer Key:
   1. False   2. False   3. True   4. False

C. Read the question. Write the answer.

1. Students read each question and answer it based on the reading in exercise A.

2. Check answers by reading each question and having students read the answer they wrote.

   Answer Key:
   1. When did the first ice cream shop open? The first ice cream shop opened in 1876.
   2. Who invented the first ice cream churn? Nancy Johnson invented the first ice cream churn.
   3. Where did the first ice cream factory open? The first ice cream factory opened in Baltimore.
   4. What flavors are America's favorites? America's favorite flavors are vanilla and chocolate.

Games and Activities

Note: For all Reading Time activities, students may use their Student Books for reference.

1. **Make New Phrases.** Write *ice cream cone* on the board. Strike through the word *cone*. Students replace *cone* with other words in order to create new phrases. For example: *ice cream churn, ice cream factory, ice cream shop, ice cream flavor*. Write each new phrase on the board as students say it. Then have volunteers use each new phrase in a sentence.

2. **Write the Words.** Divide the class into pairs. Write the following sentences on the board:

   1. *Nancy Johnson _____ the first ice cream churn.*
   2. *In 1851, the first _____ opened.*
   3. *One of America's favorite desserts is _____.*
   4. *My favorite flavor of ice cream is _____.*

   Students in each pair work together to complete each sentence. Check answers by having volunteers take turns reading a sentence to the class.

   Answer Key:
   1. Nancy Johnson <u>invented</u> the first ice cream churn.
   2. In 1851, the first <u>ice cream factory</u> opened.
   3. One of America's favorite desserts is <u>ice cream</u>.
   4. My favorite flavor of ice cream is (<u>vanilla</u>). (*Answers will vary.*)

3. **Timeline.** Divide the class into groups of two to three. Students in each group work together to create a timeline about the history of ice cream. Once students have completed their timelines, say *1896* and have students say what happened in that year. Do the same with *1876*, *1843*, and *1851*.

   OPTIONS:

   1. Students illustrate their timelines with drawings or pictures cut from magazines.

   2. Students go to the library or use the Internet to do further research on ice cream. They then include the new information on their timelines.

> **Extra Practice**
> Explain and assign Worksheet 2, Ice Cream Sandwiches, page 189. (For instructions and answer key, see page 183.)

Finish the Lesson

1. **Use It in a Sentence.** Say *invent*. A volunteer says a sentence using *invent* (this can be either an original sentence or a sentence from the reading). Do the same with the remaining New Words from the lesson.

2. Explain and assign Workbook page 5. (For instructions, see Teacher's Book pages 158–159.)

Your Time

Language Focus: Personalizing location language

Materials Needed: CD/cassette and player; Unit 1 Word Time Picture Cards, 1 set (see Picture and Word Card Book page 1)

For general information on Your Time, see pages 18–19.

Warm-Up and Review

1. **Reading Review: Find the Facts.** Say *one of America's favorite desserts*. Students look at Student Book page 5 to find those words. When they do, they read or say the sentence containing the words out loud (*Ice cream is now one of America's favorite desserts*). Do the same with *the first ice cream shop, the first ice cream churn, the first ice cream cone, the first ice cream factory, America's favorite flavors, you can buy ice cream, a lot of flavors*.

2. Check Workbook page 5. (For instructions and answer key, see Teacher's Book pages 158–159.)

Introduce the Lesson

Write *Is there a drugstore beside our school?* on the board. Point to the question and have students read it. Quickly review meaning if necessary. Then ask students five to six questions relating to location (see Suggested Questions below).

Suggested Questions:
Is there a lizard beside (Bob)?
Is (Mari) behind (Ken)?
Am I near my desk?
Is there a bridge across from your house?
Are there any books in your bookbag?
Is there a hotel in front of our school?

Practice the Lesson

Students open their Student Books to page 6.

A. Listen and answer the questions.

1. Play the recording. For each number, students listen to the question and answer it based on their own knowledge.

   1. *Is there a library near your house?*
   2. *Is there a library near your school?*
   3. *Is there a theater beside your house?*
   4. *Is there a bank across from your school?*

2. Check answers by dividing the class into pairs and having students in each pair read one question and answer to the class.

   Answer Key:
   Answers will vary.

B. Pairwork. Fill in the chart. Then tell your partner about your town.

Divide the class into pairs. Each student fills in the names of any buildings he/she wants in the *You* column on his/her chart. Then a student in each pair (S1) tells his/her partner about his/her "town," using the sentence cues and information from his/her chart. For example: A student writes *bridge* and *library* in his/her chart for *a* and *b*. So for number 1, he/she says *There's a bridge beside the library*. S2 fills in the information he/she receives from S1. S1 continues in the same way for numbers 2–4. S2 then takes a turn in the same way.

C. Review. Read and write the answers.

1. Students read each question and write an answer based on their own knowledge and experience.

2. Check answers by dividing the class into pairs and having students in each pair read one question and answer to the class.

   Answer Key:
   Answers will vary.

Games and Activities

1. **Draw a Map.** Divide the class into groups of two to three. Give each group ten minutes to draw and label a map of either their town or the neighborhood around their school. Once students have finished their maps, have groups take turns standing up and telling the class about their maps.

2. **Follow the Directions.** Arrange students' desks to create several "city blocks." Set Unit 1 Word Time Picture Cards on the desks to represent buildings on the city blocks. Then bring all students to the front of the classroom and give them directions to get to different buildings. For example: *Walk straight for two blocks. Turn right. It's on the left.* Students follow your directions and then name the building they come to, saying *It's the (library).* Continue in the same way for six to seven minutes, having a volunteer take on the teacher's role after several minutes.

3. **Questions.** Ask students six to seven questions about which buildings they would visit in order to do certain activities (see Suggested Questions below).

   Suggested Questions:
   You want to mail a letter. Where do you go? (post office)
   You want to get a book. Where do you go? (library)
   You want to take a train. Where do you go? (train station)
   You want to get a haircut. Where do you go? (barbershop)
   You want to go to sleep. Where do you go? (hotel)
   You want to see a show. Where do you go? (theater)
   You want to get money. Where do you go? (bank)

Finish the Lesson

1. **When Did You Go?** Say *library*. A volunteer says *I went to the library on (Tuesday). I (read a book).* Continue in the same way with different building names, having volunteers say the last time they went to the building and what they did there.

2. Explain and assign Workbook page 6. (For instructions, see Teacher's Book page 159.)

> **Assessment**
> Explain and assign the Unit 1 Test, page 216. (For instructions and answer key, see page 208.)

2 At the Diner

Conversation Time

Language Focus: Ordering food in a restaurant
Materials Needed: CD/cassette and player; Wall Chart 3

For general information on Conversation Time, see pages 8–9.

Warm-Up and Review

1. **Review: In My Town.** Write *Is there a bakery beside your house?* on the board. Point to the question and have students read it. Quickly review meaning if necessary. Then ask students five to six questions relating to location (see Suggested Questions below).

   Suggested Questions:
   Is there a puppy beside (Kim)?
   Is (Mari) in front of (Ken)?
   Am I above my desk?
   Is there a sidewalk in front of your house?
   Are there any pencils near your bookbag?
   Is there a restaurant across from our school?

2. Check Workbook page 6. (For instructions and answer key, see Teacher's Book page 159.)

Introduce the Conversation

1. Set the scene and clarify meaning by saying *Today's conversation is at a restaurant. A man and a woman are hungry and are going to eat some good food.* Then introduce the new words by writing each word on the board. Point to and read each word before explaining its meaning. Students repeat the word.

   order: Say *I'm at a restaurant. I'm going to order my food.* Then, pretending to talk to a waiter, say *I want a baked potato and a salad, please.*

   steak: Say *Steak is a kind of meat. It comes from a cow.*

   rare/medium/well done: Say *Rare. If you want your steak rare, cook it for seven minutes. Medium. If you want your steak medium, cook it for eleven minutes. Well done. If you want your steak well done, cook it for seventeen minutes.*

   special: Explain that often restaurants offer meals that are not on their menus. These are called specials, and usually change from day to day.

2. Bring three students to the front of the classroom. Have Student A hold a pencil and pad of paper. Students B and C should sit at a table and each should hold a "menu" (folded piece of paper). Stand behind each student and model his/her lines of the conversation with the following actions:

A: *Hello. Are you ready to order?*
Walk up to Students B and C. Speak in a friendly manner.

B: *I think so. I'll have a steak.*
Look at the menu, then nod your head and look at Student A.

A: *Rare, medium, or well done?*
Look at Student B questioningly.

B: *Medium, please. And a baked potato.*
Speak to Student A in a friendly manner.

A: *How about a salad?*
Look at Student B questioningly.

B: *Sounds good.*
Nod and smile at Student A.

C: *What's today's special?*
Look at the menu, then look at Student A.

A: *Spaghetti and meatballs.*
Speak to Student C in a friendly, slightly enthusiastic manner.

C: *Good! I'm in the mood for spaghetti. I'll have that.*
Nod and smile happily. Speak to Student A.

A: *Here you are.*
Turn around and walk away. Then come back to the table while pretending to hold two plates. Set the "plates" down in front of Students B and C.

C: *Thanks. It looks delicious.*
Look at Student A and smile. Speak enthusiastically.

3. Divide the class into Groups A, B, and C. Model the conversation again using facial expressions and body language. Group A repeats the first line of the conversation, Group B repeats line two, and so on. Encourage students to copy your facial expressions and body language. Groups change roles and say the conversation again in the same way. Continue until each group has taken on each role.

4. Attach Wall Chart 3 to the board or open a Student Book to page 7. Students then open their Student Books to page 7. Ask the following questions:

> Where are these people?
> What are they going to do?
> What's the woman sitting at the table going to eat?
> What's the man at the table going to eat?
> What's today's special?
> Who's in the mood for spaghetti and meatballs?

Practice the Conversation

A. Listen and repeat. Point to the speakers. Then listen again.

1. Play the recording (first version of the conversation). Students listen and repeat, pointing to each speaker.

   1. Waitress: *Hello. Are you ready to order?*
      Woman: *I think so. I'll have a steak.*
   2. Waitress: *Rare, medium, or well done?*
      Woman: *Medium, please. And a baked potato.*
   3. Waitress: *How about a salad?*
      Woman: *Sounds good.*
   4. Man: *What's today's special?*
      Waitress: *Spaghetti and meatballs.*
   5. Man: *Good! I'm in the mood for spaghetti. I'll have that.*
   6. Waitress: *Here you are.*
      Man: *Thanks. It looks delicious.*

2. Play the recording (second version of the conversation). Students listen.

B. Role-play the conversation.

Divide the class into groups of three. Using their Student Books for reference, students in each group role-play the conversation. They then switch roles and role-play the conversation again. Groups continue until each student has taken on each role.

Games and Activities

Note: For all Conversation Time activities, students may use their Student Books for reference.

1. **Responses.** Divide the class into pairs. A student in each pair (S1) begins by saying the first line of dialogue in any of the scenes (except for the fifth scene). His/Her partner (S2) responds accordingly. Pairs continue in the same way with the remaining scenes. S2 then says the first lines of the dialogue in the same way and S1 responds.

2. **At a Restaurant.** Divide the class into groups of three. Each group takes five to seven minutes to create a menu. Students in each group then role-play the conversation, substituting items from their menus. Groups continue until each student has been the waitperson.

3. **Make It Your Own.** Write the following on the board:

   A: *Hello. Are you ready to order?*
   B: <u>*I think so. I'll have a steak.*</u>

   Students read the dialogue on the board. Then divide the class into pairs and write the following on the board:

   1. *No, not yet. I need a few more minutes.*
   2. *Yes! I'd like a steak, please.*
   3. *Yes, but first I have a question about your specials.*

   Students read each new response. Quickly clarify meaning if necessary. Then students in each pair role-play the dialogue on the board, substituting the new responses into the underlined part of the target conversation.

Finish the Lesson

1. **Finish the Phrase.** Say the beginning words of a phrase from the lesson (see Suggested Phrases below) and have students compete to be the first to complete the phrase. Any reasonable answer is okay.

   Suggested Phrases:
   Are you _____
   How about _____
   Sounds _____
   Rare, medium _____
   What's today's _____
   I'm in the mood _____
   Here you _____

2. Explain and assign Workbook page 7. (For instructions, see Teacher's Book page 159.)

Word Time

Language Focus: Food and drink (*root beer, lemonade, roast beef, ham, chicken soup, fruit salad, iced tea, coffee, garlic bread, apple pie*)

Materials Needed (excluding materials for optional activities):
CD/cassette and player; Wall Chart 4; Unit 2 Word Time Picture Cards, 1 set per 3 students; Unit 2 Word Time Word Cards, 1 set per 3 students (see Picture and Word Card Book pages 5 and 6)

For more general information on Word Time, see pages 10–11.

Warm-Up and Review

1. **Conversation Review: True/False/I Don't Know.** Play the recording of the Unit 2 conversation, having students take notes if necessary to remember the information they hear. Say four to five statements about the Unit 2 conversation (see Suggested Statements below). Students say *True* if the statement is true, and *False* if it is false. If a statement is false, choose a volunteer to make it true. If students don't have enough information to determine if the statement is true or false, they say *I don't know*.

   Suggested Statements:
   The woman's favorite food is steak.
   The man is in the mood for spaghetti.
   The woman wants her steak medium.
   The restaurant's special is steak.
   The woman is going to have a baked potato and corn.

2. Check Workbook page 7. (For instructions and answer key, see Teacher's Book page 159.)

Introduce the Words

1. Hold up and name each of the Unit 2 Word Time Picture Cards. Students listen. Hold up and name the cards again, and have students repeat. Hold up the cards in random order and have students name them.

2. Attach the Unit 2 Word Time Picture Cards in a row to the board. Stand the Unit 2 Word Time Word Cards on the chalktray under the corresponding picture cards. Point to each picture/word card pair and read the word. Students repeat. Then reposition the word cards so they are no longer directly below the corresponding picture cards. Volunteers come to the board one by one and place a word card under its corresponding picture card, then point to and read the word. Seated students repeat.

Talk About the Picture

1. Students open their Student Books to page 8. They look at the large scene and use complete sentences to identify anything they can.

2. Attach Wall Chart 4 to the board or open a Student Book to page 8. Read the following "story" while pointing to or touching the pictures (**bold** words) and pantomiming the actions (*italicized* words).

   Lots of people are *eating* and *drinking* at this restaurant. The cook has **coffee**. Digger is outside. No pets in the restaurant! **These two people** are looking at **menus**. There is **lemonade** on their table. On the next table there is **root beer** and **apple pie**. The waiter is bringing **garlic bread**. What's at these two tables? There's **ham** and **chicken soup**, and at the next table is **fruit salad, coffee,** and **roast beef**. It all looks delicious!

3. Ask the following questions while pointing to or touching the pictures (**bold** words).

   (**lemonade**) What's this?
   (**apple pie**) What's this?
   Does the **waiter** have water? What does he have?
   Is there any spaghetti and meatballs? How about fruit salad?
   What's across the table from the **fruit salad**? What drink is near the fruit salad?

Practice the Words

A. Listen and repeat.

1. Play the recording. Students listen and repeat, pointing to each word in the vocabulary box.

   1. *root beer*   2. *lemonade*
   3. *roast beef*   4. *ham*
   5. *chicken soup*   6. *fruit salad*
   7. *iced tea*   8. *coffee*
   9. *garlic bread*   10. *apple pie*

36   Unit 2

2. Say the words in random order. Students point to them in the vocabulary box.

B. Point and say the words.

Students point to each of the target vocabulary items in the large scene and name them.

C. 🔊 **Listen and point.**

Play the recording. Students listen to the words. For the vocabulary, they point to the named item; for the conversations, they point to the speakers. (References are shown in parentheses.) Play the recording as many times as necessary for students to complete the task.

> *Roast beef.*
> *Coffee.*
> *Lemonade.*
> *Iced tea.*
> *Fruit salad.*
> *Garlic bread.*
> *Chicken soup.*
> *Root beer.*
> *Apple pie.*
> *Ham.*
>
> *Now listen and point to the speakers.*
>
> A: *What are you going to have?* (boyfriend and girlfriend)
> B: *I don't know.*
> A: *I'm going to have some french fries and a hot dog.*
> B: *That sounds good. I'll have that, too.*
>
> A: *I rented a video. Do you want to watch it tonight?* (Annie and Ted)
> B: *I can't. I'm going to see a movie with my family. How about tomorrow?*
> A: *Sure!*
>
> A: *Here you are.* (waiter and woman)
> B: *Thanks. It looks delicious.*
> A: *How about some more water?*
> B: *No, thanks.*

Games and Activities

1. **Describe the Restaurant Table.** Bring four volunteers (S1–S4) to the front of the classroom and have them sit around a desk. Place the Unit 2 Word Time Picture Cards on the desk so that their location can be described in terms of *across from, beside, near,* and *in front of.* Ask seated students the following questions: *What's in front of S1? What's near the (coffee)? What's beside the (ham)? What's beside the (fruit salad)? Who is sitting across from (S3)?*

   Then divide the class into groups of four and give each group a set of Unit 2 Word Time Picture Cards. Each group does the activity as above, asking each other appropriate questions about their own "restaurant table."

2. **Survey.** Students create a survey on a sheet of paper by writing *Name* and *Do you like* _____? in a row at the top of the paper. They then write a list of five different food and drink items along the left side of the paper. Students then go around the classroom and ask their classmates *Do you like (root beer)?* Students respond *Yes, I like (root beer)* or *No, I don't like (root beer).* Students record the answers they hear. Continue until all students have asked five other students the question. Students sit down. Then ask students questions about the survey. For example: Ask *Does Bill like root beer?* Students who know this information respond either *Yes, he does* or *No, he doesn't.*

3. **Place Your Orders, Please**. Divide the class into groups of three to four and give each group a set of Unit 2 Word Time Picture Cards and Word Cards. Each group will role-play a restaurant scene, with one student acting as the waiter, one student acting as the cook, and the rest acting as customers in the restaurant. The customers lay the word cards faceup on a desk to make a menu. The waiter comes to the group and says to each student *Hello. Are you ready to order?* Each customer replies *I think so. I'll have some (chicken soup).* The waiter then walks to the cook. The cook asks *What's (she) going to have?* about each customer. The waiter answers *(She's) going to have some (chicken soup).* The cook then finds the Unit 2 Word Time Picture Card to fill each order and gives it to the waiter, who "serves" it to the customer, saying *Here you are.* Students then change roles and do the activity again. Groups continue until each student has been both the waiter and the cook.

4. **Option: Personalize the Vocabulary.** Students look through old magazines or newspapers and cut out pictures of any food items they can name in English. They then create a collage by gluing all their pictures on a large sheet of paper and labeling each picture. Students then take turns showing their collages to the class, pointing to each picture and saying *I want (ham). I don't want (fruit salad)* or asking their classmates *Do you like (ham)?* Volunteers respond either *Yes, I do* or *No, I don't.* Hang the collages on the walls for future reference.

Finish the Lesson

1. **Slow Reveal.** (See Game 15, page 155.) Play the game using Unit 2 Word Time Picture Cards.

2. Explain and assign Workbook page 8. (For instructions, see Teacher's Book page 159.)

Focus Time

Language Focus: Food quantities (*a bottle of root beer, a can of lemonade, a slice of ham, a piece of apple pie, a bowl of chicken soup, a glass of iced tea, a cup of coffee, a loaf of garlic bread*)

Wh- questions with *how much/many* [*How much (root beer) did (she) have? (She) had (one) (bottle) of (root beer)./How many (bottles) of (root beer) did (she) have? (She) had (three) (bottles) of (root beer).*]

Function: Expressing quantities of food and drink

Materials Needed: CD/cassette and player; Unit 2 Word Time Picture Cards, 1 set; Unit 2 Word Time Word Cards, 1 set per 2 students; Unit 2 Focus Time Picture Cards, 1 set per 2 students; Unit 2 Focus Time Word Cards, 1 set per 2 students; *I, You, He, She, They, I, we, he, she,* and *they* grammar cards, 1 set per 2 students; Unit 2 Grammar Cards, 1 set per 2 students (see Picture and Word Card Book pages 5, 6, 7, 8, 43, 46, and 47)

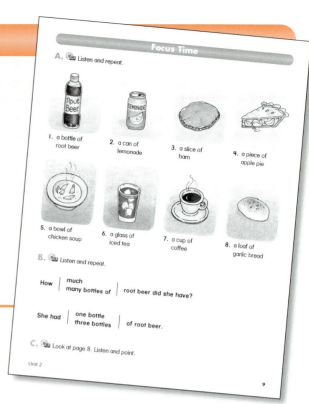

For general information on Focus Time, see pages 12–13.

Warm-Up and Review

1. **Vocabulary Review: Eating and Drinking.** Hold up each Unit 2 Word Time Picture Card and have students name it. Then divide the board into two vertical columns. Write *We eat _____* at the top of the first column, and *We drink _____* at the top of the second. Say *roast beef* and have a volunteer point to the corresponding column on the board. A different volunteer says *We eat roast beef*. Write *roast beef* in the *We eat _____* column. Do the same with the remaining Unit 2 food items. Then point to each column and have students read the words.

2. Check Workbook page 8. (For instructions and answer key, see Teacher's Book page 159.)

This lesson is in two parts.

Part 1: Introduce the Words

1. Hold up and name each of the Unit 2 Focus Time Picture Cards. Students listen. Hold up and name the cards again, and have students repeat. Hold up the cards in random order and have students name them.

2. Attach the Unit 2 Focus Time Picture Cards in a row to the board. Stand the Unit 2 Focus Time Word Cards on the chalktray under the corresponding picture cards. Point to each picture/word card pair and read the word. Students repeat. Then reposition the word cards so they are no longer directly below the corresponding picture cards. Volunteers come to the board one by one and place a word card under its corresponding picture card, then point to and read the word. Seated students repeat.

Practice the Words

Students open their Student Books to page 9.

A. Listen and repeat.

Play the recording. Students listen and repeat each word.

1. *a bottle of root beer*   2. *a can of lemonade*
3. *a slice of ham*   4. *a piece of apple pie*
5. *a bowl of chicken soup*   6. *a glass of iced tea*
7. *a cup of coffee*   8. *a loaf of garlic bread*

Part 2: Introduce the Patterns

1. **How much (root beer) did (she) have? (She) had (one) (bottle) of (root beer).** Bring a volunteer to the front of the classroom. Pretend to hand him/her a bottle of root beer and say *Here's a bottle of root beer.* Prompt the student to pretend to drink the bottle of root beer. Point to the volunteer and ask seated students *How much root beer did (she) have?* Students repeat. Write *How much root beer did (she) have?* on the board. Point to and read each word. Students repeat. Ask the question again, point to the volunteer, and say *(She) had one bottle of root beer.* Students repeat. Write *(She) had one bottle of root beer.* on the board to the right of *How much root beer did (she) have?* Point to and read each word. Students repeat. Repeat the entire procedure, pretending to hand the volunteer two bottles of root beer and saying *Here are two bottles of root beer.* Have the student pretend to drink both bottles of root beer. Do the same with a slice of ham, a loaf of garlic bread, and a cup of coffee.

2. **How many (bottles) of (root beer) did (she) have? (She) had (one) (bottle) of (root beer).** Follow the same procedure as in Step 1, underlining *How many bottles* when writing the question on the board and using cans of lemonade, pieces of apple pie, bowls of chicken soup, and glasses of iced tea.

3. **Practice for Fluency.** Write *How much…* and *How many…* on the board. Write *root beer, lemonade, ham, apple pie,* and *garlic bread* below *How much….* Write *bottles of root beer, cans of lemonade, slices of ham, pieces of apple pie,* and *loaves of garlic bread* below *How many….* Say *they, lemonade* and point to *How much….* Students ask *How much lemonade did they have?* Say *three cans.* Students say *They had three cans of lemonade.* Then say *he, pieces of apple pie* and point to *How many….* Students ask *How many pieces of apple pie did he have?* Say *one piece.* Students say *He had one piece of apple pie.* Continue for four to six minutes, using different food items, pronouns, and quantities. After students have made several questions and answers, do not point to *How much…* and *How many….*

Note: Use *much* to ask about singular and uncountable nouns (for example: *apple pie, lemonade, coffee*). Use *many* to ask about plural nouns (for example: *pieces of apple pie, cans of lemonade, cups of coffee*).

Practice the Patterns

B. Listen and repeat.

1. Write the text from the pattern boxes on the board. Then play the recording, pointing to each word. Students listen.

   A: *How much root beer did she have?*
   B: *She had one bottle of root beer.*

   A: *How many bottles of root beer did she have?*
   B: *She had three bottles of root beer.*

2. Play the recording again. Students look at the pattern boxes in their books and repeat, pointing to each word.

3. Students work with partners to say the questions and answers, while looking at the pattern boxes in their books.

C. Look at page 8. Listen and point.

Play the recording. Students look at page 8 and listen to the words, pointing to each person being talked about. Play the recording as many times as necessary for students to complete the task.

   A: *How many slices of roast beef did she have?*
   B: *She had two slices of roast beef.*

   A: *How much lemonade did she have?*
   B: *She had one can of lemonade.*

   A: *How many slices of ham did he have?*
   B: *He had four slices of ham.*

Games and Activities

1. **Plurals.** Divide the class into pairs and give each pair a set of Unit 2 Focus Time Picture Cards. Students in each pair work together to write on each picture card both the singular and plural form of each illustrated item. For example: On the *root beer* card, students would write both *a bottle of root beer* and *(two) bottles of root beer*. Once pairs have labeled each card, they choose four of the cards and write a sentence using each of the phrases. The sentences can use any English that students know. For example: *I drank a bottle of root beer. I like to eat four slices of ham for breakfast.*

2. **How Much/How Many.** Divide the class into pairs and write the following on the board:

   1. How _____ ham did you have? (three slices)
   2. How _____ cups of coffee did she have? (one cup)
   3. How _____ chicken soup did they have? (two bowls)
   4. How _____ garlic bread did he have? (four loaves)
   5. How _____ pieces of apple pie did you have? (two pieces)

   Students in each pair work together to fill in the blank in each question using *much* or *many*. They then use the words in parentheses to write the answer to each question. Check answers by saying *Number 1* and having a volunteer read both the question and answer he/she wrote. Do the same for numbers 2–5.

   Answer Key:
   1. How <u>much</u> ham did you have? <u>I had three slices of ham.</u>
   2. How <u>many</u> cups of coffee did she have? <u>She had one cup of coffee.</u>
   3. How <u>much</u> chicken soup did they have? <u>They had two bowls of chicken soup.</u>
   4. How <u>much</u> garlic bread did he have? <u>He had four loaves of garlic bread.</u>
   5. How <u>many</u> pieces of apple pie did you have? <u>I had two pieces of apple pie.</u>

3. **Make the Sentences.** (See Game 17, pages 155–156.) Do the activity using *I, You, He, She, They, I, we, he, she,* and *they* grammar cards and Unit 2 Word Time Word Cards, Focus Time Word Cards, and Grammar Cards.

Finish the Lesson

1. **Special Menus.** Elicit the name of a famous gymnast or model and the name of a famous boxer or weightlifter. Write the two names on the board and have seated students ask and answer the target questions about the two people with special diet needs.

2. Explain and assign Workbook page 9. (For instructions, see Teacher's Book pages 159–160.)

Practice Time

Language Focus: Wh- questions with *how much/many* [*How much (garlic bread) did (he) have? (He) had (six) (loaves) of (garlic bread).*]

Function: Expressing quantities of food and drink

Materials Needed: CD/cassette and player; Unit 2 Word Time Picture Cards, 1 set per 4–6 students; Unit 2 Focus Time Picture Cards, 1 set per 4–6 students (see Picture and Word Card Book pages 5 and 7)

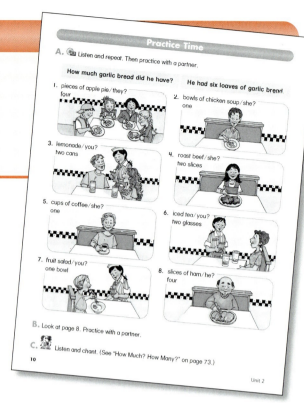

For general information on Practice Time, see pages 14–15.

Warm-Up and Review

1. **Pattern Review: Match the Cards.** Hold up each Unit 2 Focus Time Picture Card and have students name it. Then write *How much root beer did he have?/How many bottles of root beer did he have? He had two bottles of root beer.* on the board. Point to each sentence and have students read it. Then say *they, ham* and elicit the target question. Say *two slices* and elicit the target answer. Continue for four to six minutes, using different food items, pronouns, and quantities.

2. Check Workbook page 9. (For instructions and answer key, see Teacher's Book pages 159–160.)

Practice the Patterns

Students open their Student Books to page 10.

A. Listen and repeat. Then practice with a partner.

1. Play the recording. Students listen and repeat, pointing to each picture in their books.

   A: *How much garlic bread did he have?*
   B: *He had six loaves of garlic bread.*

   1. *How many pieces of apple pie did they have?*
      They had four pieces of apple pie.
   2. *How many bowls of chicken soup did she have?*
      She had one bowl of chicken soup.
   3. *How much lemonade did you have?*
      We had two cans of lemonade.
   4. *How much roast beef did she have?*
      She had two slices of roast beef.
   5. *How many cups of coffee did she have?*
      She had one cup of coffee.
   6. *How much iced tea did you have?*
      I had two glasses of iced tea.
   7. *How much fruit salad did you have?*
      I had one bowl of fruit salad.
   8. *How many slices of ham did he have?*
      He had four slices of ham.

2. Students practice numbers 1–8 in pairs. (S1 in each pair asks the questions, and S2 answers.) Students then change roles and repeat the activity.

B. Look at page 8. Practice with a partner.

Students remain in pairs and look at page 8. They then take turns asking and answering questions about people and food items in the large scene, using the target patterns and vocabulary items. For example: S1 (pointing to the woman with coffee): *How many cups of coffee did she have?* S2: *She had one cup of coffee.*

C. Listen and chant.

1. Students turn to the *How Much? How Many?* chant on page 73. They cover up the text, look at the picture, and talk about what they see. Read the lyrics line by line. Students repeat each line. Play the recording. Students listen and follow along in their books.

   How Much? How Many?

   How much roast beef did you have?
       I had one slice.
   How many slices?
       One slice. I had one slice of roast beef.

   How much chicken soup did you have?
       I had two bowls.
   How many bowls?
       Two bowls. I had two bowls of chicken soup.

How much root beer did you have?
  I had three bottles.
How many bottles?
  Three bottles. I had three bottles of root beer.

How much iced tea did you have?
  I had four glasses.
How many glasses?
  Four glasses. I had four glasses of iced tea.

2. Play the recording again. Students listen and chant, using their books for reference. Play the recording as many times as necessary for students to become familiar with the chant.

3. Divide the class into Groups A and B. Play the karaoke version. Group A chants the questions and Group B chants the answers, holding up one finger in the first verse, two in the second, three in the third, and four in the fourth verse. Groups switch roles and chant again.

Games and Activities

1. **How Many Did He Have?** Divide students into groups of four to six, and give each group a set of Unit 2 Word Time Picture Cards and Unit 2 Focus Time Picture Cards. Students shuffle the cards and turn them facedown. Each group then numbers slips of paper from 1–8 and turns these facedown. A student in each group (S1) begins by picking up a number card that he/she doesn't show to the others. S2 turns over a picture card, points to S1, and asks S3 *How (many) (slices of) (ham) did (he) have?* S3 looks at S1's number card and answers *(He) had (three) (slices of) (ham)*. Groups continue in the same way with the remaining cards, changing roles each time. Remind students that if they turn over a Word Time Picture Card, they ask *How much...* and if they turn over a Focus Time Picture Card, they ask *How many...*.

2. **What Did You Eat?** Each student makes a list of the ten Unit 2 target foods. They then write down how many of each item they have eaten in the last week. Divide the class into pairs and have students in each pair take turns using the target patterns to ask each other about what they have eaten (students can take notes if necessary to remember what their partner says). Pairs continue for four to five minutes. Then ask students questions about what they found out. For example: Ask *How many cans of lemonade did Kim have?* Kim's partner responds *Kim had one can of lemonade.*

OPTIONS:
1. Quickly teach students the word *about* so that they can approximate quantities that they're not sure of. For example: *I had about four slices of roast beef.*

2. Quickly teach students the pattern *I didn't have any (garlic bread).*

3. **Survey.** Write *How much?* and *How many?* in a row at the top of the board. Under *How much?* write *candy (pieces of)*, *soda pop (bottles of)*, *glue (bottles of)*, *tape (rolls of)*, and *paper (pieces of)* in a column. Under *How many?* write *pencils, sisters, brothers, books, eyes, ears,* and *hands*. Point to each word and have students read it. Quickly review meaning if necessary. Then divide the class into groups of three to four. Students in each group take turns asking each other *How many/How much* questions about the items on the board. For example: *How many pencils do you have?* Students can take notes if necessary to remember what their classmates say. Groups continue for five to six minutes. Then ask students questions about what they found out. For example: Ask *How much paper does Ron have?* Students who know this information respond *Ron has ten pieces of paper.*

OPTIONS:
1. Quickly teach students the word *about* so that they can approximate quantities that they're not sure of. For example: *I have about ten pieces of paper.*

2. Quickly teach students the pattern *I don't have any (paper).*

> **Extra Practice**
> Explain and assign Worksheet 3, How Many?/How Much?, page 190. (For instructions and answer key, see page 183.)

Finish the Lesson

1. **Share the Answer.** Ask a student *How many fingers do you have?* Continue around the classroom for three to four minutes, asking students questions about body parts they can name in English.

2. Explain and assign Workbook page 10. (For instructions, see Teacher's Book page 160.)

Reading Time

Language Focus: Reading a restaurant review

Materials Needed: CD/cassette and player; copies of reading, 1 per 6–8 students; Unit 2 Word Time Word Cards, 1 set; Unit 2 Focus Time Word Cards, 1 set (see Picture and Word Card Book pages 6 and 8)

For general information on Reading Time, see pages 16–17.

Warm-Up and Review

1. **Pattern Review: What Did You Have for Dinner?** Attach the Unit 2 Word Time Word Cards in a row to the board, then write *How much _____ did you have?* and *I had _____.* below the cards. Attach the Unit 2 Focus Time Word Cards in another row to the board, then write *How many _____ of _____ did you have?* and *I had _____.* below the cards. Pairs of volunteers read one of the questions and answers, filling in the blanks with different food items and quantities. Continue until most students have taken a turn.

2. Check Workbook page 10. (For instructions and answer key, see Teacher's Book page 160.)

Introduce the Reading

Note: Students may learn the new vocabulary within the context of the reading, or each new word can be taught before students encounter it in the reading. Follow the steps below to introduce the new vocabulary and/or introduce the reading content.

1. Write the new words in a column on the board. Point to and read each word before explaining its meaning.

   new: Explain that when you buy something in a store it is new. If you have had something for a while, it is old.

   Italian: Explain that people or things that come from Italy are called Italian.

   downtown: Explain that downtown refers to the main business area of a town, and usually has stores, restaurants, banks, and other businesses.

   owner: Explain that the person who has paid for and is in charge of something is called the owner.

   real: Write *real = true* on the board.

   chef: Say *A chef is a person who cooks food at a restaurant.*

   best: Enthusiastically say *Chocolate cake is my favorite. I like it best.*

   price: Write $2 on the back of a notebook. Show students and say *This costs two dollars. The price is two dollars.*

   A.M./P.M.: Explain that A.M. is used to denote times between midnight and noon. For times between noon and midnight, P.M. is used.

   serve: Say *There's a restaurant that serves breakfast and lunch. This means that you can eat breakfast and lunch there.*

2. Students open their Student Books to page 11. They look at the reading and pictures and talk about what they see. For example: *This is from a newspaper. Here is a restaurant.* Ask students what they think the reading will be about.

Practice the Reading

Students read the article silently to themselves.

A. Listen and read along.

1. Play the recording. Students listen and read along in their Student Books.

   Papa Joe's Restaurant Opens
   by Shawn Long

   Papa Joe's is a new Italian restaurant in downtown Sunnyville. It opened on May 5th. Who is Papa Joe? Is it the owner, Mr. Minelli? No! The real Papa Joe is Mr. Minelli's father. Papa Joe is the chef at Papa Joe's Restaurant.

   Last Saturday, Kelly Jones and her friend DeeDee Smith had lunch at Papa Joe's. "Their pizza is the best pizza in town," Kelly said. DeeDee said, "I'm going to bring my children here. Kids under five eat free!"

   Papa Joe's is clean and the prices are good. The address is 12 Pine Street. They're open daily from 11:00 A.M. to 10:00 P.M. They serve lunch and dinner.

New Words
new
Italian
downtown
owner
real
chef
best
price
A.M./P.M.
serve

2. Play the recording again, stopping it after each sentence. Students listen and repeat each sentence.

3. Divide the class into pairs. Students in each pair take turns reading the article aloud to their partner.

B. Listen and circle True or False.

1. Play the recording. For each number, students listen and circle *True* if the statement is true, and *False* if it is not.

   1. *Papa Joe's is a bakery.*
   2. *Kelly Jones said, "Their pasta is the best pasta in town."*
   3. *Kids under five eat free.*
   4. *Papa Joe's serves breakfast and lunch.*

2. Check answers by saying *Number 1. Papa Joe's is a bakery.* Students say *True* if they circled *True*, and *False* if they circled *False*. If the statement is false, choose a volunteer to make it true. Do the same for numbers 2–4.

   Answer Key:
   1. False   2. False   3. True   4. False

C. Read the question. Write the answer.

1. Students read each question and answer it based on the reading in exercise A.

2. Check answers by reading each question and having students read the answer they wrote.

   Answer Key:
   1. What is the name of the restaurant? <u>The name of the restaurant is Papa Joe's.</u>
   2. Where is Papa Joe's? <u>Papa Joe's is in downtown Sunnyville.</u> or <u>Papa Joe's is at 12 Pine Street.</u>
   3. Who is Papa Joe? <u>Papa Joe is Mr. Minelli's father. He is the chef at Papa Joe's restaurant.</u>
   4. When is Papa Joe's open? <u>Papa Joe's is open daily from 11:00 A.M. to 10:00 P.M.</u>

Games and Activities

Note: For all Reading Time activities, students may use their Student Books for reference.

1. **Sentence Strips.** Divide the class into groups of six to eight and give each group a copy of the reading. Students in each group cut the reading so that each sentence is on a separate strip of paper. They then shuffle the strips. Play the recording. Students in each group work together to put the strips in order. Play the recording as many times as necessary for students to complete the task. Then have each group read a paragraph to the class.

   OPTION: Give students enlarged photocopies of the reading.

2. **Definitions.** Divide the class into Teams A and B. Then say *People eat there*. The first student to name the corresponding word from the reading, *restaurant,* wins a point for his/her team. Do the same with six to seven other words from the reading (see Suggested Definitions below). The team with the most points at the end wins.

   Suggested Definitions:
   not old (new)
   this person owns a restaurant (owner *or* Mr. Minelli)
   this person cooks at the restaurant (chef *or* Papa Joe)
   children (kids)
   an Italian food (pizza)
   not dirty (clean)
   every day (daily)

3. **Use It in a Sentence.** Say *new*. A volunteer says a sentence using *new* (this can be either an original sentence or a sentence from the reading). Do the same with the remaining new words from the lesson.

> **Extra Practice**
> Explain and assign Worksheet 4, Annie's Diary, page 191. (For instructions and answer key, see page 183.)

Finish the Lesson

1. **Please Correct Me.** Read sentences or parts of sentences from the reading, replacing one word in each utterance. Students follow in their Student Books and repeat each utterance, putting the word from the reading back in. For example: Say *Papa Joe's is an old Italian restaurant.* Students say *Papa Joe's is a new Italian restaurant.* Continue for three to four minutes.

2. Explain and assign Workbook page 11. (For instructions, see Teacher's Book page 160.)

Your Time

Language Focus: Personalizing food and quantity language

Materials Needed: CD/cassette and player

For general information on Your Time, see pages 18–19.

Warm-Up and Review

1. **Reading Review: In Your Own Words.** Students open their Student Books to page 11 and take two to three minutes to read the restaurant review. Then have students take turns telling the class—in their own words—something about the reading. For example: *This reading is about a new restaurant.* Continue until most students have taken a turn. It is okay if more than one student tells the same information.

2. Check Workbook page 11. (For instructions and answer key, see Teacher's Book page 160.)

Introduce the Lesson

Ask students five to six questions relating to food (see Suggested Questions below).

Suggested Questions:
What's your favorite food?
Do you like Italian food?
How much lemonade did you drink yesterday?
How many bowls of chicken soup can you eat?
Do you like ice cream?
What's your favorite flavor of ice cream?

Practice the Lesson

Students open their Student Books to page 12.

A. Listen and answer the questions.

1. Play the recording. For each number, students listen to the question and answer it based on their own knowledge and experience.

   1. *How many glasses of iced tea can you drink?*
   2. *How many slices of roast beef can you eat?*
   3. *How much lemonade can you drink?*
   4. *How much fruit salad can you eat?*

2. Check answers by dividing the class into pairs and having students in each pair read one question and answer to the class.

   Answer Key:
   Answers will vary.

B. Ask your classmates. Write their names and circle Yes or No.

Quickly review the following patterns: *Do you want (a slice of ham) for dinner? Yes, I do./No, I don't.* Students then go around the classroom and ask their classmates *Do you want (a slice of ham) for dinner?* Students respond *Yes, I do* or *No, I don't.* Students record their classmates' names and answers on their surveys. Continue until all students have asked four other students the questions. Students sit down. Then ask students questions about the survey. For example: Ask *Does Bill want a bowl of fruit salad for dinner?* Students who know this information respond either *Yes, he does* or *No, he doesn't.*

C. Review. Read and write the answers.

1. Students read each question and write an answer based on their own knowledge and experience.

2. Check answers by dividing the class into pairs and having students in each pair read one question and answer to the class.

   Answer Key:
   Answers will vary.

Games and Activities

1. **Memory Chain.** (See Game 18, page 156.) Play the game using *My favorite food is (pizza)*.

   OPTION: Play the game using *I want a (slice) of (ham) for dinner*.

2. **What Will You Eat?** Students write down how much of various types of food they plan to eat in the next week. They then get together with a partner. Each student asks his/her partner *How much (pizza) will you eat?* and records the answers.

3. **Alien Interview.** Divide the class into groups of four to six. One student in each group is an alien from outer space visiting the planet Earth. The other group members interview the alien, asking him/her questions like *What's your favorite food?/What did you have (this morning)?/How much (cake) can you eat/drink?* and writing down the answers. Then each group reports to the class on their alien.

Finish the Lesson

1. **Alien Pets.** Elicit names of eight animals/pets from the class and write the words in a row at the top of the board. Bring four volunteers (aliens) to the front of the classroom. Each volunteer stands below a word on the board. Seated students take turns asking the aliens questions about their animals/pets. For example: *How much milk can your chimpanzee drink?/How many slices of roast beef can your cheetah eat?* The volunteers answer. Encourage students to use a variety of food items in their questions and allow volunteers to give exaggerated answers. Continue with another four volunteers.

2. Explain and assign Workbook page 12. (For instructions, see Teacher's Book page 160.)

3. Do Chapter 1 of Storybook 5, *Digger and the Thief*. (For instructions and answer key, see Teacher's Book pages 180 and 181.)

> **Assessment**
> Explain and assign the Unit 2 Test, page 217. (For instructions and answer key, see page 208.)

3 Daily Activities

Conversation Time

Language Focus: Shopping for a pie at a bakery

Materials Needed: CD/cassette and player; Wall Chart 5

For general information on Conversation Time, see pages 8–9.

Warm-Up and Review

1. **Review: Food.** Ask students questions about what they ate yesterday. For example: *Who ate fruit on (Tuesday)? (Mari), how much fruit did you have?* Continue for three to four minutes.

2. Check Workbook page 12. (For instructions and answer key, see Teacher's Book page 160.)

Introduce the Conversation

1. Set the scene and clarify the meaning by saying *Today's conversation is at a bakery. A man wants to buy a pie.* Then introduce the new words by writing each word on the board. Point to and read each word before explaining its meaning. Students repeat the word.

   expensive: Write $1 on the back of a notebook and $1,000 on the back of another notebook. Hold up the $1 notebook and say *This is cheap.* Then hold up the $1,000 notebook and say *This is expensive!*

   fresh: Draw two vases of flowers on the board, one with fresh, perky flowers, and the other with droopy, wilted flowers. Point to the vase of fresh flowers and say *fresh.* Point to the wilted flowers and say *not fresh.*

2. Bring two students to the front of the classroom. Stand behind each student and model his/her lines of the conversation with the following actions:

   A: *Good morning. Can I help you?*
   Speak pleasantly and smile.

   B: *Yes, please. What kinds of pie do you have today?*
   Speak quizzically.

   A: *We have lemon, peach, and blueberry.*
   Speak pleasantly.

   B: *Do you have any cherry pies?*
   Speak quizzically. Stress *cherry.*

   A: *Sorry. We're out of cherry. But the blueberry pies are very nice.*
   Shake your head and look a little sad. Then smile and speak a little more happily.

   B: *How much are they?*
   Speak quizzically.

   A: *They're ten dollars each.*
   Hold up ten fingers.

   B: *Oh, that's too expensive. How much are the peach pies?*
   Speak a little sadly.

   A: *They're five dollars each.*
   Hold up five fingers.

   B: *Okay. I'll take one.*
   Nod and smile. Reach into your pocket as if to take out money.

   A: *Great! I'll get a fresh pie for you.*
   Speak enthusiastically. Then turn and start to walk away.

3. Divide the class into Groups A and B. Model the conversation again using facial expressions and body language. Group A repeats the first line of the conversation, Group B repeats line two, and so on. Encourage students to copy your facial expressions and body language. Groups change roles and say the conversation again in the same way.

4. Attach Wall Chart 5 to the board or open a Student Book to page 13. Students then open their Student Books to page 13. Ask the following questions:

   What kinds of pie do you see?
   Does the baker have any lemon pies?
   What kind of pie does the man want? Does the baker have any cherry pies?
   How much are the blueberry pies? Is that expensive?
   How much are the peach pies?
   What kind of pie does the customer buy?

Practice the Conversation

A. Listen and repeat. Point to the speakers. Then listen again.

1. Play the recording (first version of the conversation). Students listen and repeat, pointing to each speaker.

   1. Baker: *Good morning. Can I help you?*
      Customer: *Yes, please. What kinds of pie do you have today?*
   2. Baker: *We have lemon, peach, and blueberry.*
   3. Customer: *Do you have any cherry pies?*
      Baker: *Sorry. We're out of cherry. But the blueberry pies are very nice.*
   4. Customer: *How much are they?*
      Baker: *They're ten dollars each.*
   5. Customer: *Oh, that's too expensive. How much are the peach pies?*
      Baker: *They're five dollars each.*
   6. Customer: *Okay. I'll take one.*
      Baker: *Great! I'll get a fresh pie for you.*

2. Play the recording (second version of the conversation). Students listen.

B. Role-play the conversation.

Students choose a partner and, using their Student Books for reference, role-play the conversation. They then change roles and role-play the conversation again.

Games and Activities

Note: For all Conversation Time activities, students may use their Student Books for reference.

1. **Listen Carefully.** Write the following sentences on the board. Play the recording of the conversation. Students listen and write the missing words to complete each sentence.

   1. The bakery has lemon, _____ , and blueberry pies.
   2. They're out of _____ pies.
   3. The blueberry pies are _____ dollars each.
   4. The peach pies are _____ dollars each.

   Check answers by saying *Number 1.* A volunteer reads the complete sentence. Do the same for numbers 2–4.

   Answer Key:
   1. The bakery has lemon, <u>peach</u>, and blueberry pies.
   2. They're out of <u>cherry</u> pies.
   3. The blueberry pies are <u>ten</u> dollars each.
   4. The peach pies are <u>five</u> dollars each.

2. **Match the Halves.** Divide the class into pairs. Students in each pair write the contents of each speech bubble from the conversation on a separate piece of paper and then cut each piece of paper in half. Pairs shuffle the pieces of paper and place them facedown. Say *Go!* Pairs try to be the first to turn over the pieces of paper, match each half, and put the complete speech bubbles in the correct order. The first pair to do so raises their hands and says the conversation they have put together. If it is correct, they come to the front of the classroom and role-play the conversation for the rest of the class. If it is not correct, all pairs continue to work until one pair has put together the correct conversation. Students then change partners and do the activity again.

3. **Make It Your Own.** Write the following on the board:

   A: *Can I help you?*
   B: <u>*Yes, please. What kinds of pie do you have today?*</u>

   Students read the dialogue on the board. Then divide the class into pairs and write the following on the board:

   1. *Yes, please. Can you tell me where the skirts are?*
   2. *No, thank you. I'm just looking.*
   3. *Yes. Do you have this shirt in red?*

   Students read each new response. Quickly clarify meaning if necessary. Then students in each pair role-play the dialogue on the board, substituting the new responses into the underlined part of the target conversation.

Finish the Lesson

1. **Discussion.** Have a short discussion (for about three to four minutes) with the class, talking about when and where they might have a conversation in which they are talking to a store clerk about buying something.

2. Explain and assign Workbook page 13. (For instructions, see Teacher's Book page 161.)

Word Time

Language Focus: Daily activities (*walk to school, go to the dentist, do laundry, chop vegetables, iron a shirt, slice fruit, take a bus, wash my hair, stay home, buy groceries*)

Materials Needed (excluding materials for optional activities):
CD/cassette and player; Wall Chart 6; Unit 3 Word Time Picture Cards, 1 card per student; Unit 3 Word Time Word Cards, 1 set (see Picture and Word Card Book pages 9 and 10)

For more general information on Word Time, see pages 10–11.

Warm-Up and Review

1. **Conversation Review: Say the Next Word.** Play the recording of the Unit 3 conversation. Students listen. Then, using a Student Book for reference if necessary, a volunteer says the first word of the conversation. The student sitting behind him/her says the next word. Continue around the class with each student saying the next word in the conversation, until the entire conversation has been said.

2. Check Workbook page 13. (For instructions and answer key, see Teacher's Book page 161.)

Introduce the Words

1. Hold up and name each of the Unit 3 Word Time Picture Cards. Students listen. Hold up and name the cards again, and have students repeat. Hold up each card in random order and have students name it and then pretend to be doing the action.

2. Attach the Unit 3 Word Time Picture Cards in a row to the board. Stand the Unit 3 Word Time Word Cards on the chalktray under the corresponding picture cards. Point to each picture/word card pair and read the word. Students repeat. Then reposition the word cards so they are no longer directly below the corresponding picture cards. Volunteers come to the board one by one and place a word card under its corresponding picture card, then point to and read the word. Seated students repeat.

Talk About the Picture

1. Students open their Student Books to page 14. They look at the large scene and use complete sentences to identify anything they can.

2. Attach Wall Chart 6 to the board or open a Student Book to page 14. Read the following "story" while pointing to or touching the pictures (**bold** words) and pantomiming the actions (*italicized* words).

   What are people doing today? The **little girl** is *staying home* with her **father**. **This boy** is *chopping vegetables*. In the bathroom, **this boy's mom** is *washing his hair*. **These boys** are *doing laundry*. **Grandpa Day** is *ironing a shirt*. **This girl** is *slicing fruit*. Others are out in the town: going to the dentist, buying **groceries**. Ted and Matt are taking a **bus**.

3. Ask the following questions while pointing to or touching the pictures (**bold** words).

   (**girl slicing fruit**) What's she doing?
   (**banana**) What's this?
   Can you point to the boy buying groceries?
   Who's taking the bus? Point to them.
   (**boys doing the laundry**) What are they doing?
   Do you like to do laundry?
   Do you like taking the bus?

Practice the Words

A. Listen and repeat.

1. Play the recording. Students listen and repeat, pointing to each word in the vocabulary box.

   1. *walk to school*
   2. *go to the dentist*
   3. *do laundry*
   4. *chop vegetables*
   5. *iron a shirt*
   6. *slice fruit*
   7. *take a bus*
   8. *wash my hair*
   9. *stay home*
   10. *buy groceries*

2. Say the words in random order. Students point to them in the vocabulary box.

B. Point and say the words

Students point to each of the target vocabulary items in the large scene and name them.

C. 🔊 Listen and point.

Play the recording. Students listen to the words. For the vocabulary, they point to the person doing the named action; for the conversations, they point to the speakers. (References are shown in parentheses.) Play the recording as many times as necessary for students to complete the task.

> *Do laundry.*
> *Take a bus.*
> *Go to the dentist.*
> *Slice fruit.*
> *Iron a shirt.*
> *Buy groceries.*
> *Walk to school.*
> *Wash my hair.*
> *Chop vegetables.*
> *Stay home.*
>
> *Now listen and point to the speakers.*
>
> A: *Was there a mouse beside that tree?* (Ted and friend)
> B: *Where?*
> A: *Beside that tree, on the sidewalk.*
> B: *I don't know.*
>
> A: *Hi, Mr. Clay. How much is a medium apple juice?* (clerk and girl at juice stand)
> B: *It's two dollars.*
> A: *Great! I'll take one, please.*
> B: *Here you are.*
>
> A: *Look! My apple is bigger than your apple.* (Annie and friend)
> B: *But I'm so hungry.*
> A: *Here. You can have mine.*
> B: *Thanks!*

Games and Activities

1. **Charades.** Divide the class into groups of five to six and give each group a set of Unit 3 Word Time Picture Cards. A student in each group begins by looking at a picture card and then pantomiming the action. The first student to correctly name the action, saying *You're (ironing a shirt)*, is next to pantomime an action. Groups continue in this way for five to seven minutes.

2. **When Do You…?** Have students stand in two parallel lines and give each student a Unit 3 Word Time Picture Card. Each student faces the student directly across from him/her and holds up his/her picture card. Partners ask and answer *When do you (wash your hair)? I (wash my hair) (in the morning)*. Then students in each line pass their card to the right and repeat the exchange. Continue until students receive their starting card.

3. **Survey.** Students create a survey on a sheet of paper by writing *Name* and *Do you like to _____?* in a row at the top of the paper. Then they write a list of six activities along the left side of the paper. They then go around the classroom and ask their classmates *Do you like to (do laundry)?* Students respond *Yes, I like to (do laundry)* or *No, I don't like to (do laundry)*. Students record their classmates' names and answers on their surveys. Continue until all students have asked six students the questions. Students sit down. Then ask students questions about the survey. For example: Ask *Does Bill like to do laundry?* Students who know this information respond either *Yes, he does* or *No, he doesn't*.

4. **Option: Personalize the Vocabulary.** Divide the class into pairs and give them three to four minutes to talk with their partner about the activities they plan to do in the next week (students can take notes if necessary to remember what their partner says). Then each pair joins with another pair and each student tells the others about his/her partner's plans.

   OPTION: Do the activity as above, also having students draw pictures to illustrate their partner's plans.

Finish the Lesson

1. **Categorize.** Divide the board into two columns. Write *at home* at the top of the first column, and *not at home* at the top of the second column. Say *buy groceries* and have a volunteer point to the corresponding column on the board. A different volunteer says *We don't buy groceries at home*. Write *buy groceries* in the *not at home* column. Do the same with the remaining target actions. Then point to each column and have students read the words.

2. Explain and assign Workbook page 14. (For instructions, see Teacher's Book page 161.)

Focus Time

Language Focus: By + reflexive pronouns (*by myself, by himself, by herself, by yourself, by yourselves, by themselves, by ourselves*)

Simple past, affirmative and negative statements [*I (ironed a shirt) by (myself)./I didn't (iron a shirt) by (myself).*]

Function: Expressing activities in the past

Materials Needed: CD/cassette and player; Unit 3 Word Time Picture Cards, 1 card per student; Unit 3 Word Time Word Cards, 1 set per 2 students; Unit 3 Focus Time Picture Cards, 1 set; Unit 3 Focus Time Word Cards, 1 set per 2 students; *I, You, He, She, We,* and *They* grammar cards, 1 set per 2 students; Unit 3 Grammar Cards, 1 set per 2 students (see Picture and Word Card Book pages 9, 10, 11, 12, 43, 44, 48, and 53)

For general information on Focus Time, see pages 12–13.

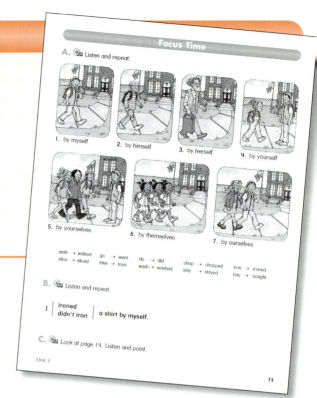

Warm-Up and Review

1. **Vocabulary Review: Slow Reveal.** (See Game 15, page 155.) Hold up each Unit 3 Word Time Picture Card and have students name it. Then play the game using the cards.
2. Check Workbook page 14. (For instructions and answer key, see Teacher's Book page 161.)

This lesson is in two parts.

Part 1: Introduce the Words

Bring three volunteers (at least one should be a boy) to the front of the classroom. Ask them to walk around the classroom, with two of them walking together, and the third volunteer (a boy) walking by himself. Point to the two volunteers walking together and say *They're walking together*. Point to the volunteer walking by himself and say *by himself. He's walking by himself*. Students repeat *by himself*. Write *by himself* on the board. Point to and read each word. Students repeat. Do the same with a girl for *herself*. Then hold up and name each Unit 3 Focus Time Picture Card. Students listen. Hold up and name each card again and have students repeat.

Practice the Words

Students open their Student Books to page 15.

A. Listen and repeat.

Play the recording. Students listen and repeat each word.

1. *by myself*
2. *by himself*
3. *by herself*
4. *by yourself*
5. *by yourselves*
6. *by themselves*
7. *by ourselves*

walk, walked
go, went
do, did
chop, chopped
iron, ironed
slice, sliced
take, took
wash, washed
stay, stayed
buy, bought

Part 2: Introduce the Patterns

1. **(I) (walked/didn't walk to school) by (myself).** Have a volunteer (S1) walk to the classroom door. After he/she reaches the door, have him/her stop. Point to him/her and say *(She) walked by (herself)*. Students repeat. Write *She walked by herself.* on the board. Point to and read each word. Students repeat. Then have another volunteer walk with S1 to the door. Point to S1 and say *(She) didn't walk by (herself)*. Students repeat. Write *She didn't walk by herself.* on the board. Point to and read each word. Students repeat. Do the same with *iron a shirt, chop vegetables,* and *buy groceries*, having the volunteers pantomime each action.

2. **Practice for Fluency.** Say *stay home, they*. Students say *They stayed home by themselves*. Then shake your head *no*. Students say *They didn't stay home by themselves*. Do the same with different actions and pronouns for three to four minutes.

50   Unit 3

Practice the Patterns

B. 🔊 Listen and repeat.

1. Write the text from the pattern boxes on the board. Then play the recording, pointing to each word. Students listen.

   I ironed a shirt by myself.
   I didn't iron a shirt by myself.

2. Play the recording again. Students listen, look at the pattern boxes in their books, and repeat, pointing to each word.

3. Students work with partners to say the sentences, while looking at the pattern boxes in their books.

C. 🔊 Look at page 14. Listen and point.

Play the recording. Students look at page 14 and listen to the words, pointing to the person/people doing each action they hear named. Play the recording as many times as necessary for students to complete the task.

   She cut fruit by herself.
   She didn't wash her hair by herself.
   They took a bus by themselves.

Games and Activities

1. **Write the Word.** Write the following sentences on the board. Students write each one, filling in the blanks with the appropriate emphatic pronoun.

   1. I sliced fruit by _____.
   2. You sliced fruit by _____. (one person)
   3. He sliced fruit by _____.
   4. She sliced fruit by _____.
   5. We sliced fruit by _____.
   6. You sliced fruit by _____. (two people)
   7. They sliced fruit by _____.

   Check answers by saying *Number 1* and having a volunteer read the whole sentence. Do the same for numbers 2–7.

   Answer Key:
   1. I sliced fruit by <u>myself</u>.
   2. You sliced fruit by <u>yourself</u>. (one person)
   3. He sliced fruit by <u>himself</u>.
   4. She sliced fruit by <u>herself</u>.
   5. We sliced fruit by <u>ourselves</u>.
   6. You sliced fruit by <u>yourselves</u>. (two people)
   7. They sliced fruit by <u>themselves</u>.

2. **Pantomime.** Say *walk*. Students say its simple past form, *walked*. Do the same with the remaining target verbs. Then bring four volunteers to the front of the classroom. Ask one of them (S1) to step away from the other volunteers, pantomime slicing fruit, and then stop. Seated students point to S1 and say *(He) sliced fruit (by himself)*. Then have all four volunteers pantomime taking a bus together. Point to S1 and elicit *(He) didn't take the bus by (himself)*. Do the same with different actions for four to five minutes, sometimes having S1 do the action by (himself) and sometimes with the other volunteers. Each time, seated students say the target pattern about S1.

3. **Make the Sentences.** (See Game 17, pages 155–156.) Do the activity using *I, You, He, She, We,* and *They* grammar cards and Unit 3 Word Time Word Cards, Focus Time Word Cards, and Grammar Cards.

Finish the Lesson

1. **Family Chart.** Draw a ten-column/five-row chart on the board. On top of each column attach one of the Unit 3 Word Time Picture Cards. To the left of the rows write names of family members: *my baby sister, my big brothers, my mother, my father,* and *my grandmother*. Above the chart write YESTERDAY. Students take turns making sentences about each family member. For example: *My baby sister didn't stay home by herself yesterday. My big brothers went to the dentist by themselves yesterday.* A volunteer checks the appropriate box for each positive statement and crosses out the appropriate box for each negative statement. Continue until most students have made a sentence.

2. Explain and assign Workbook page 15. (For instructions, see Teacher's Book page 161.)

Practice Time

Language Focus: By + reflexive pronouns; simple past, affirmative and negative statements [(You) (walked to school) by (yourselves).]

Function: Expressing activities in the past

Materials Needed: CD/cassette and player; Unit 3 Word Time Picture Cards, 1 set per 3–4 students (see Picture and Word Card Book page 9)

For general information on Practice Time, see pages 14–15.

Warm-Up and Review

1. **Pattern Review: True Sentences.** Write *They did laundry by themselves. They didn't slice fruit by themselves.* on the board. Point to each sentence and have students read it. Then have each student say a true sentence about something he/she or somebody in his/her family did or did not do by themselves yesterday.

2. Check Workbook page 15. (For instructions and answer key, see Teacher's Book page 161.)

Practice the Patterns

Students open their Student Books to page 16.

A.  **Listen and repeat. Then practice with a partner.**

1. Play the recording. Students listen and repeat, pointing to each picture in their books.

   You walked to school by yourselves.

   1. *I sliced fruit by myself.*
   2. *You didn't wash your hair by yourself.*
   3. *He bought groceries by himself.*
   4. *We took a bus by ourselves.*
   5. *She didn't go to the dentist by herself.*
   6. *You chopped vegetables by yourself.*
   7. *They did laundry by themselves.*
   8. *She didn't stay home by herself.*

2. Students practice numbers 1–8 in pairs. They then change partners and repeat the activity.

B. Look at page 14. Practice with a partner.

Students remain in pairs and look at page 14. They then take turns making statements about the large scene using the target patterns and vocabulary items. For example: S1 (pointing to the little girl with her father in the doorway): *She didn't stay home by herself.* S2 (pointing to the boy chopping vegetables): *He chopped vegetables by himself.*

C. **Listen and sing along.**

1. Students turn to the *I Stayed Home By Myself* song on page 74. They cover up the text, look at the pictures, and talk about what they see. Read the lyrics line by line. Students repeat each line. Play the recording. Students listen and follow along in their books.

   I Stayed Home By Myself
   (Melody: *Michael, Row the Boat Ashore*)

   I stayed home by myself.
     By yourself.
   She stayed home by herself.
     By herself.
   We did laundry by ourselves.
     By yourselves.
   They did laundry by themselves.
     By themselves.

   I walked to school by myself.
     By yourself.
   He walked to school by himself.
     By himself.
   We took a bus by ourselves.
     By yourselves.
   They took a bus by themselves.
     By themselves.

2. Play the recording again. Students listen and sing along, using their books for reference. Play the recording as many times as necessary for students to become familiar with the song.

3. Divide the class into Groups A and B. Play the karaoke version. Group A sings the un-indented lines, pantomiming each action as they sing it. Group B sings the indented lines. Groups switch roles and sing the song again.

Games and Activities

1. **True Sentences.** Divide the class into groups of three to four, and give each group a set of Unit 3 Word Time Picture Cards. A student in each group begins by picking up a picture card and using the verb phrase in a true sentence. For example: *I didn't buy groceries by myself on Friday* or *On Tuesday, I chopped vegetables by myself.* The other students in the group point to the volunteer and say *(He) (didn't) (buy groceries) by (himself) on (Friday)* or *On (Tuesday), (he) (chopped vegetables) by (himself).* Groups continue in the same way for four to five minutes.

2. **Chart.** Divide the class into pairs and write the following chart on the board:

	stay home	do laundry	buy groceries
Past	They stayed home by themselves.		
Present	They stay home by themselves.		
Future	They'll stay home by themselves.		

   Each pair copies the chart onto a piece of paper and completes it, using the example sentences as guides.

3. **Talking.** Divide the class into pairs and give them three to four minutes to talk with their partners about things they did by themselves in the last week (students can take notes if necessary to remember what their partner says). Then each pair joins with another pair and each student tells the others about his/her partner's activities. Students can use any vocabulary they know.

   OPTION: Do the activity as above, also having students draw pictures to illustrate their partner's activities.

   Extra Practice
   Explain and assign Worksheet 5, Play a Game, page 192. (For instructions and answer key, see page 184.)

Finish the Lesson

1. **Present to Past.** Say *I go to the dentist by myself.* A volunteer changes the sentence into the past tense, saying *I went to the dentist by myself.* Continue in this way until all of the target verb phrases have been changed from present to past.

2. Explain and assign Workbook page 16. (For instructions, see Teacher's Book pages 161–162.)

Reading Time

Language Focus: Reading a short story

Materials Needed: CD/cassette and player; Unit 3 Word Time Picture Cards, 1 card per student (see Picture and Word Card Book page 9)

For general information on Reading Time, see pages 16–17.

Warm-Up and Review

1. **Pattern Review: Activities in the Past.** Write *I went to the dentist by myself. I didn't take a bus by myself.* on the board. Point to each sentence and have students read it. Then give each student a Unit 3 Word Time Picture Card. A volunteer (S1) begins by standing up, showing the class his/her card, and saying *I (walked to school) by myself.* The student behind him/her stands up, shows the class his/her card, and says *I didn't (walk to school) by myself. I (went to the dentist) by myself.* Continue in this way until all students have taken a turn.

2. Check Workbook page 16. (For instructions and answer key, see Teacher's Book pages 161–162.)

Introduce the Reading

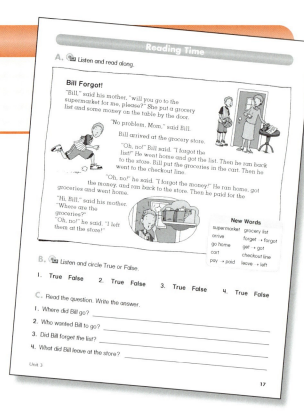

Note: Students may learn the new vocabulary within the context of the reading, or each new word can be taught before students encounter it in the reading. Follow the steps below to introduce the new vocabulary and/or introduce the reading content.

1. Write the new words in a column on the board. Point to and read each word before explaining its meaning.

   supermarket: Say *A supermarket is a big store where you can buy groceries.*

   grocery list: Say *I need to buy groceries. I write down the food I want to buy on a grocery list so that I remember what I need to buy.*

   arrive: Ask students *What time do you arrive at school?* Prompt them to answer.

   forget → forgot: Say *Yesterday when I was at the supermarket, I forgot my change. Forgot is the past tense of forget.*

   go home: Say *When I'm finished with class, I will go home.*

   get → got: Say *My hair was long, so yesterday I got a haircut. Now my hair is short. Got is the past tense of get.*

   cart: Pantomime putting groceries into a cart and pushing the cart. Say *When you're at the supermarket, you put your groceries in a cart.*

   checkout line: Pantomime putting groceries into a cart, pushing the cart, and then standing in the checkout line. Then pretend to put the groceries on the checkout counter. Say *You go to the checkout line so that you can give the cashier money for your groceries.*

   pay → paid: Say *When you give the cashier money for your groceries, you pay for them. Paid is the past tense of pay.*

   leave → left: Say *Yesterday I got up, ate breakfast, and then left my house at seven A.M. Left is the past tense of leave.*

2. Ask students about their own experiences with buying groceries (see Suggested Questions below).

   Suggested Questions:
   Is there a supermarket near your house?
   What is it called?
   Do you buy groceries by yourself?
   Do you go to the supermarket with your mother and father?
   Do you like going to the supermarket?
   What do you like to buy?

3. Students open their Student Books to page 17. They look at the pictures and talk about what they see. For example: *This is a story. Here is a grocery list. Here's some money. This boy is running.* Ask students what they think the reading will be about.

Practice the Reading

Students read the story silently to themselves.

A. Listen and read along.

1. Play the recording. Students listen and read along in their Student Books.

   Bill Forgot!

   "Bill," said his mother, "will you go to the supermarket for me, please?" She put a grocery list and some money on the table by the door.

   "No problem, Mom," said Bill.

Bill arrived at the grocery store.

"Oh, no!" Bill said. "I forgot the list!" He went home and got the list. Then he ran back to the store. Bill put the groceries in the cart. Then he went to the checkout line.

"Oh, no!" he said. "I forgot the money!" He ran home, got the money, and ran back to the store. Then he paid for the groceries and went home.

"Hi, Bill," said his mother. "Where are the groceries?"

"Oh, no!" he said. "I left them at the store!"

New Words
supermarket
grocery list
arrive
forget, forgot
go home
get, got
cart
checkout line
pay, paid
leave, left

2. Play the recording again, stopping it after each sentence. Students listen and repeat each sentence.

3. Divide the class into pairs. Students in each pair take turns reading the story aloud to their partner.

B. Listen and circle True or False.

1. Play the recording. For each number, students listen and circle *True* if the statement is true, and *False* if it is not.

   1. *Bill went to the supermarket with his mother.*
   2. *Bill ran to the bookstore.*
   3. *Bill forgot the money.*
   4. *Bill didn't pay for the groceries.*

2. Check answers by saying *Number 1. Bill went to the supermarket with his mother.* Students say *True* if they circled *True*, and *False* if they circled *False*. If the statement is false, choose a volunteer to make it true. Do the same for numbers 2–4.

   Answer Key:
   1. False   2. False   3. True   4. False

C. Read the question. Write the answer.

1. Students read each question and answer it based on the reading in exercise A.

2. Check answers by reading each question and having students read the answer they wrote.

   Answer Key:
   1. Where did Bill go? <u>Bill went to the grocery store.</u>
   2. Who wanted Bill to go? <u>Bill's mother wanted him to go.</u>
   3. Did Bill forget the list? <u>Yes, he did.</u>
   4. What did Bill leave at the store? <u>He left the groceries at the store.</u>

Games and Activities

Note: For all Reading Time activities, students may use their Student Books for reference.

1. **Use It in a Sentence.** Say *checkout line*. A volunteer says a sentence using *checkout line* (this can be either an original sentence or a sentence from the reading). Do the same with the remaining new words from the lesson.

2. **Act It Out.** Divide the class into groups of four to five. Two students in each group, "Bill's mother" and "Bill," stand up. The other students in the group read the narration. Bill and Bill's mother pantomime the sentences they hear and say the dialogue lines. Groups go through the entire story two to three times, changing roles each time.

3. **What Happened?** Divide the class into pairs. Students in each pair work together to write down the things Bill did, in chronological order. Students' lists may vary somewhat but should include most of the following information:

   1. Bill said he would go to the grocery store.
   2. Bill arrived at the grocery store.
   3. Bill went home and got the list.
   4. Bill ran back to the store.
   5. Bill put the groceries in the cart.
   6. Bill went to the checkout line.
   7. Bill ran home, got the money, and ran back to the store.
   8. Bill paid for the groceries.
   9. Bill went home.
   10. Bill told his mother that he left the groceries at the store.

> **Extra Practice**
> Explain and assign Worksheet 6, The Cashier's Tale, page 193. (For instructions and answer key, see page 184.)

Finish the Lesson

1. **Discussion.** Ask students to talk about tasks their parents have asked them to do. Ask them if they have ever forgotten anything they were supposed to do. Continue the discussion for four to five minutes.

2. Explain and assign Workbook page 17. (For instructions, see Teacher's Book page 162.)

Your Time

Language Focus: Personalizing daily activity language

Materials Needed: CD/cassette and player

For general information on Your Time, see pages 18–19.

Warm-Up and Review

1. **Reading Review: Changing Words.** Students open their Student Books to page 17. Read the story, changing one word in each sentence. Students raise their hands each time they hear a different word and then make the necessary correction. Then choose a volunteer to retell the story in his/her own words.

2. Check Workbook page 17. (For instructions and answer key, see Teacher's Book page 162.)

Introduce the Lesson

Ask five to six questions about students' daily activities (see Suggested Questions below).

Suggested Questions:
Do you like to do laundry?
What do you like to do on Saturdays and Sundays?
Do you take a bus in the morning?
Can you iron a shirt by yourself?
Are you going to buy groceries on Saturday?
What did you do yesterday?

Practice the Lesson

Students open their Student Books to page 18.

A. Listen and answer the questions.

1. Play the recording. For each number, students listen to the question and answer it based on their own knowledge and experience.

   1. *Did you do laundry on Tuesday?*
   2. *Did you wash your hair this morning?*
   3. *Will you eat breakfast by yourself tomorrow?*
   4. *Are you going to walk to school by yourself tomorrow?*
   5. *Can you chop vegetables by yourself?*

2. Check answers by dividing the class into pairs and having students in each pair read one question and answer to the class.

   Answer Key:
   Answers will vary.

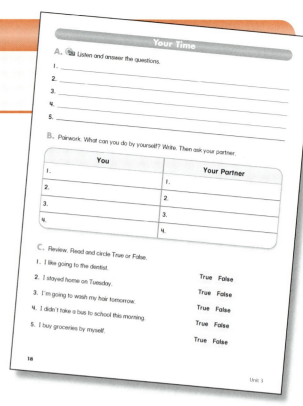

B. Pairwork. What can you do by yourself? Write. Then ask your partner.

Divide the class into pairs. Each student writes four things he/she can do by himself/herself in the *You* column of the chart. Next, each student asks his/her partner *What can you do by yourself?* and fills in the *Your Partner* column. Finally, each student tells the class about his/her partner, using the information from his/her chart. For example: *(Mari) can (do laundry) by (herself).*

C. Review. Read and circle True or False.

1. Students read each statement and circle *True* or *False* based on their own knowledge and experience.

2. Check answers by having volunteers say whether they circled *True* or *False* for each statement.

   Answer Key:
   Answers will vary.

Games and Activities

1. **Yesterday's Actions.** Divide the class into pairs. A student in each pair (S1) begins by pantomiming four different actions he/she did yesterday. His/Her partner (S2) writes down the actions he/she thinks S1 is pantomiming. Once S1 has finished pantomiming, S2 checks his/her list, asking *Did you (do laundry) yesterday?* S1 says either *Yes, I did* or *No, I didn't*. Pairs continue until S2 has an accurate list of S1's activities. Pairs then change roles and do the activity again.

2. **What Did You Do by Yourself?** Divide the class into four groups. Have students in the first group make a list of things they did and did not do by themselves when they were two years old. Students in the second group list things they did and did not do by themselves when they were four. Students in the third group make a list about when they were eight. Students in the fourth group list things they do and do not do by themselves now. Then have each group tell the class about their lists, saying, for example, *When I was two, I didn't slice fruit by myself.*

3. **Drawing.** Give students five to six minutes to draw pictures of themselves doing activities they like to do by themselves. Once students have finished drawing, divide the class into pairs. Students tell their partners about their drawings. For example: *This is me. I like to (take the bus) by myself.*

Finish the Lesson

1. **What Did They Do Yesterday?** Volunteers tell the class activities their mother and/or father did yesterday. Then other volunteers say what they will do by themselves when they are older and live by themselves.

2. Explain and assign Workbook page 18. (For instructions, see Teacher's Book page 162.)

Assessment
Explain and assign the Unit 3 Test, page 218. (For instructions and answer key, see page 209.)

Unit 3

4 Visiting a Movie Studio

Conversation Time

Language Focus: Making a telephone call and leaving a message

Materials Needed: CD/Cassette and player; Wall Chart 7; a ball

For general information on Conversation Time, see pages 8–9.

Warm-Up and Review

1. **Review: Daily Activities.** Ask *What did you do yesterday?* and have several students respond. Then ask *What can you do by yourself?* and have several students respond. Do the same with *What will you do tomorrow?*

2. Check Workbook page 18. (For instructions and answer key, see Teacher's Book page 162.)

Introduce the Conversation

1. Set the scene and clarify meaning by saying *In today's conversation, two people are talking on the telephone. One person, Barbara, wants to talk to Robert. But he's not there. So Barbara leaves a message for Robert.*

2. Bring two students to the front of the classroom. Stand behind each student and model his/her lines of the conversation with the following actions. Each student should pretend to be holding a telephone receiver.

   A: *Hello?*
   Speak in a friendly, neutral voice.

   B: *Hello. May I speak to Robert, please?*
   Speak in a friendly, neutral voice.

   A: *He's not in right now.*
   Speak with a bit of regret in your voice.

   B: *What time will he be back?*
   Speak in a friendly, questioning voice.

   A: *I'm sorry. I don't know.*
   Speak with a bit of regret in your voice.

   B: *Can you take a message?*
   Speak in a friendly, questioning voice.

   A: *Sure. Who's calling?*
   Pick up a pencil and paper.

   B: *This is Barbara White. I'm going to be late for lunch today. I'll see him at 1:00.*
   Speak very clearly. Look at your watch (wrist) and frown slightly.

   A: *Got it. What's your number?*
   Nod while writing.

   B: *917-555-1839.*
   Speak slowly and clearly.

   A: *Okay. I'll give him your message.*
   Finish writing and speak in a friendly manner.

   B: *Thanks.*
   Smile. Wait for Student A to "hang up" the phone, then pretend to hang up the phone.

   A: *You're welcome.*
   Smile and pretend to hang up the phone.

3. Divide the class into Groups A and B. Model the conversation again using facial expressions and body language. Group A repeats the first line of the conversation, Group B repeats line two, and so on. Encourage students to copy your facial expressions and body language. Groups change roles and say the conversation again in the same way.

4. Attach Wall Chart 7 to the board or open a Student Book to page 19. Students then open their Student Books to page 19. Ask the following questions:

   Who is calling Robert?
   Is Robert in? When will he be back?
   What does Barbara want the receptionist to do?
   What's the message? Did the receptionist understand it?
   Who will the receptionist give the message to?

Practice the Conversation

A. Listen and repeat. Point to the speakers. Then listen again.

1. Play the recording (first version of the conversation). Students listen and repeat, pointing to each speaker.

   1. Man: *Hello?*
      Woman: *Hello. May I speak to Robert, please?*
      Man: *He's not in right now.*

   2. Woman: *What time will he be back?*
      Man: *I'm sorry. I don't know.*

   3. Woman: *Can you take a message?*
      Man: *Sure. Who's calling?*

   4. Woman: *This is Barbara White. I'm going to be late for lunch today. I'll see him at 1:00.*

   5. Man: *Got it. What's your number?*
      Woman: *917-555-1839.*

   6. Man: *Okay. I'll give him your message.*
      Woman: *Thanks.*
      Man: *You're welcome.*

2. Play the recording (second version of the conversation). Students listen.

B. Role-play the conversation.

Students choose a partner and, using their Student Books for reference, role-play the conversation. They then change roles and role-play the conversation again.

Games and Activities

Note: For all Conversation Time activities, students may use their Student Books for reference.

1. **Responses.** Divide the class into pairs. A student in each pair (S1) begins by saying the first line of dialogue in any of the scenes (except for the fourth scene). His/Her partner (S2) responds accordingly. Pairs continue in the same way with the remaining scenes. S2 then says the first lines of the dialogue in the same way and S1 responds.

2. **True/False/I Don't Know.** Say five to six statements about the conversation (see Suggested Statements below). Students say *True* if the statement is true, and *False* if it is false. If a statement is false, choose a volunteer to make it true. If students don't have enough information to determine if the statement is true or false, they say *I don't know*.

Suggested Statements:
Robert will be back at his office at 1:00.
Barbara can't meet Robert for lunch.
Barbara will be late because she has to take out the garbage.
Barbara's phone number is 917-555-1839.
Barbara wants Robert to call her back.
The man on the telephone is Robert.

3. **Make It Your Own.** Write the following on the board:

   A: *Can you take a message?*
   B: *Sure. Who's calling?*
   A: <u>*This is Barbara White.*</u>

Students read the dialogue on the board. Then divide the class into pairs and write the following on the board:

   1. *This is his friend (Sam). Could you ask Tim to call me back?*
   2. *This is his brother (Sam). I'm calling to see if Tim can meet me at 10:00 rather than 2:00.*
   3. *This is his teacher (Sam). I'm calling to remind Tim to bring his book to class.*

Students read each new response. Quickly clarify meaning if necessary. Then students in each pair role-play the dialogue on the board, substituting the new responses into the underlined part of the target conversation.

Finish the Lesson

1. **Toss the Ball.** (See Game 5, page 154.) Play the game using the target conversation.

2. Explain and assign Workbook page 19. (For instructions, see Teacher's Book pages 162–163.)

Word Time

Language Focus: Activities (*wear a wig, drive a sports car, put on makeup, fall in love, get a sunburn, listen to pop music, take a nap, talk on the phone, sign autographs, have an accident*)

Materials Needed (excluding materials for optional activities):
CD/cassette and player; Wall Chart 8; bingo markers, 12 per student; Unit 4 Word Time Picture Cards, 16 cards per student; Unit 4 Word Time Word Cards, 1 set (see Picture and Word Card Book pages 13 and 14)

For general information on Word Time, see pages 10–11.

Warm-Up and Review

1. **Conversation Review: Say It Together.** Play the recording of the Unit 4 conversation. Students listen. Then, using their Student Books for reference if necessary, students on the right and left sides of the classroom say alternate lines of the conversation.

2. Check Workbook page 19. (For instructions and answer key, see Teacher's Book pages 162–163.)

Introduce the Words

1. Hold up and name each of the Unit 4 Word Time Picture Cards. Students listen. Hold up and name the cards again, and have students repeat. Hold up the cards in random order and have students name them.

2. Attach the Unit 4 Word Time Picture Cards in a row to the board. Stand the Unit 4 Word Time Word Cards on the chalktray under the corresponding picture cards. Point to each picture/word card pair and read the word. Students repeat. Then reposition the word cards so they are no longer directly below the corresponding picture cards. Volunteers come to the board one by one and place a word card under its corresponding picture card, then point to and read the word. Seated students repeat.

Talk About the Picture

1. Students open their Student Books to page 20. They look at the large scene and use complete sentences to identify anything they can.

2. Attach Wall Chart 8 to the board or open a Student Book to page 20. Read the following "story" while pointing to or touching the pictures (**bold** words) and pantomiming the actions or adjectives (*italicized* words).

This is **Big Star Movie Studios**. The **visitors** see **a woman** *listening to pop music* and **people** *wearing wigs*. **One star** is *signing autographs*. **This actor** wants *to put on makeup* by himself. **The monster** is *tired* and is *taking a nap*. **This woman** is *trying to talk on the phone!* **She** *isn't happy* about *getting a sunburn*, but **they're** *happy* about *falling in love*. **He's** *driving a sports car* and **they** just *had an accident!* Oh! So much to see!

3. Ask the following questions while pointing to or touching the pictures (**bold** words) and pantomiming the actions or adjectives (*italicized* words).

(**people wearing wigs**) What are they wearing on their heads?
(**girl getting a sunburn**) Why isn't she *happy*?
(**man signing autographs**) What's he doing?
(**girl listening to pop music**) What's she *listening* to?
What color is the sports car?
Can you *drive* a sports car?
(**people having an accident**) What happened?
(**person taking a nap**) Is he *putting on makeup*?

60   Unit 4

Practice the Words

A. 🔊 Listen and repeat.

1. Play the recording. Students listen and repeat, pointing to each word in the vocabulary box.

   1. wear a wig
   2. drive a sports car
   3. put on makeup
   4. fall in love
   5. get a sunburn
   6. listen to pop music
   7. take a nap
   8. talk on the phone
   9. sign autographs
   10. have an accident

2. Say the words in random order. Students point to them in the vocabulary box.

B. Point and say the words.

Students point to each of the target vocabulary items in the large scene and name them.

C. 🔊 Listen and point.

Play the recording. Students listen to the sound effects and words. For the vocabulary, they point to the person/people doing the named action; for the conversations, they point to the speakers. (References are shown in parentheses.) Play the recording as many times as necessary for students to complete the task.

Take a nap.
Fall in love.
Drive a sports car.
Talk on the phone.
Sign autographs.
Get a sunburn.
Put on makeup.
Wear a wig.
Have an accident.
Listen to pop music.

Now listen and point to the speakers.

A: *I'll have a bottle of root beer, please.* (man and woman at refreshments table)
B: *Sorry. We're out of root beer. But the lemonade is very nice.*
A: *Okay. I'll take a can of lemonade and some chips.*

A: *What are you going to do this weekend?* (woman with badminton racket and man)
B: *I'm going to play badminton. How about you?*
A: *I'm going to stay home.*

A: *Can you do it by yourself?* (man and woman in makeup area)
B: *Yes, I can do it by myself!*
A: *Okay.*

Games and Activities

1. **TV Game Show.** Bring a volunteer to the front of the classroom to act as a TV game show host. Divide the class into Teams A and B. The host calls two players, one from each team, to the front of the classroom. The host secretly shows each player a different Unit 4 Word Time Word Card. The host asks *Are you ready? Go!* The players then pantomime their actions to their own team. The first team to name their player's action correctly, saying *You're (talking on the phone)*, wins a point. Continue in the same way until all students have taken a turn pantomiming. The team with the most points at the end wins.

2. **Bingo.** (See Game 9, pages 154–155.) Play the game using Unit 4 Word Time Picture Cards.

3. **Draw the Picture.** (See Game 13, page 155.) Play the game using Unit 4 Word Time Picture Cards.

4. **Option: Personalize the Vocabulary.** Give each student a large piece of paper and crayons or markers. Students make postcards of themselves and friends or family at a movie studio, doing the target activities. Students then take turns holding up their postcards for the rest of the class to see, and using complete sentences to describe the activities the people on the postcards are doing. Display the postcards on the wall for future reference.

Finish the Lesson

1. **Name the Card.** Hold up a Unit 4 Word Time Picture Card and have a volunteer name the card, pantomime the action, and use the verb phrase in a sentence. Continue in the same way with the remaining Unit 4 Word Time Picture Cards.

2. Explain and assign Workbook page 20. (For instructions, see Teacher's Book page 163.)

Focus Time

Language Focus: Adverbs of frequency (*always, usually, often, sometimes, hardly ever, never*)

Yes/No questions with *do* and *does* [(Do) (you) ever (fall in love)? Yes, (I) (always) (fall in love)./No, (I) (never) (fall in love).]

Function: Exchanging information about the frequency of activities in the present

Materials Needed: CD/cassette and player; Unit 3 Word Time Picture Cards, 1 set; Unit 4 Word Time Picture Cards, 1 set; Unit 4 Word Time Word Cards, 1 set per 2 students; Unit 4 Focus Time Picture Cards, 1 set; Unit 4 Focus Time Word Cards, 1 set per 2 students; *I, you, he, she, we,* and *they* grammar cards, 2 sets per 2 students; Unit 4 Grammar Cards, 1 set per 2 students (see Picture and Word Card Book pages 9, 13, 14, 15, 16, 43, 48, 54, and 55)

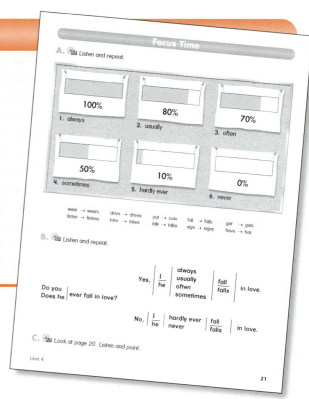

For general information on Focus Time, see pages 12–13.

Warm-Up and Review

1. **Vocabulary Review: True Sentences.** Attach the Units 3 and 4 Word Time Picture Cards to the board, and number them from 1 to 20. Say a number. Students say the corresponding verb phrase. Do the same with the remaining cards. Then have volunteers take turns using the verbs on the board to make two true sentences, one affirmative and one negative. For example: *I walk to school by myself. I don't drive a sports car.* Continue for four to five minutes.

2. Check Workbook page 20. (For instructions and answer key, see Teacher's Book page 163.)

This lesson is in two parts.

Part 1: Introduce the Words

Hold up and name each Unit 4 Focus Time Picture Card. Students listen. Hold up and name each card again and have students repeat. Hold up the cards in random order and have students name them.

Practice the Words

Students open their Student Books to page 21.

A. **Listen and repeat.**
Play the recording. Students listen and repeat each word.

1. *always*
2. *usually*
3. *often*
4. *sometimes*
5. *hardly ever*
6. *never*

wear, wears   *drive, drives*
put, puts   *fall, falls*
get, gets   *listen, listens*
take, takes   *talk, talks*
sign, signs   *have, has*

Part 2: Introduce the Patterns

1. **Do (you) ever (listen to pop music)? Yes, (I) (always) (listen to pop music).** Bring a volunteer to the front of the classroom and hand him/her a set of Unit 4 Focus Time Picture Cards (minus the *hardly ever* and *never* cards). Ask him/her *Do you ever listen to pop music?* Seated students repeat. Write *Do you ever listen to pop music?* on the board. Point to and read each word. Students repeat. Ask the question again, and prompt the volunteer to hold up and name the picture card that corresponds to how often he/she listens to pop music. Look at the card and say *Yes, I (always) listen to pop music.* The volunteer repeats. Write *Yes, I (always) listen to pop music.* on the board to the right of *Do you ever listen to pop music?* Do the same with *get a sunburn, talk on the phone,* and *take a nap.*

2. **Does (he) ever (wear a wig)? No, (he) (hardly ever) (wears a wig).** Do the same as in Step 1, using *he* and the appropriate gestures to demonstrate the pronoun. Use only the *hardly ever* and *never* picture cards and *wear a wig, drive a sports car, have an accident,* and *sign autographs.*

3. **Practice for Fluency.** Say *she, fall in love* and have students say the corresponding target question. Then say *sometimes* and have students say the target answer. Do the same with different pronouns and actions for three to four minutes.

Practice the Patterns

B. Listen and repeat.

1. Write the text from the pattern boxes on the board. Play the recording, pointing to each word. Students listen.

    A: *Do you ever fall in love?*
    B: *Yes, I always fall in love.*
    C: *Yes, I usually fall in love.*
    D: *Yes, I often fall in love.*
    E: *Yes, I sometimes fall in love.*
    F: *No, I hardly ever fall in love.*
    G: *No, I never fall in love.*

    A: *Does he ever fall in love?*
    B: *Yes, he always falls in love.*
    C: *Yes, he usually falls in love.*
    D: *Yes, he often falls in love.*
    E: *Yes, he sometimes falls in love.*
    F: *No, he hardly ever falls in love.*
    G: *No, he never falls in love.*

2. Play the recording again. Students look at the pattern boxes in their books and repeat, pointing to each word.

3. Students try to say the patterns on their own, while looking at the pattern boxes in their books.

C. Look at page 20. Listen and point.

Students look at page 20. Play the recording. Students listen to the patterns and point to the person/people doing each activity they hear named. Play the recording as many times as necessary for students to complete the task.

    A: *Do they ever have an accident?*
    B: *No, they hardly ever have an accident.*

    A: *Does he ever sign autographs?*
    B: *Yes, he often signs autographs.*

    A: *Does he ever wear a wig?*
    B: *Yes, he sometimes wears a wig.*

Games and Activities

1. **Draw It Out.** Divide the class into pairs. Give students in each pair seven minutes to work together to make pictorial representations of each adverb of frequency. For example: students might draw pie graphs or calendars. After seven minutes, have students in each pair stand up, show their pictures, and use each word in a sentence.

2. **Find Someone Who...** Each student writes the Unit 4 target activities in a column on a piece of paper. They then write one adverb of frequency next to each target activity. For example: *take a nap/hardly ever.* Students then circulate around the classroom, asking their classmates *Do you ever (take a nap)?* Once they find someone who (takes a nap) with the frequency listed on their paper, they write down that person's name next to the activity. Students continue for six to eight minutes. Then asks students questions about what they found out. For example: Ask *Does Bill ever take a nap?* Students who know this information respond either *Yes, he often takes a nap* or *No, he hardly ever takes a nap.*

3. **Make the Sentences.** (See Game 17, pages 155–156.) Do the activity using *I, you, he, she, we,* and *they* grammar cards and Unit 4 Word Time Word Cards, Focus Time Word Cards, and Grammar Cards.

Finish the Lesson

1. **Talk Show: The (Pop) Singers.** Bring three to four volunteers to the front of the classroom and have them assume the names of members of a popular performing group. Seated students use the target patterns to ask individual volunteers questions. Encourage students to use any verbs they are familiar with that make sense in this context. Play several times, with several groups of volunteers, changing the names of the performers every time.

2. Explain and assign Workbook page 21. (For instructions, see Teacher's Book page 163.)

Practice Time

Language Focus: Adverbs of frequency; Yes/No questions with *do* and *does* [*(Do) (you) ever (sign autographs)? (No), (I) (hardly ever) (sign autographs).*]

Function: Exchanging information about the frequency of activities in the present

Materials Needed: CD/cassette and player; copy of Unit 4 chant with 1 word from each line deleted, 1 per student; Unit 3 Word Time Word Cards, 1 set per 6–8 students; Unit 4 Word Time Picture Cards, 1 set; Unit 4 Word Time Word Cards, 1 set per 6–8 students; Unit 4 Focus Time Picture Cards, 1 set per 6–8 students; Unit 4 Focus Time Word Cards, 1 set (see Picture and Word Card Book pages 10, 13, 14, 15, and 16)

For general information on Practice Time, see pages 14–15.

Warm-Up and Review

1. **Pattern Review: Do You Ever…?** Hold up each of the Unit 4 Focus Time Picture Cards and have students name them. Then write *Do you ever drive a sports car? Yes, I often drive a sports car./No, I hardly ever drive a sports car.* on the board. Point to the sentences and have students read them. Then ask a student *Do you ever talk on the phone?* Continue asking students questions about different actions until most students have answered.

2. Check Workbook page 21. (For instructions and answer key, see Teacher's Book page 163.)

Practice the Patterns

A. Listen and repeat. Then practice with a partner.

1. Play the recording. Students listen and repeat, pointing to each picture in their books.

   A: *Do you ever sign autographs?*
   B: *No, I hardly ever sign autographs.*

   1. *Do you ever listen to pop music?*
      Yes, I usually listen to pop music.
   2. *Does she ever talk on the phone?*
      Yes, she always talks on the phone.
   3. *Does he ever drive a sports car?*
      Yes, he often drives a sports car.
   4. *Do they ever have an accident?*
      No, they hardly ever have an accident.
   5. *Does she ever get a sunburn?*
      Yes, she always gets a sunburn.
   6. *Do you ever put on makeup?*
      No, I never put on makeup.
   7. *Does he ever wear a wig?*
      Yes, he sometimes wears a wig.
   8. *Does he ever take a nap?*
      Yes, he usually takes a nap.

2. Students practice numbers 1–8 in pairs. (S1 in each pair asks the question and S2 answers.) Students then change roles and repeat the activity.

B. Look at page 20. Practice with a partner.

Students remain in pairs and look at page 20. They then take turns making statements about the large scene using the target patterns and vocabulary items. For example: S1 (pointing to the actor taking a nap): *Does he ever take a nap?* S2: *Yes, he always takes a nap.*

C. Listen and chant.

1. Students turn to the *Do You Ever Drive a Sports Car?* chant on page 74. They cover up the text, look at the pictures, and talk about what they see. Read the lyrics line by line. Students repeat each line. Play the recording. Students listen and follow along in their books.

Do You Ever Drive a Sports Car?

Do you ever drive a sports car?
   Yes, I often drive a sports car.
Do you ever have an accident?
   No, I never have an accident.

Do you ever put on makeup?
   Yes, I usually put on makeup.
Do you ever wear a wig?
   No, I hardly ever wear a wig.

Do you ever talk on the phone?
   Yes, I always talk on the phone.
Do you ever get a sunburn?
   Yes, I sometimes get a sunburn.

2. Play the recording again. Students listen and chant along, using their books for reference. Play the recording as many times as necessary for students to become familiar with the chant.

3. Give each student a copy of the chant that has one word from each line deleted. Play the chant again and have students listen and fill in the missing words. Play the chant as many times as necessary for students to complete the task.

Games and Activities

1. **True Sentences.** Divide the class into groups of six to eight. Give each group a set of Units 3 and 4 Word Time Word Cards and a set of Unit 4 Focus Time Picture Cards. Each group forms a circle and places their cards faceup in front of them. A student in each group (S1) begins by pointing to a word card. The other group members ask S1 *Do you ever (put on makeup)?* S1 points to a picture card and makes a true sentence, saying *(No), I (never) (put on makeup)*. Groups continue the activity until each student has answered two to three questions.

2. **Information Gap.** Divide the class into pairs. Give one student in each pair a piece of paper with the following sentences written on it:

    1. *Jan _____ takes a nap.*
    2. *Tom never talks on the phone.*
    3. *Sue often falls in love.*
    4. *Kate _____ gets a sunburn.*
    5. *Bob _____ drives a sports car.*
    6. *Dave usually signs autographs.*

   Give the other student in each pair a piece of paper with the following sentences written on it:

    1. *Jan always takes a nap.*
    2. *Tom _____ talks on the phone.*
    3. *Sue _____ falls in love.*
    4. *Kate hardly ever gets a sunburn.*
    5. *Bob sometimes drives a sports car.*
    6. *Dave _____ signs autographs.*

   Students in each pair ask their partner the target questions in order to get the information necessary to fill in the blanks.

3. **Talking.** Write the following on the board: *eat garlic bread, drink lemonade, go to the beach, go skiing, take a bus, go to the dentist, buy groceries*. Divide the class into pairs and give them three to four minutes to talk with their partners about if they ever do the activities listed on the board (students can take notes if necessary to remember what their partner says). Then each pair joins with another pair and each student tells the others about his/her partner's activities.

   OPTION: Do the activity as above, also having students draw pictures to illustrate their partner's actions.

Extra Practice
Explain and assign Worksheet 7, Do You Ever...?, page 194. (For instructions and answer key, see page 184.)

Finish the Lesson

1. **Famous People Survey.** Draw a 6×6 chart on the board. Elicit names of six famous people and write them in a column to the left of the chart, then attach the Unit 4 Focus Time Word Cards in a row above the chart. Stand the Unit 4 Word Time Picture Cards on the chalktray and bring two volunteers (S1 and S2) to the board. S1 holds up the *(wear a wig)* picture card, points to a name on the chart, and asks S2 *Does (Debra Pillman) ever (wear a wig)?* S2 says *(No), she (never) (wears a wig)*. Then S2 attaches the *(wear a wig)* picture card to the *(Debra Pillman/never)* square on the chart. Continue in the same way with four to six new pairs of volunteers.

2. Explain and assign Workbook page 22. (For instructions, see Teacher's Book page 163.)

Reading Time

Language Focus: Reading a postcard

Materials Needed: CD/cassette and player

For general information on Reading Time, see pages 16–17.

Warm-Up and Review

1. **Pattern Review: Chant Along.** Play the Unit 4 chant, *Do You Ever Drive a Sports Car?* Students listen. Play the chant again and have students chant along.

2. Check Workbook page 22. (For instructions and answer key, see Teacher's Book page 163.)

Introduce the Reading

Note: Students may learn the new vocabulary within the context of the reading, or each new word can be taught before students encounter it in the reading. Follow the steps below to introduce the new vocabulary and/or introduce the reading content.

1. Write the new words in a column on the board. Point to and read each word before explaining its meaning.

   have a good time: Write *have a good time = have fun* on the board. Point to and read each word.

   family: Say *I have a mother, a father, and a sister. They are my family.*

   yesterday: Write yesterday's date on the board. Point to it and say *Yesterday was (Monday).*

   today: Write today's date on the board. Point to it and say *Today is (Tuesday).*

   movie studio: Say *People make movies at a movie studio.*

   adventure: Name a popular adventure movie, then say *This is an adventure movie.*

   actor: Name two or three popular actors, then say *These people are actors.*

   rehearse: Write *rehearse = practice* on the board. Point to and read each word.

   movie star: Name a very popular movie star, then say *This person is a movie star.*

   tonight: Say *Now I'm at school. Tonight, at eight o'clock P.M., I'll be at home.*

2. Ask students the following questions:
   Is today Monday?
   Was yesterday Friday?
   Who's your favorite movie star?
   Do we learn English at a movie studio?
   Do you ever go to see adventure movies with your family?
   Do you like adventure movies?
   Which actors are in your favorite adventure movie?
   Do you have a good time at the movies?
   Are you going to a movie tonight?

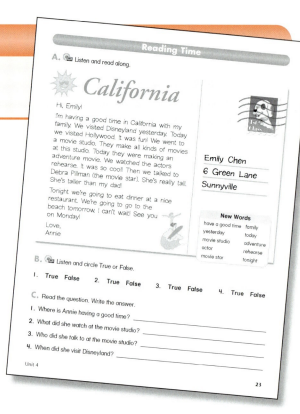

3. Students open their Student Books to page 23. They look at the pictures and talk about what they see. For example: *This is a postcard. It is from California.* Ask students what they think the reading will be about.

Practice the Reading

Students read the postcard silently to themselves.

A. Listen and read along.

1. Play the recording. Students listen and read along in their Student Books.

   Hi, Emily!

   I'm having a good time in California with my family. We visited Disneyland yesterday. Today we visited Hollywood. It was fun! We went to a movie studio. They make all kinds of movies at this studio. Today they were making an adventure movie. We watched the actors rehearse. It was so cool! Then we talked to Debra Pillman (the movie star). She's really tall. She's taller than my dad!

   Tonight we're going to eat dinner at a nice restaurant. We're going to go to the beach tomorrow. I can't wait! See you on Monday!

   Love,
   Annie

New Words
have a good time
family
yesterday
today
movie studio
adventure
actor
rehearse
movie star
tonight

2. Play the recording again, stopping it after each sentence. Students listen and repeat each sentence.

3. Divide the class into pairs. Students in each pair take turns reading the postcard aloud to their partners.

B. **Listen and circle True or False.**

1. Play the recording. For each number, students listen and circle *True* if the statement is true, and *False* if it is not.

   1. *Annie was in Florida.*
   2. *Annie went to a movie theater.*
   3. *Annie talked to a movie star.*
   4. *Annie went to Disneyland and Hollywood.*

2. Check answers by saying *Number 1. Annie was in Florida.* Students say *True* if they circled *True* and *False* if they circled *False*. If the statement is false, choose a volunteer to make it true. Do the same for numbers 2–4.

   Answer Key:
   1. False
   2. False
   3. True
   4. True

C. Read the question. Write the answer.

1. Students read each question and answer it based on the reading in exercise A.

2. Check answers by reading each question and having students read the answer they wrote.

   Answer Key:
   1. Where is Annie having a good time? <u>Annie is having a good time in California.</u>

   2. What did she watch at the movie studio? <u>She watched the actors rehearse at the movie studio.</u>

   3. Who did she talk to at the movie studio? <u>She talked to Debra Pillman (the movie star).</u>

   4. When did she visit Disneyland? <u>She visited Disneyland yesterday.</u>

Games and Activities

Note: For all Reading Time activities, students may use their Student Books for reference.

1. **Use It in a Sentence.** Say *family*. A volunteer says a sentence using *family* (this can be either an original sentence or a sentence from the reading). Do the same with the remaining new words from the lesson.

2. **One Sentence at a Time.** Divide the class into groups of five to six. Students in each group tell Annie's story, one sentence per student. Make sure students use appropriate pronouns. For example: *She's having a good time in California with her family. They visited Disneyland yesterday. Today they visited Hollywood.*

   Note: Students can do the activity directly from the reading, just changing the pronouns, or they can tell the story in their own words, also changing the pronouns.

3. **Our Own Trip.** Divide the class into groups of three to four and have each group write, then tell about, an imaginary trip they took to a place of their choice. Provide any words students need, but have them primarily use words they know. Set a time limit of ten minutes.

   OPTION: If students need additional help, write key structures on the board. For example: *(Yesterday) we visited _____. We went to a _____. We watched/saw _____ there. We talked to _____. We had lots of fun.*

   Extra Practice
   Explain and assign Worksheet 8, Movie Stars, page 195. (For instructions and answer key, see page 184.)

Finish the Lesson

1. **Please Correct Me.** Read sentences or parts of sentences from the reading, replacing one word in each utterance. Students follow in their Student Books and repeat each utterance, putting the word from the reading back in. For example: say *I'm having a good time in New York with my family.* Students say *I'm having a good time in California with my family.* Continue for three to four minutes.

2. Explain and assign Workbook page 23. (For instructions, see Teacher's Book pages 163–164.)

Your Time

Language Focus: Personalizing language related to frequency and activities

Materials Needed: CD/cassette and player; Unit 4 Focus Time Word Cards, 1 card per student (see Picture and Word Card Book page 16)

For general information on Your Time, see pages 18–19.

Warm-Up and Review

1. **Reading Review: In Your Own Words.** Students open their Student Books to page 23 and take two to three minutes to review the postcard. Then have students take turns telling the class—in their own words—something about the postcard. For example: *This is about Annie's visit to California.* Continue until most students have taken a turn. It is okay if more than one student tells the same information.

2. Check Workbook page 23. (For instructions and answer key, see Teacher's Book pages 163–164.)

Introduce the Lesson

Ask students five to six questions relating to movies (see Suggested Questions below).

Suggested Questions:
What's your favorite movie?
Do you like adventure movies?
Do you ever wear a wig?
Do you ever put on makeup?
Do you like meeting movie stars?
Did you watch actors rehearse this morning?

Practice the Lesson

Students open their Student Books to page 24.

A. Listen and answer the questions.

1. Play the recording. For each number, students listen to the question and answer it based on their own knowledge and experience.

   1. *Do you ever sign autographs?*
   2. *Do you ever talk on the phone?*
   3. *Do your friends ever listen to pop music?*
   4. *Do you ever drive a sports car?*

2. Check answers by dividing the class into pairs and having students in each pair read one question and answer to the class.

   Answer Key:
   Answers will vary.

B. Pairwork. Write. Then ask your partner.

Divide the class into pairs. Each student fills in the *You* column on his/her chart. Then each student asks his/her partner the target questions and fills in the *Your Partner* column on his/her chart. Next, each student tells the class about his/her partner, using the sentence cues and information from his/her chart. For example: *(Ken) (usually) (takes a nap)*, or *(Ken) (never) (takes a nap)*.

C. Review. Read and write the answers.

1. Students read each question and write an answer based on their own knowledge and experience.

2. Check answers by dividing the class into pairs and having students in each pair read one question and answer to the class.

   Answer Key:
   Answers will vary.

Games and Activities

1. **What Do You Do?** Write *eat apple pie, do laundry by yourself, stay home by yourself, drink root beer,* and *iron a shirt by yourself* on the board. Then divide the class into pairs. Students in each pair ask each other *Do you ever...?* questions about the activities listed on the board (students can take notes if necessary to remember what their partner says). Then each pair joins with another pair and each student tells the others about his/her partner's activities.

2. **Draw, Write, and Tell.** Each student writes *often, sometimes,* and *never* in a column on a piece of paper. Then give students seven minutes to draw a picture of themselves or a friend next to each word, to illustrate actions they do often, sometimes, and never. Once students have finished drawing, have them write a sentence to describe each picture. Each student then tells a partner about his/her pictures.

3. **Talking.** Divide the class into pairs and give them three to four minutes to talk with their partners about the last time they saw a movie (students can take notes if necessary to remember what their partner says). Then each pair joins with another pair and each student tells the others about his/her partner's experience at the movies.

   OPTION: Do the activity as above, also having students draw pictures to illustrate their partner's experience at the movies.

Finish the Lesson

1. **True Sentences.** Give each student a Unit 4 Focus Time Word Card. Students take turns standing up and using the word on their card to make a true sentence about themselves or someone in their family. For example, *My sister always sets the table.* Continue until most students have taken a turn.

2. Explain and assign Workbook page 24. (For instructions, see Teacher's Book page 164.)

3. Do Chapter 2 of Storybook 5, *Digger and the Thief.* (For instructions and answer key, see Teacher's Book pages 180 and 181.)

> **Assessment**
> Explain and assign the Unit 4 Test, page 219. (For instructions and answer key, see page 209.)

5 In Town

Conversation Time

Language Focus: Talking about the weather and inquiring after family

Materials Needed: CD/cassette and player; Wall Chart 9; Unit 4 Focus Time Word Cards, 1 set (see Picture and Word Card Book page 16)

For general information on Conversation Time, see pages 8–9.

Warm-Up and Review

1. **Review: I Always Ride a Bicycle.** Place the Unit 4 Focus Time Word Cards along the chalktray. Point to each word and have students read it. Then say *always* and have several volunteers name actions they always do, saying *I always (ride a bicycle)*. Do the same with the remaining word cards.
2. Check Workbook page 24. (For instructions and answer key, see Teacher's Book page 164.)

Introduce the Conversation

1. Set the scene and clarify meaning by saying *In today's conversation, two people meet in the park. They're friends, so they stop and talk.* Then introduce the new words by writing each word on the board. Point to and read each word before explaining its meaning. Students repeat the word.

   92 degrees: Explain that degrees are a way to measure temperature, and that 92 degrees Fahrenheit equals 33 degrees Celsius.

   getting cloudy: Draw a simple outdoor scene on the board—a tree, some flowers, and a sun. Say *There aren't any clouds in the sky.* Then begin to draw clouds in the sky and say *It's getting cloudy.*

   flu: Grimace in pain and say *My head hurts and I have a fever.* Then pretend to sneeze and cough. Say *I have the flu.*

   better: Say *I wasn't good at playing the piano. But then I practiced and practiced. Now I'm better.*

2. Bring two students to the front of the classroom. Have Student B sit down on a chair. Set another chair beside Student B. Stand behind each student and model his/her lines of the conversation with the following actions:

   A: *Hi, Mr. Day!*
   Walk up to Student B and wave happily.

   B: *Hello, Charlie. Have a seat.*
   Smile and nod. Gesture for Student A to sit down on the chair.

A: *Thanks. Phew! It's hot today.*
Sit down. Wipe your forehead.

B: *That's right. It's 92 degrees!*
Nod in agreement. Speak enthusiastically.

A: *Wow! Do you think it's going to rain?*
Look up (at the sky) with a questioning expression.

B: *Maybe. It's getting cloudy. So, how's your family, Charlie?*
Look up and shrug your shoulders. Then look at Student A and speak in a friendly tone.

A: *They're fine. But my sister has the flu.*
Speak a little bit sadly.

B: *I'm sorry to hear that.*
Look concerned.

A: *It's not serious. She's doing better today.*
Shake your head on *not serious*. Nod on *doing better*.

B: *Good!*
Smile and nod.

A: *Look! It's starting to rain.*
Look up and hold out your hand as if feeling raindrops.

B: *I'd better go home. Take care, Charlie.*
Stand up and begin to walk away from the chairs. Wave to Student A.

A: *Bye, Mr. Day.*
Stand up and begin to walk away from Student B. Wave to Student B.

3. Divide the class into Groups A and B. Model the conversation again using facial expressions and body language. Group A repeats the first line of the conversation, Group B repeats line two, and so on. Encourage students to copy your facial expressions and body language. Groups change roles and say the conversation again in the same way.

4. Attach Wall Chart 9 to the board or open a Student Book to page 25. Students then open their Student Books to page 25. Ask the following questions.

   Where are Charlie and Mr. Day?
   What is Charlie holding?
   How does Charlie feel?
   How hot is it?
   How is Charlie's family? Is his sister sick? What's the matter?
   Is it raining here today?

Practice the Conversation

A. Listen and repeat. Point to the speakers. Then listen again.

1. Play the recording (first version of the conversation). Students listen and repeat, pointing to each speaker.

   1. Charlie: *Hi, Mr. Day!*
      Mr. Day: *Hello, Charlie. Have a seat.*
   2. Charlie: *Thanks. Phew! It's hot today.*
      Mr. Day: *That's right. It's 92 degrees!*
   3. Charlie: *Wow! Do you think it's going to rain?*
      Mr. Day: *Maybe. It's getting cloudy.*
   4. Mr. Day: *So, how's your family, Charlie?*
      Charlie: *They're fine. But my sister has the flu.*
   5. Mr. Day: *I'm sorry to hear that.*
      Charlie: *It's not serious. She's doing better today.*
      Mr. Day: *Good!*
   6. Charlie: *Look! It's starting to rain.*
      Mr. Day: *I'd better go home. Take care, Charlie.*
      Charlie: *Bye, Mr. Day.*

2. Play the recording (second version of the conversation). Students listen.

B. Role-play the conversation.

Students choose a partner and, using their Student Books for reference, role-play the conversation. They then change roles and role-play the conversation again.

Games and Activities

Note: For all Conversation Time activities, students may use their Student Books for reference.

1. **Responses.** Divide the class into pairs. A student in each pair (S1) begins by saying the first line of dialogue in any of the scenes. His/Her partner (S2) responds accordingly. Pairs continue in the same way with the remaining scenes. S2 then says the first lines of the dialogue in the same way and S1 responds.

2. **Back-to-Back.** Divide the class into pairs. Students sit with their backs to their partners and role-play the conversation without looking at each other. Partners then change roles and repeat the activity.

3. **Make It Your Own.** Write the following on the board:

   A: *So, how's your family?*
   B: *They're fine. But my sister has the flu.*

   Students read the dialogue on the board. Then divide the class into pairs and write the following on the board:

   1. *Everybody's fine. We're all busy.*
   2. *They're doing well. We leave next week for our vacation!*
   3. *We're all fine. Thanks for asking!*

   Students read each new response. Quickly clarify meaning if necessary. Then students in each pair role-play the dialogue on the board, substituting the new responses into the underlined part of the target conversation.

Finish the Lesson

1. **Discussion.** Have a short discussion (for about three to four minutes) with the class, talking about what Mr. Day and Charlie might do next, once they have left each other. For example, Mr. Day might go home and fix himself a cold glass of lemonade. Charlie might go to the drugstore to get medicine and tissues for his sister.

2. Explain and assign Workbook page 25. (For instructions, see Teacher's Book page 164.)

Word Time

Language Focus: Activities (*feed the birds, read a newspaper, take medicine, go on a date, visit a museum, take the subway, give a speech, take a math test, bake bread, get a haircut*)

Materials Needed (excluding materials for optional activities):
CD/cassette and player; Wall Chart 10; Units 4 and 5 Word Time Picture Cards, 1 set per 3–4 students; Unit 5 Word Time Word Cards, 1 set (see Picture and Word Card Book pages 13, 14, 17, and 18)

For general information on Word Time, see pages 10–11.

Warm-Up and Review

1. **Conversation Review: True/False/I Don't Know.** Play the recording of the Unit 5 conversation. Students listen. Then say five to six statements about the conversation (see Suggested Statements below). Students say *True* if the statement is true, and *False* if it is false. If a statement is false, choose a volunteer to make it true. If students don't have enough information to determine if the statement is true or false, they say *I don't know.*

   Suggested Statements:
   Mr. Day and Charlie are talking.
   It's a cold day.
   There aren't any clouds.
   Charlie's sister doesn't like to be sick.
   Charlie's sister will be better in two days.
   Mr. Day is going to go home.

2. Check Workbook page 25. (For instructions and answer key, see Teacher's Book page 164.)

Introduce the Words

1. Hold up and name each of the Unit 5 Word Time Picture Cards. Students listen. Hold up and name the cards again, and have students repeat. Hold up the cards in random order and have students name them.

2. Attach the Unit 5 Word Time Picture Cards in a row to the board. Stand the Unit 5 Word Time Word Cards on the chalktray under the corresponding picture cards. Point to each picture/word card pair and read the word. Students repeat. Then reposition the word cards so they are no longer directly below the corresponding picture cards. Volunteers come to the board one by one and place a word card under its corresponding picture card, then point to and read the word. Seated students repeat.

Talk About the Picture

1. Students open their Student Books to page 26. They look at the large scene and use complete sentences to identify anything they can.

2. Attach Wall Chart 10 to the board or open a Student Book to page 26. Read the following "story" while pointing to or touching the pictures (**bold** words) and pantomiming the actions (*italicized* words).

   In the park, the **man** is *reading a newspaper*, and the **boy** is *feeding the birds*. The **mother and child** are *taking the subway*. In town, **Bill** is *getting a haircut* and the **baker** is *baking bread*. The **young man and woman** are *on a date*. **This man** is *giving a speech*. Here, **Penny** is *taking medicine*. The **students** are *taking a math test*. **This man** is *visiting a museum* and *looking at paintings*.

3. Ask the following questions while pointing to or touching the pictures (**bold** words) and pantomiming the actions (*italicized* words).

   (**man with newspaper**) Is the man *reading a book*?
   (**boy feeding birds**) What's the boy doing in the park?
   How will the **mother and child** go home?
   (**girl taking medicine**) Does she like to take medicine?
   What are the **students** at school doing?
   (**man at museum**) Where is he *looking at paintings*?
   Were you at a museum yesterday?
   Do you ever take the subway by yourself?

Practice the Words

A. 🔊 **Listen and repeat.**

1. Play the recording. Students listen and repeat, pointing to each word in the vocabulary box.

   1. *feed the birds*
   2. *read a newspaper*
   3. *take medicine*
   4. *go on a date*
   5. *visit a museum*
   6. *take the subway*
   7. *give a speech*
   8. *take a math test*
   9. *bake bread*
   10. *get a haircut*

2. Say the words in random order. Students point to them in the vocabulary box.

B. Point and say the words.

Students point to each of the target vocabulary items in the large scene and name them.

C. 🔊 **Listen and point.**

Play the recording. Students listen to the sound effects and words. For the vocabulary, they point to the person/people doing the named action; for the conversations, they point to the speakers. (References are shown in parentheses.) Play the recording as many times as necessary for students to complete the task.

Take the subway.
Take medicine.
Read a newspaper.
Visit a museum.
Take a math test.
Feed the birds.
Bake bread.
Get a haircut.
Go on a date.
Give a speech.

Now listen and point to the speakers.

A: *May I speak to Dan, please?* (man on cell phone by birds)
B: *I'm sorry. He's not in right now.*
A: *Can you take a message?*
B: *Sure. Who's calling?*
A: *This is Len. I'll be late for lunch today. I'll see him at two o'clock.*

A: *What are you doing?* (girl on blanket and boy)
B: *I'm writing a letter to Gabby Landers.*

A: *How much root beer did you have?* (waiter and man at café)
B: *We had two bottles of root beer.*
A: *How many pieces of apple pie did you have?*
B: *We had two pieces of apple pie.*

Games and Activities

1. **Concentration.** (See Game 10, page 155.) Play the game using Units 4 and 5 Word Time Picture Cards.

2. **Ask and Answer.** Write *always, usually, often, sometimes, hardly ever,* and *never* on the board. Point to each word and have students read it. Then quickly review the *Do you ever (get a haircut)?* pattern. Divide the class into groups of three to four and give each group a set of Units 4 and 5 Word Time Picture Cards. Groups place the cards faceup in front of them. A student in each group begins by asking *Does (Kim) ever (give a speech)?* The first student to touch the named card asks (Kim) *Do you ever give a speech?* (Kim) answers truthfully and then takes a turn asking a *Does (Tom) ever…* question. Groups continue in the same way for five to seven minutes.

3. **Categorizing.** Divide the class into groups of two to three. Students in each group work together to make two lists. One list should contain the target actions that people generally do by themselves. The other list should contain the target actions that people generally do not do by themselves. Once each group has made their lists, have students share their lists with the class. Work with the class as a whole to come to a consensus about what should be on each list. Write the final lists on the board.

4. **Option: Personalize the Vocabulary.** Divide the class into groups of two to three and give each group a magazine. Members of each group work together to find pictures of people doing the target actions. Groups cut out the pictures and make a collage. Groups then take turns showing the class their collages and talking about the people doing the activities, saying, for example, *He's taking the subway. They like to bake bread.* Display the collages on the wall for future reference.

Finish the Lesson

1. **Slow Reveal.** (See Game 15, page 155.) Play the game using Unit 5 Word Time Picture Cards.

2. Explain and assign Workbook page 26. (For instructions, see Teacher's Book page 164.)

Focus Time

Language Focus: Adverbial phrases of frequency (*once a day, twice a week, three times a month, four times a year*)

Wh- questions with *how often* [*How often (do) (you) (read a newspaper)? (I) (read a newspaper) (once) a (month).*]

Function: Asking about the frequency of actions

Materials Needed: CD/cassette and player; Unit 5 Word Time Picture Cards, 1 card per student; Unit 5 Word Time Word Cards, 1 set per 2 students; Unit 5 Focus Time Picture Cards, 1 set; Unit 5 Focus Time Word Cards, 1 set per 2 students; *I, He, She, We, They, I, you, he, she, we,* and *they* grammar cards, 1 set per 2 students; Unit 5 Grammar Cards, 1 set per 2 students (see Picture and Word Card Book pages 17, 18, 19, 20, 43, 46, 48, 49, 56, and 57)

For general information on Focus Time, see pages 12–13.

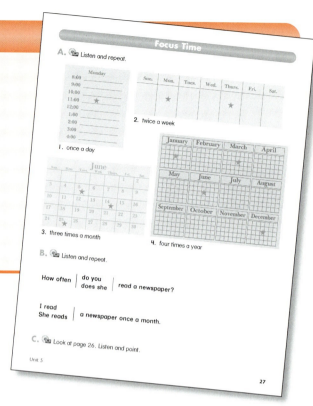

Warm-Up and Review

1. **Vocabulary Review: How Many Verbs?** Stand the Unit 5 Word Time Picture Cards on the chalktray. Point to each of the cards and have students name them. Then say one of the nouns illustrated on a card (for example: *the birds*). Several volunteers take turns using *(the birds)* in different sentences. For example: S1 says *I see the birds.* Then S2 says *I hear the birds.* S3 says *I like the birds.* Then say another noun. Continue with the remaining Unit 5 target vocabulary. Allow students to repeat verbs. For example: *I hear the birds. I hear a speech.*

   OPTION: Give students a list of verbs to choose from.

2. Check Workbook page 26. (For instructions and answer key, see Teacher's Book page 164.)

This lesson is in two parts.

Part 1: Introduce the Words

1. Hold up and name each Unit 5 Focus Time Picture Card. Students listen. Hold up and name each card again and have students repeat. Hold up the cards in random order and have students name them.

2. Attach the Unit 5 Focus Time Picture Cards in a row to the board. Stand the Unit 5 Focus Time Word Cards on the chalktray under the corresponding picture cards. Point to each picture/word card pair and read the word. Students repeat. Then reposition the word cards so they are no longer directly below the corresponding picture cards. Volunteers come to the board one by one and place a word card under its corresponding picture card, then point to and read the word. Seated students repeat.

Practice the Words

Students open their Student Books to page 27.

A. Listen and repeat.

Play the recording. Students listen and repeat each word.

1. *once a day*
2. *twice a week*
3. *three times a month*
4. *four times a year*

Part 2: Introduce the Patterns

1. **How often do (you) (read a newspaper)? (I) (read a newspaper) (once) a (day).** Place the Unit 5 Word Time Picture Cards on the chalktray and bring a volunteer to the front of the classroom. Pick up the *get a haircut* card and say *I get a haircut once a month.* Students repeat. Write *I get a haircut once a month.* on the board. Point to and read each word. Students repeat. Then turn to the volunteer and ask *How often do you get a haircut?* Students repeat. Write *How often do you get a haircut?* on the board to the left of *I get a haircut once a month.* Point to and read each word. Students repeat. Then ask the question again and prompt the volunteer to respond *I get a haircut (twice) a (month).* Seated students repeat. Do the same with *take medicine, take a math test,* and *read a newspaper.*

2. **How often does (she) (read a newspaper)? (She) (reads a newspaper) (once) a (day).** Do the same as in Step 1, using appropriate gestures to demonstrate *she*.

3. **Practice for Fluency.** Say *you, take the subway*. Students ask the target question. Then say *twice a week* and have students use the target pattern to answer the question. Continue in the same way—using different pronouns, activities, and frequencies—for three to four minutes.

Practice the Patterns

B. **Listen and repeat.**

1. Write the text from the pattern boxes on the board. Then play the recording, pointing to each word. Students listen.

   A: *How often do you read a newspaper?*
   B: *I read a newspaper once a month.*

   A: *How often does she read a newspaper?*
   B: *She reads a newspaper once a month.*

2. Play the recording again. Students look at the pattern boxes in their books and repeat, pointing to each word.

3. Students work with partners to say the questions and answers, while looking at the pattern boxes in their books.

C. **Look at page 26. Listen and point.**

Students look at page 26. Play the recording. Students listen to the patterns and point to the person doing each activity they hear named. Play the recording as many times as necessary for students to complete the task.

   A: *How often does he get a haircut?*
   B: *He gets a haircut twice a month.*

   A: *How often do they take the subway?*
   B: *They take the subway five times a week.*

   A: *How often does he give a speech?*
   B: *He gives a speech four times a year.*

Games and Activities

1. **Around the Circle.** Divide the class into groups of four to six and give each student a Unit 5 Word Time Picture Card. Each group forms a circle. A student in each group (S1) begins by looking at the card of the student to his/her right (S2) and asking *How often do you (take medicine)?* S2 uses the target pattern to reply truthfully. Then S2 looks at his/her neighbor's card and asks the question in the same way, and so on around the circle. Once each student has asked a question, they exchange cards and do the activity again.

2. **Match and Draw.** Divide the class into pairs and write the following questions and answers in two columns on the board:

   1. How often does she go on a date?
   2. How often do you bake bread?
   3. How often does he get a haircut?
   4. How often do they feed the birds?

   He gets a haircut twice a month.
   She goes on a date once a week.
   They feed the birds once a day.
   I bake bread three times a year.

   Students in each pair work together to match each question in the left-hand column to the corresponding answer in the right-hand column, writing each question/answer pair on a piece of paper. Students also quickly draw a small calendar beside each match to show the frequency they are talking about. Check answers by having students take turns reading the questions and answers they matched.

3. **Make the Sentences.** (See Game 17, pages 155–156.) Do the activity using *I, He, She, We, They, I, you, he, she, we,* and *they* grammar cards and Unit 5 Word Time Word Cards, Focus Time Word Cards, and Grammar Cards.

Finish the Lesson

1. **Talk Show: The (Pop) Singers.** Bring several volunteers to the front of the classroom and have them assume the names of members of a popular performing group. Seated students ask individual members of the group target questions, and the "performers" respond using the target patterns. Encourage students to use any verbs they are familiar with that make sense in the context. Play several times, with several groups of volunteers, changing the names of the performers each time.

2. Explain and assign Workbook page 27. (For instructions, see Teacher's Book page 165.)

Practice Time

Language Focus: Adverbial phrases of frequency; Wh- questions with *how often* [*How often (do) (you) (visit a museum)? (I) (visit a museum) (four times) a (year).*]

Function: Asking about the frequency of actions

Materials Needed: CD/cassette and player; two balls; Unit 5 Focus Time Picture Cards, 1 set (see Picture and Word Card Book page 19)

For general information on Practice Time, see pages 14–15.

Warm-Up and Review

1. **Pattern Review: Ask and Answer.** Write *How often do you bake bread? I bake bread once a day.* on the board. Point to the sentences and have students read them. Then stand the Unit 5 Focus Time Picture Cards on the chalktray for reference. Ask several students *How often do you (give a speech)?* Point to various volunteers and ask the rest of the class *How often does (she) (give a speech)?* Students answer the question. Continue in the same way for four to five minutes.

2. Check Workbook page 27. (For instructions and answer key, see Teacher's Book page 165.)

Practice the Patterns

Students open their Student Books to page 28.

A. Listen and repeat. Then practice with a partner.

1. Play the recording. Students listen and repeat, pointing to each picture in their books.

   A: *How often do you visit a museum?*
   B: *I visit a museum four times a year.*

   1. *How often do you get a haircut?*
      I get a haircut twice a month.
   2. *How often does she take medicine?*
      She takes medicine three times a day.
   3. *How often does he feed the birds?*
      He feeds the birds once a day.
   4. *How often do they go on a date?*
      They go on a date twice a week.
   5. *How often do you take the subway?*
      We take the subway five times a week.
   6. *How often does she bake bread?*
      She bakes bread once a day.
   7. *How often do they take a math test?*
      They take a math test three times a month.
   8. *How often does he give a speech?*
      He gives a speech four times a year.

2. Students practice numbers 1–8 in pairs. (S1 in each pair asks the question, S2 says the answer.) Students then change roles and repeat the activity.

B. Look at page 26. Practice with a partner.

Students remain in pairs and look at page 26. They then take turns asking and answering questions about the large scene using the target patterns and vocabulary items. For example: S1 (pointing to the baker): *How often does she bake bread?* S2: *She bakes bread twice a day.*

C. Listen and sing along.

1. Students turn to the *How Often Do You Give a Speech?* song on page 75. They cover up the text, look at the pictures, and talk about what they see. Read the lyrics line by line. Students repeat each line. Play the recording. Students listen and follow along in their books.

   How Often Do You Give a Speech?
   (Melody: *When the Saints Go Marching In*)

   How often do you give a speech?
     I give a speech three times a year.
   How often do you get a haircut?
     I get a haircut once a month.

   How often does he feed the birds?
     He feeds the birds four times a month.
   How often does he take a math test?
     He takes a math test twice a week.

   How often do they bake bread?
     They bake bread three times a day.
   How often do they take the subway?
     They take the subway twice a day.

2. Play the recording again. Students listen and sing along, using their books for reference. Play the recording as many times as necessary for students to become familiar with the song.

3. Divide the class into Groups A and B. Play the karaoke version. Group A sings the questions and Group B sings the answers. Everyone pantomimes each action as they sing. Groups then switch roles and sing the song again.

Games and Activities

1. **Survey.** Students create a survey on a sheet of paper by writing *Name* and *How often do you _____?* in a row at the top of the paper. They write *bake bread, take the subway, visit a museum, feed the birds,* and *get a haircut* along the left side of the paper. Students then go around the classroom and ask their classmates *How often do you (bake bread)?* Students respond *I (bake bread) (twice) a (year).* Students record their classmates' names and answers on the survey. Continue until all students have asked at least five other students questions. Students sit down. Then ask students questions about the survey. For example: Ask *How often does Jane bake bread?* Students who know this information respond *Jane bakes bread twice a year.*

    OPTIONS:
    1. Quickly teach students the word *about* so that they can approximate frequency. For example: *I take the subway about three times a month.*

    2. Remind students that they can use the patterns *I never (take the subway)* and *I hardly ever (take the subway).*

2. **Talking.** Write the following on the board: *go fishing, pick apples, feed the pets, play cards, cook breakfast by yourself, walk to school by yourself, talk on the phone.* Divide the class into pairs and give them three to four minutes to talk with their partners about how often they do the activities listed on the board (students can take notes if necessary to remember what their partner says). Then each pair joins with another pair and each student tells the others about his/her partner's activities.

    OPTIONS:
    1. Quickly teach students the word *about* so that they can approximate frequency. For example: *I cook breakfast by myself about three times a month.*

    2. Remind students that they can use the patterns *I never (cook breakfast by myself)* and *I hardly ever (cook breakfast by myself).*

3. **Listen Carefully.** Read the following paragraph to students, having them take notes as necessary.

    I'm going to tell you about my good friend, Ginger. Ginger loves to do so many things! Once a day, she goes swimming. She practices the violin once a day, too. She likes to bake, so twice a week she bakes four loaves of bread. Her family says, "Yum! Ginger, your bread is great!" Sometimes—about three times a month—she makes cookies, too. Chocolate cookies are her favorite. My friend Ginger is busy doing so many fun things!

    Ask the following questions about the above reading, having students refer to their notes for reference. If necessary, read the paragraph several times.

    How often does Ginger bake bread?
    How many loaves of bread does she bake?
    Does her family like Ginger's bread?
    How often does Ginger go swimming?
    How often does she play the violin?

    Extra Practice
    Explain and assign Worksheet 9, How Often?, page 196. (For instructions and answer key, see page 185.)

Finish the Lesson

1. **How Often?** Bring two volunteers to the front of the classroom and give each one a ball. The first volunteer tosses the ball to a seated student (S1) and asks *How often do you (take medicine)?* S1 replies using the target pattern, then throws the ball back. The second volunteer tosses the ball to another seated student (S2), points to S1, and asks *How often does (he) (take medicine)?* S2 replies using the target pattern, then throws the ball back. After two to four questions, bring two new volunteers to the front of the classroom to toss the balls and ask questions.

2. Explain and assign Workbook page 28. (For instructions, see Teacher's Book page 165.)

Reading Time

Language Focus: Reading a newspaper advice column

Materials Needed: CD/cassette and player; copies of reading, 1 per 6–8 students

For general information on Reading Time, see pages 16–17.

Warm-Up and Review

1. **Pattern Review: Sing Along.** Play the Unit 5 song *How Often Do You Give a Speech?* Students listen. Play the song again and have students sing along.

2. Check Workbook page 28. (For instructions and answer key, see Teacher's Book page 165.)

Introduce the Reading

Note: Students may learn the new vocabulary within the context of the reading, or each new word can be taught before students encounter it in the reading. Follow the steps below to introduce the new vocabulary and/or introduce the reading content.

1. Write the new words in a column on the board. Point to and read each word before explaining its meaning.

   pest: Walk up to a student. Tap him/her on the shoulder, pull at his/her sleeve, and generally be bothersome about getting attention. Say *I'm being a pest.*

   bother: Walk up to a student. Tap him/her on the shoulder, pull at his/her sleeve, and generally be bothersome about getting attention. Say *I'm bothering you.*

   without: Say *You came to class without your book. You don't have your book. Now you have to share with your friend.*

   tell: Point to a student and say *Please tell me your name.* Prompt the student to tell you his/her name. Do the same with three to four different students.

   patient: Ask a student to find a picture of Annie in his/her Student Book. As he/she is looking, impatiently tap your foot and say *Hurry up!* Then say *I'm not being patient.*

   fair: Say *My sister always goes to the movies with her friends. I can't go to the movies with my friends. It's not fair.*

   crazy: Explain that in this context, crazy means agitated, frustrated, and at one's wit's end.

   attention: Ask students to quietly talk to the students seated around them. Then say *I want you to stop what you're doing and listen to me. I want your attention.*

   spend time: Say *I like my sister a lot! We always do lots of fun things together. I like to spend time with her.*

   grow up: Ask a student *Do you want to be a nurse when you grow up?* Prompt him/her to answer. Do the same with three to four different students.

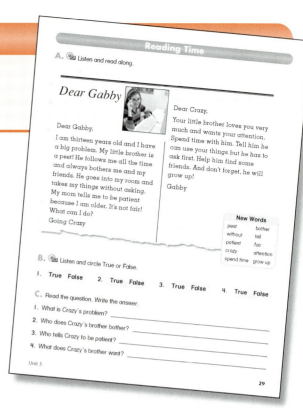

2. Students open their Student Books to page 29. They look at the reading and picture and talk about what they see. For example: *This is from a newspaper. Maybe this woman is the writer.* Ask students what they think the reading will be about.

Practice the Reading

Students read the article silently to themselves.

A. Listen and read along.

1. Play the recording. Students listen and read along in their Student Books.

Dear Gabby

Dear Gabby,

I am thirteen years old and I have a big problem. My little brother is a pest! He follows me all the time and always bothers me and my friends. He goes into my room and takes my things without asking. My mom tells me to be patient because I am older. It's not fair! What can I do?

Going Crazy

Dear Crazy,

Your little brother loves you very much and wants your attention. Spend time with him. Tell him he can use your things but he has to ask first. Help him find some friends. And don't forget, he will grow up!

Gabby

78   Unit 5

New Words
pest
bother
without
tell
patient
fair
crazy
attention
spend time
grow up

2. Play the recording again, stopping it after each sentence. Students listen and repeat each sentence.

3. Divide the class into pairs. Students in each pair take turns reading the story aloud to their partner.

B. **Listen and circle True or False.**

1. Play the recording. For each number, students listen and circle *True* if the statement is true, and *False* if it is not.

   1. *Crazy is thirteen years old.*
   2. *Crazy is younger than her brother.*
   3. *Her brother bothers their mother.*
   4. *Her brother borrows her things without asking.*

2. Check answers by saying *Number 1. Crazy is thirteen years old*. Students say *True* if they circled *True*, and *False* if they circled *False*. If the statement is false, choose a volunteer to make it true. Do the same for numbers 2–4.

   Answer Key:
   1. True   2. False   3. False   4. True

C. Read the question. Write the answer.

1. Students read each question and answer it based on the reading in exercise A.

2. Check answers by reading each question and having students read the answer they wrote.

   Answer Key:
   1. What is Crazy's problem? <u>Her little brother is a pest.</u>
   2. Who does Crazy's brother bother? <u>Crazy's brother bothers Crazy and her friends.</u>
   3. Who tells Crazy to be patient? <u>Crazy's mom tells her to be patient.</u>
   4. What does Crazy's brother want? <u>Crazy's brother wants her attention.</u>

Games and Activities

Note: For all Reading Time activities, students may use their Student Books for reference.

1. **Listen Carefully.** Write the following sentences on the board. Then play the recording. Students listen and write the missing words to complete each sentence.

   1. *My little brother is a _____!*
   2. *He always _____ me and my friends.*
   3. *He takes my things _____ asking.*
   4. *My mom tells me to be _____ because I am older.*
   5. *It's not _____! What can I do?*

   Check answers by saying *Number 1*. A volunteer reads the complete sentence. Do the same for numbers 2–5.

   Answer Key:
   1. My little brother is a <u>pest</u>!
   2. He always <u>bothers</u> me and my friends.
   3. He takes my things <u>without</u> asking.
   4. My mom tells me to be <u>patient</u> because I am older.
   5. It's not <u>fair</u>! What can I do?

2. **Sentence Strips.** Divide the class into groups of six to eight and give each group a copy of the reading. Students in each group cut the reading so that each sentence is on a separate strip of paper. They then shuffle the strips. Play the recording. Students in each group work together to put the strips in order. Play the recording as many times as necessary for students to complete the task. Then have each group read a paragraph to the class.

3. **Ten Years Later.** Divide the class into three groups and ask each group to write, then read to the class, a letter that Crazy might write ten years in the future to thank Gabby for her good advice. Write the beginning and the ending of the letter on the board, and ask students to use the past tense in their letter. Suggested beginning: *When I was thirteen years old, I had a big problem….* Suggested ending: *I spent time with my brother and helped him find some friends. He did grow up and I love him very much!* When students have finished, each group reads its letter to the class.

Extra Practice
Explain and assign Worksheet 10, *Am I a Pest?*, page 197. (For instructions and answer key, see page 185.)

Finish the Lesson

1. **Tell Me About It.** Ask students three to four questions about the form (rather than the content) of the reading (see Suggested Questions below).

   Suggested Questions:
   What is this reading about?
   How do you know that these are letters?
   Who do you think Gabby is?
   Where can you find letters like these?
   Do you like reading letters like these? Why or why not?

2. Explain and assign Workbook page 29. (For instructions, see Teacher's Book page 165.)

Your Time

Language Focus: Personalizing activity and frequency language

Materials Needed: CD/cassette and player; Unit 5 Word Time Word Cards, 1 card per 2 students (see Picture and Word Card Book page 18)

For general information on Your Time, see pages 18–19.

Warm-Up and Review

1. **Reading Review: In Your Own Words.** Students open their Student Books to page 29 and take two to three minutes to review the article. Then have students take turns telling the class—in their own words—something about the reading. For example: *This reading is about Crazy. Her brother is a pest.* Continue until most students have taken a turn. It is okay if more than one student tells the same information.

2. Check Workbook page 29. (For instructions and answer key, see Teacher's Book page 165.)

Introduce the Lesson

Write *How often do you take medicine? I take medicine once a day.* on the board. Point to the sentences and have students read them. Quickly review meaning if necessary. Then ask students five to six questions relating to how often they do certain actions (see Suggested Questions below).

Suggested Questions:
How often do you give a speech?
How often do you go to the dentist?
How often do you drink lemonade?
Do you ever get a sunburn?
Do you ever bake bread?

Practice the Lesson

Students open their Student Books to page 30.

A. Listen and answer the questions.

1. Play the recording. For each number, students listen to the question and answer it based on their own knowledge.

    1. *How often do you read a newspaper?*
    2. *How often do you get a haircut?*
    3. *How often do you visit a museum?*
    4. *How often do you feed the birds?*

2. Check answers by dividing the class into pairs and having students in each pair read one question and answer to the class.

    Answer Key:
    Answers will vary.

B. Ask your classmates. Write their names and circle Yes or No.

Students ask three classmates *Do you (take medicine) (once) a (day)?* using the word cues from the chart. They record the answers in the chart. Then ask students questions about what they found out. For example: Ask *Does (Ken) take medicine once a day?* Students who know this information respond *Yes, he does* or *No, he doesn't.*

C. Review. Read and write the answers.

1. Students read each question and write an answer based on their own knowledge and experience.

2. Check answers by dividing the class into pairs and having students in each pair read one question and answer to the class.

    Answer Key:
    Answers will vary.

Games and Activities

1. **Cut and Paste.** Cut the Unit 5 Word Time Word Cards in half after the verb (for example: *go/on a date*, *take/the subway*). Then give each student one of the card halves. Students walk around the classroom, looking for the other half of their card. Once they find a student with the other half of their card, the two

students work together to write two different sentences about themselves or people they know, using their verb phrase. For example: *I often take the subway. My brother takes the subway three times a week.* Pairs then take turns reading their sentences to the class. Student then exchange cards and do the activity again.

2. **Schedules.** Divide the class into pairs and give them three to four minutes to talk with their partners about their weekly/monthly schedules (students can take notes if necessary to remember what their partner says). Then each pair joins with another pair and each student tells the others about his/her partner's weekly/monthly schedule. For example: *My partner, Jim, washes the pots and pans once a day. He hardly ever practices the piano.*

3. **Drawing.** Give students five to six minutes to draw pictures of themselves doing activities they do just once or twice a week. Once students have finished drawing, divide the class into pairs. Students tell their partners about their drawings. For example: *This is me. I practice the violin twice a week.*

Finish the Lesson

1. **Sentence Contest.** Divide the class into Teams A and B. Write *always, often, hardly ever, once a week, twice a month, three times a day, walk to school, buy groceries, visit a museum,* and *bake bread* on the board. S1 from Team A makes a sentence about himself/herself or people he/she knows, including a verb phrase and a frequency word/phrase from the board. For example: *I buy groceries once a week.* S1 from Team B does the same with another verb phrase and a frequency word/phrase. Each contestant gets a point for a grammatically correct sentence. Continue for four to five minutes. The team with the most points at the end wins.

   Note: Students may use verbs other than the ones on the board.

2. Explain and assign Workbook page 30. (For instructions, see Teacher's Book page 165.)

3. Do Chapter 3 of Storybook 5, *Digger and the Thief.* (For instructions and answer key, see Teacher's Book pages 180 and 181.)

> **Assessment**
> Explain and assign the Unit 5 Test, page 220. (For instructions and answer key, see page 210.)

Review 1

Conversation Time Review

Review Focus: Units 1–5 conversations
Materials Needed: CD/cassette and player

Warm-Up

1. **Review Units 1–5 Conversations.** Students turn to each Conversation Time page (pages 1, 7, 13, 19, and 25). Elicit each conversation.
2. Check Workbook page 30. (For instructions and answer key, see Teacher's Book page 165.)

Practice the Language

Students open their Student Books to page 31.

A. **Listen and circle the correct picture.**

1. Play the recording. Students listen and, for each number, they circle the picture that corresponds to the conversation they hear.

    1. Clerk: *Good morning, Sunnyville Museum. How can I help you?*
       Ted: *Hi. Do you have a special exhibit today?*
       Clerk: *Yes, we do. It's an exhibit of old photographs of Sunnyville.*
       Ted: *Are there any tours?*
       Clerk: *Yes. Tours are at 11:00, 2:30, and 5:00.*
       Ted: *Thanks for your help.*
       Clerk: *You're welcome.*

    2. Waiter: *Hello. Are you ready to order?*
       Ms. Day: *I think so. I'll have a bowl of chicken soup.*
       Waiter: *I'm sorry. We don't have chicken soup today. We have garlic soup.*
       Ms. Day: *Oh, I don't like garlic. Hmm. What's today's special?*
       Waiter: *Spaghetti and meatballs.*
       Ms. Day: *Sounds good. I'll have spaghetti and iced tea.*
       Waiter: *Okay. Spaghetti and meatballs, and a glass of iced tea. I'll be right back.*

    3. Baker: *Hi. Can I help you?*
       Man: *Yes, please. What kinds of pie do you have?*
       Baker: *We have lemon, peach, and cherry.*
       Man: *How about apple? I love apple pie.*
       Baker: *Sorry, we're out of apple.*
       Man: *Oh. How much are the cherry pies?*
       Baker: *They're $10 each.*
       Man: *Okay, I'll take a cherry pie.*
       Baker: *Great!*

    4. Ms. Day: *Hello?*
       Woman: *Hello. May I speak to Annie, please?*
       Ms. Day: *I'm sorry. She's not in right now.*
       Woman: *Can you take a message?*
       Ms. Day: *Sure. Who's calling?*
       Woman: *This is Mrs. Brown at the Sunnyville Library. We have* Sports in Sunnyville *now.*
       Ms. Day: *Is that a book?*
       Woman: *No. It's a video.*
       Ms. Day: *Okay. I'll give her the message.*

5. Matt: *Hi, Ted!*
   Ted: *Hi, Matt. How are you?*
   Matt: *Fine, thanks. How are you?*
   Ted: *I'm good. How's your family?*
   Matt: *My mother and sister are sick.*
   Ted: *I'm sorry to hear that. What's the matter?*
   Matt: *They have the flu.*
   Ted: *Oh. Is your brother sick, too?*
   Matt: *No, he isn't sick.*
   Ted: *Good!*
   Matt: *Well, I'll see you later, Ted!*
   Ted: *Okay. Bye!*

2. Check answers by having students listen to the conversations again. Stop the recording after each conversation and have students say the letter of the picture they have circled.

   Answer Key:
   1. b   2. b   3. a   4. b   5. c

B. Listen and circle the correct answer.

1. Play the recording. Students listen and, for each number, they circle the number or words that they hear discussed in the conversation.

   1. Clerk: *Sunnyville Theater. How can I help you?*
      Annie: *Hi. What time is the movie today?*
      Clerk: *4:15.*
      Annie: *4:50?*
      Clerk: *No. 4:15.*
      Annie: *Oh. Thank you.*

   2. Waiter: *Hello. Are you ready to order?*
      Ms. Day: *I think so. I'll have a piece of apple pie and a glass of iced tea.*
      Dr. Day: *I'll have a piece of apple pie, too, and a cup of coffee.*
      Annie: *I'll have a piece of apple pie and a glass of iced tea.*
      Waiter: *All right. That's three pieces of apple pie, one glass of iced tea, and two cups of coffee.*
      Ms. Day: *No, no. We want two glasses of iced tea and one cup of coffee.*
      Waiter: *Okay. I'll be right back.*

   3. Baker: *Hi. Can I help you?*
      Woman: *Yes, please. I'd like a lemon pie and a blueberry pie.*
      Baker: *Okay. That's 30 dollars.*
      Woman: *13 dollars?*
      Baker: *No, 30 dollars.*
      Woman: *Okay. Here you are.*
      Baker: *Thank you.*

   4. Ms. Day: *Hello?*
      Girl: *Hello. May I speak to Annie, please?*
      Ms. Day: *She's not in right now.*
      Girl: *Can you take a message, please? This is Tim Jones. My number is 987-9876.*
      Ms. Day: *Did you say 987-9867?*
      Girl: *No, it's 987-9876.*
      Ms. Day: *Got it. I'll give her the message.*

2. Check answers by having students listen to the conversations again. Stop the recording after each conversation and have students say the number or words they have circled.

   Answer Key:
   1. 4:15
   2. 2 glasses
   3. 30
   4. 987-9876

Games and Activities

1. **Role Play.** Write the third conversation from exercise A on the board. Point to each line and have students read it. Then divide the class into pairs and have students in each pair role-play the conversation. Students change roles and role-play the conversation again.

2. **Act It Out.** Divide the class into pairs. Students in each pair work together to write out a mini-dialogue (approximately four to five lines long) between two friends meeting in the park. Once students have created their dialogues, choose volunteers to role-play their dialogues for the class.

3. **Illustrators.** Read the third conversation from exercise B. Students listen and then draw pictures to illustrate the conversation. Volunteers then take turns showing their pictures to the class and explaining them.

Finish the Lesson

1. **Who Says It?** Read the second conversation from exercise B. Discuss with students where they think the conversation is being held, and who the speakers might be.

2. Explain and assign Workbook page 31. (For instructions, see Teacher's Book page 166.)

Digger and Max

Review Focus: Units 1–5 conversations, vocabulary, and patterns

Materials Needed: CD/cassette and player

Warm-Up

1. **Review Units 1–5 Vocabulary and Patterns.** Turn to each Word Time page (pages 2, 8, 14, 20, and 26) and Focus Time page (pages 3, 9, 15, 21, and 27). Elicit each vocabulary item and pattern.
2. Check Workbook page 31. (For instructions and answer key, see Teacher's Book page 166.)

Work with the Pictures

Students open their Student Books to pages 32 and 33.

1. Divide the class into groups of three. Groups find and name any items or characters they recognize in the pictures.
2. Ask each group how many items they found. Encourage groups to name as many items or characters as they can, using complete sentences when possible.
3. When groups have finished, have each group name one item, and write a sentence using that item on the board. Once all the sentences have been written, point to and read each sentence. Students repeat, pointing to those items in their books.
4. Ask students what they think the readings will be about.

Practice the Reading

A. **Listen and read along. Then look at the pictures and write the days of the week.**

1. Play the recording. Students listen and read along.

   Today I went to a restaurant with Max. He had four slices of ham, two bowls of chicken soup, and three pieces of apple pie. Max loves eating! He eats too much. He's always in the mood for ice cream, too.

   Today I was busy. I bought groceries, did laundry, and ironed all my shirts. Then I baked bread and made dinner. Max visited me and ate all the bread. He never has dinner by himself!

   Today Max and I visited the Food School. We took the subway. There was a baking class. Max baked an apple pie. Max sliced apples by himself. He hurt his finger. It wasn't serious.

   Max and I walked to the park today. We took a nap near the lake. Max got a sunburn. Then we fed the birds and Max fell into the lake. Tomorrow I'm going to stay home by myself!

2. Play the recording again, stopping after each paragraph. Students find the picture that corresponds to each paragraph and write the corresponding day.

   Answer Key:
   Monday, Tuesday, Thursday, Friday

B. **Listen and read along. Then look at the pictures and write the days of the week.**

1. Play the recording. Students listen and read along.

   Today I went to a restaurant with Digger. He had one bowl of fruit salad and a cup of coffee. He doesn't eat enough. He's too thin. Tomorrow I'm going to go to his house and make dinner with him.

   I ate too much at Digger's house on Tuesday night. I had a stomachache this morning. I had a bowl of ice cream for lunch. It was delicious! Ice cream is the best medicine.

   There was a baking class at the Food School today. I made an apple pie. I had an accident. I hurt my finger. But my pie was delicious. Digger liked it, too. I'm happy.

84

> *It was 80 degrees today. I went to Digger's house. He wanted to stay home by himself. I went to the park by myself. It wasn't fun. Then Digger came to the park because he was bored at home. We had a good time.*
>
> 2. Play the recording again, stopping after each paragraph. Students find the picture that corresponds to each paragraph and write the corresponding day.
>
>   *Answer Key:*
>   Monday, Wednesday, Thursday, Saturday
>
> 3. Ask students to comment on the differences between Digger's and Max's accounts of their week.

Games and Activities

1. **Listen Carefully.** Play the recording of Digger's Diary again. Students listen and write down three things that Digger did on Tuesday and two things he did on Friday. Then play the recording of Max's Diary. Students listen and write down two things Digger ate on Monday, and two things Max did on Thursday.

2. **Tell the Story.** Divide the class into pairs. Students in each pair cover the text on each diary page. They then take turns looking at the pictures and telling the events to their partners.

3. **Make a New Story.** Each student divides a piece of paper in four equal parts. He/She then creates a new story about *either* Digger or Max by drawing original scenes. Students then take turns standing up and describing their story to the rest of the class.

Finish the Lesson

1. **Change the Readings.** Students take turns reading one sentence each, first from Digger's diary, then from Max's diary. They change the diaries into stories by changing the subjects from *I* to *he*. For example: *Today he was busy. He bought groceries, did laundry, and ironed all his shirts. Then he baked bread and made dinner.*

2. Explain and assign Workbook pages 32–33. (For instructions, see Teacher's Book page 166.)

Word Time and Focus Time Review

Review Focus: Units 1–5 vocabulary and patterns

Materials Needed: CD/cassette and player; Units 1–5 Word Time Word Cards, 1 set (see Picture and Word Card Book pages 2, 6, 10, 14, and 18)

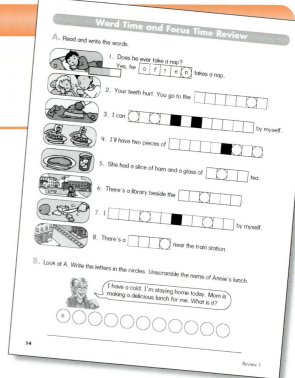

Warm-Up

1. **Questions.** Ask students *Do you ever bake bread?* Several students answer. Do the same with *Do you ever drink iced tea?* and *Is there a library near your house?*
2. Check Workbook pages 32–33. (For instructions and answer key, see Teacher's Book page 166.)

Review

Students open their Student Books to page 34.

A. Read and write the words.

1. Based on the picture and word cues, students fill in each missing word.
2. Check answers by saying *Number 1* and having a volunteer say the corresponding sentence. Do the same for numbers 2–8.

   Answer Key:
   1. Does he ever take a nap? Yes, he often takes a nap.
   2. Your teeth hurt. You go to the <u>dentist</u>.
   3. I can <u>iron a shirt</u> by myself.
   4. I'll have two pieces of <u>apple pie</u>.
   5. She had a slice of ham and a glass of <u>iced</u> tea.
   6. There's a library beside the <u>school</u>.
   7. I <u>sliced fruit</u> by myself.
   8. There's a <u>bank</u> near the train station.

B. Look at A. Write the letters in the circles. Unscramble the name of Annie's lunch.

Students write each of the circled letters from exercise A. They then unscramble the letters and write the food that Annie will have for lunch.

   Answer Key:
   chicken soup

Games and Activities

1. **Draw the Picture.** (See Game 13, page 155.) Play the game using Units 1–5 Word Time Word Cards.
2. **Classification.** Place the Units 1–3 Word Time Word Cards along the chalktray. Then make three columns on the board, one labeled *Buildings*, one labeled *Food*, and one labeled *Activities*. For students' reference, attach the *library* word card to the *Buildings* column, the *roast beef* word card to the *Food* column, and the *take a bus* word card to the *Activities* column. Volunteers then take turns coming to the board, placing one of the word cards from the chalktray in the appropriate column, naming the card, and using the word or phrase in a sentence. Once all the word cards have been attached to the board, point to each one and have students read it. If necessary, re-adjust cards so that they are in the correct columns.

Finish the Lesson

1. **True Sentences.** Students take turns saying true sentences using the pattern *I can (slice fruit) by myself.* Continue until each student has taken a turn.
2. Explain and assign Workbook page 34. (For instructions, see Teacher's Book pages 166–167.)

Pairwork

Review Focus: Personalizing Units 1–5 language

Materials Needed: CD/cassette and player

Warm-Up

1. **Questions.** Ask students *Do you ever eat garlic bread?* Several students answer. Do the same with *Do you ever do laundry?* and *How often do you talk on the phone?*
2. Check Workbook page 34. (For instructions and answer key, see Teacher's Book pages 166–167.)

Review

Divide the class into pairs. One student in each pair opens his/her Student Book to page 35. The other student in each pair opens his/her Student Book to page 36.

A. Ask your partner and fill in the chart.

1. Students in each pair ask their partner the target questions in order to get the information necessary to fill in the blanks.
2. Check answers by having pairs of students read the questions and answers to the class.

Answer Key:

	Annie	Ted
1. roast beef	one slice	two slices
2. apple pie	three pieces	one piece
3. garlic bread	two loaves	one loaf
4. root beer	one bottle	two bottles

B. Ask and answer the questions.

1. Each student fills in the *You* column of the chart. Then students in each pair ask their partner the target questions in order to get the information necessary to fill in the blanks.
2. Check answers by having pairs of students read the questions and answers to the class.

Answer Key:

	Annie	Ted	You	Your Partner
1. take a nap	sometimes	always		Answers will vary.
2. listen to pop music	often	sometimes		
3. visit a museum	hardly ever	never		
4. talk on the phone	often	usually		

C. Ask and answer the questions.

1. Each student fills in the *You* column of the chart. Then students in each pair ask their partner the target questions in order to get the information necessary to fill in the blanks.
2. Check answers by having pairs of students read the questions and answers to the class.

Answer Key:

	Annie	Ted	You	Your Partner
1. do laundry	twice a month	twice a month		Answers will vary.
2. bake bread	three times a month	once a year		
3. feed the pets	twice a day	once a day		
4. set the table	once a week	once a day		

D. Finished? Compare answers with Student A/Student B.

Students compare answers with their partners.

Games and Activities

1. **True Sentences.** Say *often*. Elicit *I often (visit a museum)* from several students. Do the same with *always*, *usually*, *hardly ever*, *never*, and *sometimes*.
2. **Option: Project.** For a week, students keep a list of actions they do once, twice, and three times a week. Then have students share their lists in class.

Finish the Lesson

1. Explain and assign Checklist 1 (see Student Book pages 78–81) for students to do at home or in class.
2. Explain and assign Workbook pages 35–36. (For instructions and answer key, see Teacher's Book page 167.)

Assessment
Explain and assign the Midterm Test, pages 221–224. (For instructions and answer key, see pages 210–211.)

6 The School Concert

Conversation Time

Language Focus: Helping a friend clean up

Materials Needed: CD/cassette and player; Wall Chart 11

For general information on Conversation Time, see pages 8–9.

Warm-Up and Review

1. **Review: Questions and Answers.** Write *How often do you feed the birds?* and *Do you ever feed the birds?* on the board. Point to each sentence and have students read it. Then say *feed the birds*. A volunteer asks you *How often do you feed the birds?* or *Do you ever feed the birds?* Answer the question. Then say *bake bread* and have a different volunteer ask you a question. Continue in the same way for three to four minutes.

2. Check Workbook pages 35–36. (For instructions and answer key, see Teacher's Book page 167.)

Introduce the Conversation

1. Set the scene and clarify meaning by saying *Ted is cleaning up the music room to help his teacher get ready for the concert. Annie wants to help. They move the heavy bass and have an accident. Ms. Apple is not happy to see the mess.* Then introduce the new words by writing each word on the board. Point to and read each word before explaining its meaning. Students repeat the word.

   concert: Say *A concert is a show where people sing, and play the piano, the violin, and other instruments.*

   move: Set your book on a student's desk. Then, while moving the book to a different student's desk, say *I'm moving the book.*

   lift: Lift up a chair and set it back down in the same place. Say *I lifted the chair.*

   look out: On the board write *look out = watch out*. Point to and read each word. Students repeat.

   What's going on?: Write *What's going on? = What are you doing?* on the board. Point to and read each word. Students repeat.

2. Bring three students to the front of the classroom. Have one of them (Student C) stand off to the side. Stand behind each student and model his/her lines of the conversation with the following actions:

   A: *Hi, Ted! What are you doing?*
   Walk up to Student B. Speak in a friendly, questioning voice.

B: *I'm helping Mr. Tune clean up the music room. He's getting ready for the concert.*
Pretend to be cleaning the room. Stop and look at Student A.

A: *Do you want some help?*
Ask Student B the question in a friendly voice.

B: *Sure. You can move the bass. Put it over there, by the window.*
Point to a pretend bass. Turn and point to the window.

A: *Ugh! I can't lift it by myself. It's so heavy.*
Pretend to begin to lift the "bass." Then heavily set it back down on the floor.

B: *Here. I'll take it.*
Walk toward Student A. Speak confidently. Pretend to pick up the bass and start to walk with it.

A: *Look out! There's a box behind you!*
Speak excitedly, with an alarmed expression on your face. Point behind Student B.

B: *Ahhhh!*
While still holding the bass, pretend to trip over a box.

C: *What's going on in here?*
Walk up to Students A and B with a slightly alarmed expression on your face.

B: *We're cleaning up.*
Speak sheepishly.

3. Divide the class into Groups A, B, and C. Model the conversation again using facial expressions and body language. Group A repeats Annie's lines, Group B repeats Ted's lines, and Group C repeats Ms. Apple's line. Encourage students to copy your facial expressions and body language. Groups change roles and say the conversation again in the same way. Continue until each group has taken on each role.

4. Attach Wall Chart 11 to the board or open a Student Book to page 37. Students then open their Student Books to page 37. Ask the following questions:

> What is Ted doing?
> Why is he cleaning the music room?
> Can Annie lift the bass?
> Why did Annie say "Look out!"?
> What did Ms. Apple ask?

Practice the Conversation

A. Listen and repeat. Point to the speakers. Then listen again.

1. Play the recording (first version of the conversation). Students listen and repeat, pointing to each speaker.

   1. Annie: Hi, Ted! What are you doing?
      Ted: I'm helping Mr. Tune clean up the music room. He's getting ready for the concert.
   2. Annie: Do you want some help?
      Ted: Sure. You can move the bass.
   3. Ted: Put it over there, by the window.
      Annie: Ugh! I can't lift it by myself.
   4. Annie: It's so heavy.
      Ted: Here. I'll take it.
   5. Annie: Look out! There's a box behind you!
      Ted: Ahhhh!
   6. Teacher: What's going on in here?
      Ted: We're cleaning up.

2. Play the recording (second version of the conversation). Students listen.

B. Role-play the conversation.

Divide the class into groups of three. Using their Student Books for reference, each group role-plays the conversation. They then change roles and role-play the conversation again. Groups continue until each student has taken on each role.

Games and Activities

Note: For all Conversation Time activities, students may use their Student Books for reference.

1. **Listen Carefully.** Write the following sentences on the board. Play the recording of the conversation. Students listen and write the missing words to complete each sentence.

   1. Ted is _____ Mr. Tune.
   2. Annie asks, "Do you want _____ help?"
   3. Ted wants Annie to put the bass by the _____.
   4. The bass is _____.

   Check answers by saying *Number 1*. A volunteer reads the complete sentence. Do the same for numbers 2–4.

   Answer Key:
   1. Ted is <u>helping</u> Mr. Tune.
   2. Annie asks, "Do you want <u>some</u> help?"
   3. Ted wants Annie to put the bass by the <u>window</u>.
   4. The bass is <u>heavy</u>.

2. **True/False/I Don't Know.** Say five to six statements about the conversation (see Suggested Statements below). Students say *True* if the statement is true, and *False* if it is false. If a statement is false, choose a volunteer to make it true. If students don't have enough information to determine if the statement is true or false, they say *I don't know*.

   Suggested Statements:
   Ted likes Mr. Tune.
   The bass is heavy.
   Annie is strong.
   Ms. Apple is happy.
   Ted wants the bass by the door.
   Annie doesn't like to play the bass.

3. **Make It Your Own.** Write the following on the board:

   A: Do you want some help?
   B: <u>Sure. You can move the bass.</u>

   Students read the dialogue on the board. Then divide the class into pairs and write the following on the board:

   1. No, thanks. Everything's under control.
   2. Well, let me think. Oh, I know! You can erase the board.
   3. Not right now, thanks. But if you come back in ten minutes, you can sweep the floor.

   Students read each new response. Quickly clarify meaning if necessary. Then students in each pair role-play the dialogue on the board, substituting the new responses into the underlined part of the target conversation.

Finish the Lesson

1. **Discussion.** Have a short discussion (for about three to four minutes) with the class, talking about what might happen next. For example: Ms. Apple helps Annie and Ted clean up the music room. Annie and Ted get sent to the principal's office for making such a mess.

2. Explain and assign Workbook page 37. (For instructions, see Teacher's Book page 167.)

Word Time

Language Focus: Musical instruments (*tuba, flute, cymbals, drums, xylophone, electric keyboard, harp, cello, recorder, trumpet*)

Materials Needed (excluding materials for optional activities): CD/cassette and player; Wall Chart 12; beanbags, 1 per 3–4 students; Unit 6 Word Time Picture Cards, 1 set per 3–4 students; Unit 6 Word Time Word Cards, 1 set; (see Picture and Word Card Book pages 21 and 22)

For general information on Word Time, see pages 10–11.

Warm-Up and Review

1. **Conversation Review: Dictation.** Say a line from the Unit 6 conversation. Students write the line on a piece of paper, using correct capitalization and punctuation. The first student to correctly write the line quickly acts it out. Continue in the same way with three to four different lines of conversation.

2. Check Workbook page 37. (For instructions and answer key, see Teacher's Book page 167.)

Introduce the Words

1. Pantomime playing a flute. Say *I'm playing a flute.* Then hold up and name the *flute* picture card. Students copy your actions and repeat the word. Continue in the same way with the remaining target instruments.

2. Attach the Unit 6 Word Time Picture Cards in a row to the board. Stand the Unit 6 Word Time Word Cards on the chalktray under the corresponding picture cards. Point to each picture/word card pair and read the word. Students repeat. Then reposition the word cards so they are no longer directly below the corresponding picture cards. Volunteers come to the board one by one and place a word card under its corresponding picture card, then point to and read the word. Seated students repeat.

   OPTION: Give each student a Unit 6 Word Time Picture Card or Word Card. A student with a picture card stands up and pantomimes playing the instrument on his/her card. The student(s) with the corresponding word card holds up and names the card. Continue in the same way for two to three minutes.

Talk About the Picture

1. Students open their Student Books to page 38. They look at the large scene and use complete sentences to identify anything they can.

2. Attach Wall Chart 12 to the board or open a Student Book to page 38. Read the following "story" while pointing to or touching the pictures (**bold** words) and pantomiming the actions (*italicized* words).

   > The students are playing a concert! Each student is playing a **musical instrument**. **Joe** has a **tuba**. **Jan** is really *hitting* the **drums**. **Kim** is *playing the* **xylophone** and **Mike** is *playing an* **electric keyboard**. **This boy and girl** are *holding* **cymbals**. **These boys** are *playing* **violins**. **Matt** and **his friend** are *playing* **flutes**. **Emily** is *blowing* into a **trumpet**. **Bob** is *playing the* **harp** and *crying*. **Ivy** is *quietly playing the* **cello**.

3. Ask the following questions while pointing to or touching the pictures (**bold** words) and pantomiming the adjectives (*italicized* words).

   > Do the **cymbals** sound *quiet*?
   > Which **instruments** can sound *quiet*?
   > Does the **harp** sound *loud*?
   > Which **instruments** can sound *loud*?
   > (**flute**) Is it a flute?
   > (**violin**) Is it a bass?
   > (**harp**) What's this?
   > Can you please raise your hand if you play the drums?
   > Can you please raise your hand if you play the recorder?
   > Can you please raise your hand if you play the cello?
   > What's your favorite instrument?

Practice the Words

A. Listen and repeat.

1. Play the recording. Students listen and repeat, pointing to each word in the vocabulary box.

   1. *tuba*
   2. *flute*
   3. *cymbals*
   4. *drums*
   5. *xylophone*
   6. *electric keyboard*
   7. *harp*
   8. *cello*
   9. *recorder*
   10. *trumpet*

2. Say the words in random order. Students point to them in the vocabulary box.

B. Point and say the words.

Students point to each of the target vocabulary items in the large scene and name them.

C. Listen and point.

Play the recording. Students listen to the words. For the vocabulary, they point to the named item; for the conversations, they point to the speakers. (References are shown in parentheses.) Play the recording as many times as necessary for students to complete the task.

Flute.
Cymbals.
Recorder.
Cello.
Xylophone.
Drums.
Trumpet.
Harp.
Electric keyboard.
Tuba.

Now listen and point to the speakers.

A: *Mom, I have a stomachache.* (boy and mother in front row of audience)
B: *How many bottles of root beer did you have at dinner?*
A: *Three.*
B: *Oh, dear.*

A: *Hi. Is Sam there? He isn't? Can you take a message? This is Kelly Beal.* (woman talking on cell phone and man in front row of audience)
B: *Sh! Be quiet!*
A: *Sorry!*

A: *I like playing the violin, but I don't practice enough.* (two boys on left playing violins)
B: *Well, practice makes perfect!*
A: *Do you want to practice together?*
B: *Sure!*

Games and Activities

1. **Beanbags.** (See Game 8, page 154.) Play the game using Unit 6 Word Time Picture Cards.

2. **Survey.** Students create a survey on a sheet of paper by writing *Name* and *Do you like to play the _____?* in a row at the top of the paper. Then they write a list of six musical instruments along the left side of the paper. Students then go around the classroom and ask their classmates *Do you like to play the (tuba)?* Students respond *Yes, I like to play the (tuba)* or *No, I don't like to play the (tuba).* Students record the answers they hear. Continue until all students have asked at least six other students the question. Students sit down. Then ask students questions about the survey. For example: Ask *Does Bill like to play the recorder?* Students who know this information respond either *Yes, he does* or *No, he doesn't.*

3. **Categorize.** Work with students to come up with two or three different categories that the instruments could be divided into. Some possibilities are: *woodwind, brass, strings, instruments you blow into, big instruments, little instruments.* Once the class has decided on a set of categories, divide the class into groups of three. Students in each group write each category on a piece of paper and list the corresponding instruments in each category.

4. **Option: Personalize the Vocabulary.** Invite one to three musicians to come to your English class. Ask them to tell students about the instrument(s) they play.

Finish the Lesson

1. **Pantomime.** Say *flute*. Students say *I'm going to play the flute* and then pantomime playing the flute. Do the same with the remaining target instruments.

2. Explain and assign Workbook page 38. (For instructions, see Teacher's Book pages 167–168.)

Focus Time

Language Focus: Adverbs of manner (*well, badly, quietly, loudly, quickly, slowly, happily, sadly*)

Wh- questions with *how*; simple past tense [*How did (he) play the (tuba)? (He) played the (tuba) (well).*]

Function: Describing how actions were performed in the past

Materials Needed: CD/cassette and player; Unit 6 Word Time Picture Cards, 1 set; Unit 6 Word Time Word Cards, 1 set per 2 students; Unit 6 Focus Time Picture Cards, 1 set per 6–8 students; Unit 6 Focus Time Word Cards, 1 set per 2 students; *I, He, She, We, They, you, he, she,* and *they* grammar cards, 1 set per 2 students; Unit 6 Grammar Cards, 1 set per 2 students (see Picture and Word Card Book pages 21, 22, 23, 24, 43, and 49)

For general information on Focus Time, see pages 12–13.

Warm-Up and Review

1. **Vocabulary Review: True Sentences.** Attach the Unit 6 Word Time Picture Cards to the board and number them from 1 to 10. Say a number. Students say the musical instrument corresponding to that number. Then volunteers make true sentences about the instruments on the board. For example: *I can play the flute. I can't play the trumpet.* Continue for three to four minutes.

2. **Check Workbook page 38.** (For instructions and answer key, see Teacher's Book pages 167–168.)

This lesson is in two parts.

Part 1: Introduce the Words

Write very neatly on the board and say *I'm writing well.* Students copy your actions and words. Then write very sloppily and say *I'm writing badly.* Students copy your actions and words. Write *well* and *badly* on the board. Then speak quietly and say *I'm talking quietly.* Students repeat. Speak very loudly and say *I'm speaking loudly.* Students repeat. Write *quietly* and *loudly* on the board. Walk across the room quickly and say *I'm walking quickly.* Students copy your actions and words. Walk slowly and say *I'm walking slowly.* Students copy your actions and words. Write *quickly* and *slowly* on the board. Read a short passage from a book very happily. Say *I'm reading happily.* Students repeat. Then read the same passage sadly and say *I'm reading sadly.* Students repeat. Write *happily* and *sadly* on the board. Point to each of the eight words on the board and have students read them.

Practice the Words

Students open their Student Books to page 39.

A. Listen and repeat.

Play the recording. Students listen and repeat each word.

1. *well*
2. *badly*
3. *quietly*
4. *loudly*
5. *quickly*
6. *slowly*
7. *happily*
8. *sadly*

good, well
bad, badly
quiet, quietly
loud, loudly
quick, quickly
slow, slowly
happy, happily
sad, sadly

Part 2: Introduce the Patterns

1. **How did (he) play the (tuba)? (He) played the (tuba) (well).** Bring a volunteer to the front of the classroom. Say *Please play the tuba quickly* and have the volunteer pretend to quickly play a tuba, then stop. Point to the volunteer, look at the class, and ask *How did he play the tuba?* Students repeat. Write *How did he play the tuba?* on the board. Point to and read each word. Students repeat. Then ask the question again and have students formulate an answer on their own. Say *He played the tuba quickly.* Students repeat. Write *He played the tuba quickly.* on the board to the right of *How did he play the tuba?* Do the same with *flute/quietly, harp/happily,* and *drums/loudly.*

2. **Practice for Fluency.** Say *they, recorder.* Students ask the corresponding target question, *How did they play the recorder?* Say *well.* Students say *They played the recorder well.* Do the same with other pronouns, instruments, and adverbs for four to five minutes.

Practice the Patterns

B. Listen and repeat.

1. Write the text from the pattern boxes on the board. Then play the recording, pointing to each word. Students listen.

   A: *How did he play the tuba?*
   B: *He played the tuba well.*

   A: *How did they play the tuba?*
   B: *They played the tuba well.*

2. Play the recording again. Students look at the pattern boxes in their books and repeat, pointing to each word.

3. Students work with partners to say the questions and answers, while looking at the pattern boxes in their books.

C. Look at page 38. Listen and point.

Play the recording. Students look at page 38 and listen to the words, pointing to the person playing each instrument they hear named. Play the recording as many times as necessary for students to complete the task.

   A: *How did she play the flute?*
   B: *She played the flute well.*

   A: *How did he play the harp?*
   B: *He played the harp sadly.*

   A: *How did he play the electric keyboard?*
   B: *He played the electric keyboard slowly.*

Games and Activities

1. **Slow, Slowly.** Say *good.* Using their Student Books for reference if necessary, students say the corresponding adverb, *well.* Do the same with the remaining target adjective/adverb pairs. Then say *slowly* and have a volunteer use the word in a sentence. For example: *I always walk to school slowly* or *I like to read slowly.* Do the same with the remaining target adverbs.

2. **How Did He Play?** Divide the class into groups of six to eight and give each group a set of Unit 6 Word Time Word Cards and Focus Time Picture Cards. The groups place the picture cards and word cards facedown in two separate piles. A student in each group (S1) begins by picking up a card from each pile (for example: *cello, sadly*). He/She then pantomimes playing the (cello) (sadly) and then stops. The student to S1's left (S2) asks another student in the group (S3) about S1's playing, *How did (he) play the (cello)?* S3 answers, *He/She played the cello sadly.* S2 then takes a turn choosing two cards and pantomiming. Groups continue until they have pantomimed all the cards.

3. **Make the Sentences.** (See Game 17, pages 155–156.) Do the activity using *I, He, She, We, They, you, he, she,* and *they* grammar cards and Unit 6 Word Time Word Cards, Focus Time Word Cards, and Grammar Cards.

Finish the Lesson

1. **Follow Directions.** Say *Please play the drums quietly.* Students on the right side of the classroom pantomime playing drums quietly. Then they stop. Students on the left side of the classroom ask *How did you play the drums?* Students on the right answer. Continue in the same way for three to four minutes, having students switch roles each time.

2. Explain and assign Workbook page 39. (For instructions, see Teacher's Book page 168.)

Practice Time

Language Focus: Adverbs of manner; Wh- questions with *how*; simple past tense [*How did (he) play the (recorder)? (He) played the (recorder) (sadly).*]

Function: Describing how actions were performed in the past

Materials Needed: CD/cassette and player; Unit 1 Word Time Picture Cards, 1 set per 3–4 students; Unit 6 Word Time Picture Cards, 1 set; Unit 6 Focus Time Picture Cards, 1 set (see Picture and Word Card Book pages 1, 21, and 23)

For general information on Practice Time, see pages 14–15.

Warm-Up and Review

1. **Pattern Review: How Did You Play the Flute?** Write *How did they play the flute? They played the flute well.* on the board. Point to each sentence and have students read it. Then say *they, drums*. Students say *How did they play the drums?* Say *loudly* and have students say *They played the drums loudly*. Continue in the same way for three to four minutes.

2. Check Workbook page 39. (For instructions and answer key, see Teacher's Book page 168.)

Practice the Patterns

Students open their Student Books to page 40.

A. Listen and repeat. Then practice with a partner.

1. Play the recording. Students listen and repeat, pointing to each picture in their books.

   A: *How did he play the recorder?*
   B: *He played the recorder sadly.*

   1. *How did she play the xylophone?*
      She played the xylophone happily.
   2. *How did you play the drums?*
      I played the drums quickly.
   3. *How did he play the harp?*
      He played the harp sadly.
   4. *How did he play the electric keyboard?*
      He played the electric keyboard slowly.
   5. *How did you play the cymbals?*
      We played the cymbals loudly.
   6. *How did she play the trumpet?*
      She played the trumpet badly.
   7. *How did they play the flute?*
      They played the flute well.
   8. *How did she play the cello?*
      She played the cello quietly.

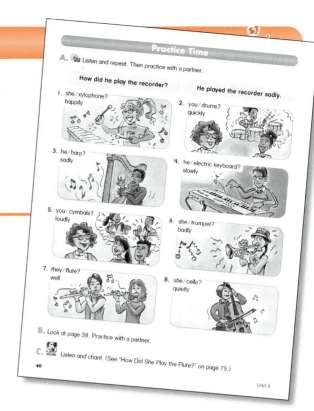

2. Students practice numbers 1–8 in pairs. (S1 in each pair asks the question, S2 answers.) Students then change roles and repeat the activity.

B. Look at page 38. Practice with a partner.

Students remain in pairs and look at page 38. They then take turns asking and answering questions about the characters in the large scene, using the target patterns and vocabulary items. For example: S1 (pointing to the girl playing the xylophone): *How did she play the xylophone?* S2: *She played the xylophone happily.*

C. Listen and chant.

1. Students turn to the *How Did She Play the Flute?* chant on page 75. They cover up the text, look at the pictures, and talk about what they see. Read the lyrics line by line. Students repeat each line. Play the recording. Students listen and follow along in their books.

   How Did She Play the Flute?

   How did she play the flute?
     She played the flute quickly.
   How did she play the cello?
     She played the cello slowly.
   How did she play the trumpet?
     She played the trumpet loudly.
   How did she play the harp?
     She played the harp quietly.

How did he play the drums?
  He played the drums happily.
How did he play the tuba?
  He played the tuba sadly.
How did he play the xylophone?
  He played the xylophone badly.
How did he play the recorder?
  He played the recorder well.

2. Play the recording again. Students listen and chant along, using their books for reference. Play the recording as many times as necessary for students to become familiar with the chant.

3. Play the karaoke version. Students chant along, pantomiming playing each instrument as they chant its name, and also pantomiming each adverb.

Games and Activities

1. **From Words to Sentences.** Write *Happy. I play the trumpet happily.* on the board. Point to the word and sentence and have students read them. Then hold up the *drums* and *loudly* picture cards. Students say *Loud. I play the drums loudly.* Continue in the same way with the remaining Unit 6 Word Time and Focus Time Picture Cards.

2. **Fill In.** Divide the class into pairs and write the following sentences on the board. Students in each pair copy the sentences onto a piece of paper and fill in the blanks with the correct forms of the word in parentheses. When they are done, each pair of students reads a pair of sentences to the class.

    1. It's my birthday today. I'm <u>happy</u>. I'm singing <u>happily</u>. (happy)
    2. The sick man is _____. He walks _____. (sad)
    3. Mother is a _____ cook. She cooks _____. (good)
    4. I can't play the flute. I'm _____ at it. I play the flute _____. (bad)
    5. The baby is sleeping. I'm being _____. I'm closing the door _____. (quiet)

    Answer Key:
    1. It's my birthday today. I'm <u>happy</u>. I'm singing <u>happily</u>.
    2. The sick man is <u>sad</u>. He walks <u>sadly</u>.
    3. Mother is a <u>good</u> cook. She cooks <u>well</u>.
    4. I can't play the flute. I'm <u>bad</u> at it. I play the flute <u>badly</u>.
    5. The baby is sleeping. I'm being <u>quiet</u>. I'm closing the door <u>quietly</u>.

3. **The Animals Came to Town.** Elicit names of animals familiar to students and write their names on the board. Divide the class into groups of three to four and give each group a set of Unit 1 Word Time Picture Cards. Each group arranges the picture cards on the floor. A student in each group begins by saying *I'm a (giraffe). I'm walking to the (library)*. He/She then pretends to be a giraffe walking to the *(library)* picture card. He/She walks in any way he/she wants to (for example: quickly, slowly, quietly). Once the (giraffe) has reached the (library), another student in the group asks the others in the group *How did the (giraffe) walk to the (library)?* Students answer *It walked to the (library) (quickly)*. Groups continue in the same way for five to seven minutes, taking turns pantomiming and asking the questions.

> **Extra Practice**
> Explain and assign Worksheet 11, Instruments, page 198. (For instructions and answer key, see page 185.)

Finish the Lesson

1. **Memory Chain.** (See Game 18, page 156.) Play the game using the pattern *I play the (electric keyboard) (happily)*.

2. Explain and assign Workbook page 40. (For instructions, see Teacher's Book page 168.)

Reading Time

Language Focus: Reading a concert review in a newspaper

Materials Needed: CD/cassette and player; Unit 6 Word Time Picture Cards, 1 card per student (see Picture and Word Card Book page 21)

For general information on Reading Time, see pages 16–17.

Warm-Up and Review

1. **Pattern Review: Questions and Answers.** Write *How did you play the tuba? I played the tuba quietly.* on the board. Point to each sentence and have students read it. Then give each student a Unit 6 Word Time Picture Card. Students take turns standing up and pretending to play the instrument on their card in a specific way (for example: happily, slowly, quietly). Then they stop. Choose different volunteers to ask *How did you play the (tuba)?* after each student has pantomimed. Continue until most students have taken a turn.

2. Check Workbook page 40. (For instructions and answer key, see Teacher's Book page 168.)

Introduce the Reading

Note: Students may learn the new vocabulary within the context of the reading, or each new word can be taught before students encounter it in the reading. Follow the steps below to introduce the new vocabulary and/or introduce the reading content.

1. Write the new words in a column on the board. Point to and read each word before explaining its meaning.

   performance: Say *I'm going to see a show on Friday night. A performance means the same thing as a show.*

   last: Say *In our last class, we studied (adverbs).*

   second: Have two students come to the front of the class. Point to each one as you say *first, second.*

   perform: Say *I performed at last night's performance. To perform is to be in a show.*

   play: Say the name of a popular play that students have seen or know about. Say *This is a play.*

   hit: Say the name of a very popular play or movie and say *Many people like it. It's a hit!*

   chorus: Say *A chorus is people singing together.*

   orchestra: Say *An orchestra is people playing the violin, tuba, flute, and other instruments together.*

   soloist: Say *A soloist is a person who plays an instrument or sings by herself at a performance.*

   after: Say *After our class today, you'll go home.*

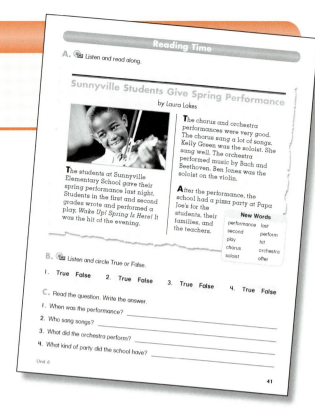

2. Students open their Student Books to page 41. They look at the picture and talk about what they see. For example: *This is from a newspaper. This boy is playing the violin.* Ask students what they think the reading will be about.

Practice the Reading

Students read the story silently to themselves.

A. Listen and read along.

1. Play the recording. Students listen and read along in their Student Books.

   Sunnyville Students Give Spring Performance
   by Laura Lakes

   The students at Sunnyville Elementary School gave their spring performance last night. Students in the first and second grades wrote and performed a play, Wake Up! Spring Is Here! It was the hit of the evening.

   The chorus and orchestra performances were very good. The chorus sang a lot of songs. Kelly Green was the soloist. She sang well. The orchestra performed music by Bach and Beethoven. Ben Jones was the soloist on the violin.

   After the performance, the school had a pizza party at Papa Joe's for the students, their families, and the teachers.

New Words
performance
last
second
perform
play
hit
chorus
orchestra
soloist
after

2. Play the recording again, stopping after each sentence. Students listen and repeat each sentence.

3. Divide the class into pairs. Students in each pair take turns reading the story aloud to their partner.

B. Listen and circle True or False.

1. Play the recording. For each number, students listen and circle *True* if the statement is true, and *False* if it is not.

   1. *The students gave their winter performance last night.*
   2. *The students in the first and second grades wrote and performed a play.*
   3. *There weren't any soloists in the performance.*
   4. *After the performance, there was an ice cream party.*

2. Check answers by saying *Number 1. The students gave their winter performance last night.* Students say *True* if they circled *True*, and *False* if they circled *False*. If the statement is false, choose a volunteer to make it true. Do the same for numbers 2–4.

   Answer Key:
   1. False   2. True   3. False   4. False

C. Read the question. Write the answer.

1. Students read each question and answer it based on the reading in exercise A.

2. Check answers by reading each question and having students read the answer they wrote.

   Answer Key:
   1. When was the performance? The performance was last night.
   2. Who sang songs? The chorus sang songs.
   3. What did the orchestra perform? The orchestra performed music by Bach and Beethoven.
   4. What kind of party did the school have? The school had a pizza party.

Games and Activities

Note: For all Reading Time activities, students may use their Student Books for reference.

1. **Please Correct Me.** Read sentences or parts of sentences from the reading, replacing one word in each utterance. Students follow in their Student Books and repeat each utterance, putting the word from the reading back in. For example: Say *The chorus and orchestra performances were very bad.* Students say *The chorus and orchestra performances were very good.* Continue for three to four minutes.

2. **Categorizing.** Divide the class into groups of two to three and write *People, Performance, Music, Time* in a row on the board. Students in each group work together to write words from the reading associated with the words on the board (see Suggested Categories below). Some words can be listed in several columns, for example *soloist (People, Performance, Music).* Once each group has made its lists, have students share their lists with the class. Work with the class as a whole to come to a consensus about what should be on each list. Write the final lists on the board.

   Suggested Categories:
   People: students, chorus, orchestra, Kelly Green, Ben Jones, Papa Joe, families, teachers
   Performance: play, perform, hit, very good
   Music: chorus, orchestra, sang, songs, soloist, music, Bach, Beethoven, violin
   Time: spring, last night, evening, after the performance

3. **End the Sentences.** Divide the class into groups of three to four and write the following sentences on the board. Students in each group work together to complete each sentence with information from the reading. Groups then take turns reading their sentences in the order in which they appear in the reading.

   The students at Sunnyville Elementary School _____.
   Students in the first and second grades _____.
   The chorus _____.
   The orchestra _____.
   Ben Jones _____.
   After the performance _____.

OPTION: Groups create their own stories by completing the sentences with original information. Then each group reads its story to the class.

Extra Practice
Explain and assign Worksheet 12, Spring Performance, page 199. (For instructions and answer key, see page 185.)

Finish the Lesson

1. **Discussion.** Ask students to talk about a show they have seen or have performed in. Continue the discussion for four to five minutes.

2. Explain and assign Workbook page 41. (For instructions, see Teacher's Book pages 168–169.)

Your Time

Language Focus: Personalizing musical language and adverbs
Materials Needed: CD/cassette and player

For general information on Your Time, see pages 18–19.

Warm-Up and Review

1. **Reading Review: Listen and Read.** Play the recording of the Unit 6 reading. Students listen. Then volunteers open their Student Books to page 41 and read the story, one sentence per student.
2. Check Workbook page 41. (For instructions and answer key, see Teacher's Book pages 168–169.)

Introduce the Lesson

Ask students five to six questions that have adverbs (see Suggested Questions below).

Suggested Questions:
Do you like to play the drums loudly?
How often do you walk to school quickly?
Can you play the piano well?
Do you like to ride your bike slowly?
Do you ever drink root beer quickly?
How often do you listen to pop music loudly?

Practice the Lesson

Students open their Student Books to page 42.

A. Listen and answer the questions.

1. Play the recording. For each number, students listen to the question and answer it based on their own knowledge and experience.

   1. *Can you ride a bike quickly?*
   2. *Do you do your homework quietly?*
   3. *What do you do well?*
   4. *Do you ever sing loudly?*

2. Check answers by dividing the class into pairs and having students in each pair read one question and answer to the class.

   Answer Key:
   Answers will vary.

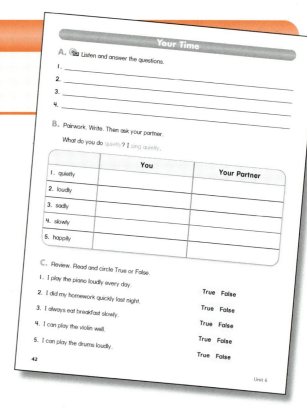

B. Pairwork. Write. Then ask your partner.

Divide the class into pairs. Each student fills in his/her chart about himself/herself. Then they ask their partners the target questions and fill in the *Your Partner* column. Next, each student tells the class about his/her partner, using the sentence cues and information from his/her chart. For example: *Ken plays the recorder loudly.*

C. Review. Read and circle True or False.

1. Students read each statement and circle *True* or *False* based on their own knowledge and experience.

2. Check answers by having volunteers say whether they circled *True* or *False* for each sentence.

   Answer Key:
   Answers will vary.

Games and Activities

1. **Find Someone Who...** Write the following on the board and have students copy it on a piece of paper:

   Find someone who...
   ...likes to play the flute.
   ...can play the electric keyboard.
   ...plays the trumpet every day.
   ...plays the tuba loudly.

   Students then circulate around the classroom, asking their classmates questions to elicit the information they are looking for. For example: *Do you like to play the flute?* Once they find someone who (likes to play the flute), they write down that person's name next to the corresponding sentence. Students continue for five to six minutes. Then ask students questions about what they found out. For example: Ask *Does Kim like to play the flute?* Students who know this information respond either *Yes, she does* or *No, she doesn't*.

2. **Drawing.** Give students five to six minutes to draw pictures of themselves doing activities they can do well. Once students have finished drawing, divide the class into pairs. Students tell their partners about their drawings. For example: *This is me. I can ride my bike well.*

3. **Writing Relay.** Each student writes a verb (phrase) and an adverb on a piece of paper and then passes it to the student sitting behind him/her. Each student then writes a true sentence using the verb phrase and adverb he/she has received. For example: *play ping pong/happily. I often play ping pong happily.* Students then read their sentences to the class. Continue in the same way, having students write new verbs and adverbs each time, for five to six minutes.

Finish the Lesson

1. **How About You?** Say *slowly* and have a volunteer use a complete sentence to say an action he/she does slowly. For example: *I do my homework slowly.* Do the same with different volunteers and *well, badly, quietly, loudly, quickly, happily,* and *sadly*.

2. Explain and assign Workbook page 42. (For instructions, see Teacher's Book page 169.)

> **Assessment**
> Explain and assign the Unit 6 Test, page 225. (For instructions and answer key, see page 211.)

7 Zoo Animals Escape!

Conversation Time

Language Focus: Making an emergency telephone call
Materials Needed: CD/cassette and player; Wall Chart 13

For general information on Conversation Time, see pages 8–9.

Warm-Up and Review

1. **Review: Quietly and Quickly.** Ask *What can you do quietly?* and have several students respond. Then ask *Do you like walking quickly?* and have several students respond. Do the same with *What do you always do happily?*
2. Check Workbook page 42. (For instructions and answer key, see Teacher's Book page 169.)

Introduce the Conversation

1. Set the scene and clarify meaning by pretending to push the buttons of a telephone and holding a telephone receiver to your ear. Say *Today's conversation is about a boy at home with his sister. His parents are at the movies. There's something wrong and he calls for help.* Then introduce the new words by writing each word on the board. Point to and read each word before explaining its meaning. Students repeat the word.

   911: Say *911 is the telephone number you call in the United States to get help from police officers or firefighters, and for a fast ride to the hospital.*

   emergency: Explain that an emergency is when something bad happens and you need to get help quickly.

   wild animal: Say *Cheetahs and snakes are wild animals. They are not pets. Cats and dogs are not wild animals.*

   calm: Say *I'm not calm* in an agitated voice. Then take a deep breath and calmly say *Now, I'm calm.*

2. Bring four students to the front of the classroom. Stand behind each student and model his/her lines of the conversation. Student C should stay off to the side until the end of the conversation. Student D should stand by Student B.

   A: *911. What's the emergency?*
   Pretend to speak into a telephone in a calm, neutral voice.

   B: *Help! There's something in my backyard!*
   Pretend to speak into a telephone in a scared, fast voice. Stare out the window.

   A: *What is it?*
   Speak into the telephone with a calm voice.

   B: *I think…I think it's a wild animal! I can see its eyes!*
   Talk into the telephone, but stare wide-eyed out the window.

   A: *What's your name and address?*
   Speak into the telephone in a calm voice.

   B: *Dan Day. 49 Maple Lane.*
   Speak into the telephone clearly and more slowly.

   A: *Are your parents home?*
   Speak into the telephone and ask the question in a kind voice.

   B: *No. They went to a movie. I'm taking care of my little sister. What should I do?*
   Shake your head *no*, point to Student D standing beside you, and speak into the telephone in a somewhat helpless and concerned tone.

   A: *Stay calm. I'm sending an officer now.*
   Speak into the telephone in a calm and helpful tone.

   C: *Is this the wild animal?*
   Walk up to Students B and D. Pretend to be holding a small dog. Ask the question in a questioning tone.

   B: *Sorry, officer. I'll take him.*
   Speak to Student C while looking embarrassed. Sound apologetic.

   D: *Oh, Digger!*
   Smile and point to the "dog" in Student C's arms.

3. Divide the class into Groups A, B, C, and D. Model the conversation again using facial expressions and body language. Group A repeats the operator's lines, Group B repeats Dan's lines, Group C repeats the officer's line, and Group D repeats Penny's line. Encourage students to copy your facial expressions and body language. Groups change roles and say the conversation again in the same way. Continue until each group has taken on each role.

4. Attach Wall Chart 13 to the board or open a Student Book to page 43. Students then open their Student Books to page 43. Ask the following questions:

> Who is calling 911?
> Why is Dan calling 911?
> Where are Dan's parents?
> What does the 911 operator do?
> Who comes to help Dan?
> Was there a wild animal in the backyard?
> What was in the backyard?

Practice the Conversation

A. Listen and repeat. Point to the speakers. Then listen again.

1. Play the recording (first version of the conversation). Students listen and repeat, pointing to each speaker.

   1. Operator: *911. What's the emergency?*
      Dan: *Help! There's something in my backyard!*
   2. Operator: *What is it?*
      Dan: *I think…I think it's a wild animal! I can see its eyes!*
   3. Operator: *What's your name and address?*
      Dan: *Dan Day. 49 Maple Lane.*
   4. Operator: *Are your parents home?*
      Dan: *No. They went to a movie. I'm taking care of my little sister.*
   5. Dan: *What should I do?*
      Operator: *Stay calm. I'm sending an officer now.*
   6. Officer: *Is this the wild animal?*
      Dan: *Sorry, officer. I'll take him.*
      Penny: *Oh, Digger!*

2. Play the recording (second version of the conversation). Students listen.

B. Role-play the conversation.

Divide the class into groups of four. Using their Student Books for reference, each group role-plays the conversation. They then change roles and role-play the conversation again. Groups continue until each student has taken on each role.

Games and Activities

Note: For all Conversation Time activities, students may use their Student Books for reference.

1. **Listen Carefully.** Write the following sentences on the board. Play the recording of the conversation. Students listen and write the missing words to complete each sentence.

   1. Dan's address is _____ Maple Lane.
   2. Dan's parents went to a _____.
   3. Dan is _____ his little sister.
   4. There wasn't a wild animal. It was _____.

   Check answers by saying *Number 1*. A volunteer reads the complete sentence. Do the same for numbers 2–4.

   Answer Key:
   1. Dan's address is <u>49</u> Maple Lane.
   2. Dan's parents went to a <u>movie</u>.
   3. Dan is <u>taking care of</u> his little sister.
   4. There wasn't a wild animal. It was <u>Digger</u>.

2. **Say the Next Line.** Using scenes 1–4 of the conversation, write the 911 operator's four questions and Dan's answers on the board. Students read the conversation. Erase Dan's answers. Divide the class into four groups. A volunteer reads the first question and Group 1 gives Dan's answer. If Group 1 answers correctly, another volunteer reads the next question and Group 2 tries to give that answer. If any group cannot answer correctly, the next group tries.

3. **Make It Your Own.** Write the following on the board:

   A: *911. What's the emergency?*
   B: <u>*Help! There's something in my backyard!*</u>

   Students read the dialogue on the board. Then divide the class into pairs and write the following on the board:

   1. Someone had an accident in front of my house.
   2. My friend fell out of a tree. He hurt his arm.
   3. There's a fire in my kitchen.

   Students read each new response. Quickly clarify meaning if necessary. Then students in each pair role-play the dialogue on the board, substituting the new responses into the underlined part of the target conversation.

Finish the Lesson

1. **Discussion.** Ask the class what the equivalent to 911 is in their own town. Then take three to four minutes to discuss which emergencies would warrant a call to 911. For example: you see a fire, or you see a bad car accident. Then ask *What do you need to tell the 911 operator?* For example: your name, address or location, and what you saw.

2. Explain and assign Workbook page 43. (For instructions, see Teacher's Book page 169.)

Word Time

Language Focus: Wild animals (*tiger, eagle, panda, bear, kangaroo, parrot, moose, camel, baboon, leopard*)

Materials Needed (excluding materials for optional activities): CD/ cassette and player; Wall Chart 14; Unit 7 Word Time Picture Cards, 1 card per student; Unit 7 Word Time Word Cards, 1 set (see Picture and Word Card Book pages 25 and 26)

For general information on Word Time, see pages 10–11.

Warm-Up and Review

1. **Conversation Review: Dictation.** Say a line from the Unit 7 conversation. Students write the line on a piece of paper, using correct capitalization and punctuation. The first student to correctly write the line quickly acts it out. Continue in the same way with three to four different lines of conversation.

2. Check Workbook page 43. (For instructions and answer key, see Teacher's Book page 169.)

Introduce the Words

1. Hold up and name each of the Unit 7 Word Time Picture Cards. Students listen. Hold up and name the cards again, and have students repeat. Hold up the cards in random order and have students name them. Then say *tiger, curry, parrot*. Students say the word that does not belong. Do the same with three to four different sets of words (see Suggested Words below).

    Suggested Words: *school, moose, camel; baboon, bank, bear; leopard, lemonade, panda; eagle, kangaroo, recorder*

2. Attach the Unit 7 Word Time Picture Cards in a row to the board. Stand the Unit 7 Word Time Word Cards on the chalktray under the corresponding picture cards. Point to each picture/word card pair and read the word. Students repeat. Then reposition the word cards so they are no longer directly below the corresponding picture cards. Volunteers come to the board one by one and place a word card under its corresponding picture card, then point to and read the word. Seated students repeat.

Talk About the Picture

1. Students open their Student Books to page 44. They look at the large scene and identify anything they can, using complete sentences wherever possible.

2. Attach Wall Chart 14 to the board or open a Student Book to page 44. Read the following "story" while pointing to or touching the pictures (**bold** words) and pantomiming the actions (*italicized* words).

    Look! These wild animals escaped from the zoo. They are in town, but the people don't see them. The people are busy *talking on the phone*, *reading a newspaper*, and *watching TV*. **Mike** is *washing the car* and a **baboon** is behind him. A **parrot** is sitting on the **roof**. There are a **camel**, a **tiger**, and a **leopard** *walking* near the **girl** who's *putting on makeup*. A **moose**, a **bear**, and a **panda** are near **Ted's house**. An **eagle** is *flying above* **the cat**, and a **kangaroo** is behind **Annie** and **Emily**. A **panda** is walking by **Mr. Lee**, but he is *sleeping*.

3. Ask the following questions while pointing to or touching the pictures (**bold** words) and pantomiming the actions and adjectives (*italicized* words).

    (**kangaroo**) What's this?
    (**moose**) What's that?
    (**eagle**) Can it *fly*?
    What's the **baboon** doing?
    Can you see a parrot? Where is it?
    Which animal is *flying*?
    Which is bigger, the **panda** or **Mr. Lee**?
    What's the *smallest* animal?
    What's the *biggest* animal?

Practice the Words

A. 🔊 Listen and repeat.

1. Play the recording. Students listen and repeat, pointing to each word in the vocabulary box.

   1. tiger
   2. eagle
   3. panda
   4. bear
   5. kangaroo
   6. parrot
   7. moose
   8. camel
   9. baboon
   10. leopard

2. Say the words in random order. Students point to them in the vocabulary box.

B. Point and say the words.

Students point to each of the target vocabulary items in the large scene and name them.

C. 🔊 Listen and point.

Play the recording. Students listen to the words. For the vocabulary, they point to the named item; for the conversations, they point to the speakers. (References are shown in parentheses.) Play the recording as many times as necessary for students to complete the task.

> Leopard.
> Eagle.
> Panda.
> Moose.
> Baboon.
> Bear.
> Camel.
> Tiger.
> Parrot.
> Kangaroo.
>
> Now listen and point to the speakers.
>
> A: Dad, do you think it's going to rain? (father and son feeding birds)
> B: Maybe. It's getting cloudy. Let's go inside.
> A: Aw. I don't want to go inside.
>
> A: Mom, where's Sarah? (mother and daughter watching TV)
> B: She's in the bathroom. She's putting on makeup.
> A: Is she going to go on a date tonight?
> B: Yes, she is.
>
> A: What did you do on Friday? (Annie and friend by trash can)
> B: I went to the beach with my dad. I got a sunburn.
> A: Did you wear any sunscreen?
> B: No. I forgot.

Games and Activities

1. **Act It Out.** Give each student a Unit 7 Word Time Picture Card. Say *The moose is walking quietly.* The student(s) with the moose picture card pretends to be a moose walking very quietly. He/She says *I'm a moose. I'm walking quietly.* Continue in the same way, using different animals and adverbs, for four to five minutes.

2. **True or False?** Say four to five comparative statements about the target animals (see Suggested Statements below). Students say *True* if the statement is true, and *False* if it is not. If the sentence is false, choose a volunteer to make it true. For example: Say *A camel is smaller than an eagle.* A volunteer corrects the statement by saying either *An eagle is smaller than a camel* or *A camel is bigger than an eagle.*

   Suggested Statements:
   A bear is bigger than a parrot.
   A leopard is faster than a camel.
   An eagle is bigger than a baboon.
   A bear is faster than a tiger.
   A kangaroo is smaller than a parrot.

3. **Descriptions.** Brainstorm with students to come up with a list of adjectives they might use to describe the target animals. Write the list of adjectives on the board, then divide the class into groups of three to four. A student in each group (S1) begins by using some of the adjectives on the board to describe one of the target animals. For example: *It's white and black.* The other students in the group try to name the animal S1 is describing. The first student to correctly name S1's animal then takes a turn describing a different animal. Groups continue until each student has described two to three animals.

4. **Option: Personalize the Vocabulary.** Divide the class into groups of five to six. Students in each group take turns telling the group about any of the target animals that they have seen. They give as many details as possible about their experiences. For example: when they saw the animal, where they saw it, who they were with, and what the animal was like (tall, short, brown, etc.).

Finish the Lesson

1. **Raise Your Hand.** Read the following passage. Students raise their hands each time they hear a target animal named.

   > *One day I was walking to school with my sister, and I saw a leopard walking down my street! I thought it was cute, but my sister thought it was scary. Then, flying in the sky above the leopard was a beautiful parrot. It was red, green, and yellow. Then, once I got to school, I saw a kangaroo, a camel, and a tiger. What were all these animals doing in my neighborhood?*

2. Explain and assign Workbook page 44. (For instructions, see Teacher's Book page 169.)

Focus Time

Language Focus: Simple past tense of movement verbs (*run → ran, walk → walked, fly → flew, hop → hopped*)

Past tense continuous; *when* clauses [*What (were) (you) doing when the (baboon) (walked) by? (We) (were) (washing the car) when the (baboon) (walked) by.*]

Function: Expressing actions that were in progress in the past

Materials Needed: CD/cassette and player; Unit 5 Word Time Picture Cards, 1 set; Unit 7 Word Time Picture Cards, 1 set; Unit 7 Word Time Word Cards, 1 set per 2 students; Unit 7 Focus Time Picture Cards, 1 set; Unit 7 Focus Time Word Cards, 1 set per 2 students; *I, He, She, We, They, you, he, she,* and *they* grammar cards, 1 set per 2 students; Unit 7 Grammar Cards, 1 set per 2 students (see Picture and Word Card Book pages 17, 25, 26, 27, 28, 43, 50, 51, and 58)

For general information on Focus Time, see pages 12–13.

Warm-Up and Review

1. **Vocabulary Review: Point and Say.** Stand the Unit 7 Word Time Picture Cards on the chalktray. Point to each card and elicit its name. Students then open their Student Books to page 44 and take turns pointing to the animals they see and making sentences about them. For example: *I can see a bear under the window. There's a baboon climbing over the fence.* Continue for three to four minutes.

2. Check Workbook page 44. (For instructions and answer key, see Teacher's Book page 169.)

This lesson is in two parts.

Part 1: Introduce the Words

1. Draw two trees, a bench, and a lake on the board. Attach the *parrot* picture card to one of the trees, the *tiger* picture card under the second tree, the *kangaroo* picture card near the bench, and the *bear* picture card near the lake. Move each animal from its original location to a new one, saying *The (parrot) is (flying)* while pantomiming (flying). When the animal has reached the new location, attach the picture card to the drawing, point to the two locations, and say *The (parrot) (flew).*

2. Hold up each Unit 7 Focus Time Picture Card and corresponding word card and have students name and read the cards.

Practice the Words

Students open their Student Books to page 45.

A. Listen and repeat.

Play the recording. Students listen and repeat each word.

1. *run, ran*   2. *walk, walked*
3. *fly, flew*   4. *hop, hopped*

wash the car, washing the car
read a newspaper, reading a newspaper
put on makeup, putting on makeup
feed the birds, feeding the birds
talk on the phone, talking on the phone
chop vegetables, chopping vegetables
take a nap, taking a nap
watch TV, watching TV
climb a tree, climbing a tree
take out the garbage, taking out the garbage

Part 2: Introduce the Patterns

1. **(He) was (reading a newspaper).** Write part of a daily schedule on the board. Say *This is what Tom did yesterday.* On the schedule show that from 5:30 to 6:30 Tom read a newspaper, from 6:30 to 7:00 Tom watched TV, and from 7:00 to 8:00 Tom talked on the phone. Then say (while pointing to the appropriate places on the schedule) *Yesterday Tom read a newspaper. At 6:00 he was reading a newspaper.* Students repeat each sentence. Then write *At 6:00 he was reading a newspaper.* on the board. Point to and read each word. Students repeat. Do the same with the following sentences: *At 6:45 he was watching TV. At 7:30 he was talking on the phone.*

Note: *At 6:00 Tom was reading a newspaper* means that by 6:00 he had begun reading a newspaper, but he had not yet finished.

2. **What was (he) doing?** Point to Tom's schedule on the board (from Step 1). Ask *What was he doing at 6:00?* Students repeat. Write *What was he doing at 6:00?* on the board. Point to and read each word. Ask the question again and elicit *He was reading a newspaper.* Do the same with the other activities on the schedule.

3. **What was (he) doing when the (tiger) (ran) by? (He) was (watching TV) when the (tiger) (ran) by.** Draw a TV on the board, and have a volunteer (S1) come to the front of the classroom and pretend to be watching TV. Give the *tiger* picture card to a different volunteer (S2), and have him/her run by S1. The students then return to their seats. Point to S1 and ask students *What was (he) doing when the tiger ran by?* Students repeat. Write *What was he doing when the tiger ran by?* on the board. Point to and read each word. Students repeat. Ask the question again and elicit *(He) was watching TV when the tiger ran by.* Prompt as necessary. Write *(He) was watching TV when the tiger ran by.* on the board. Point to and read each word. Students repeat. Do the same with *bear/walk/talk on the phone, eagle/fly/wash the car,* and *kangaroo/hop/read a newspaper.*

4. **What were (they) doing when the (tiger) (ran) by? (They) were (watching TV) when the (tiger) (ran) by.** Do the same as in Step 3 above, using two volunteers to elicit *They.*

5. **Practice for Fluency.** Say *he, baboon, walk* and elicit the target question, *What was he doing when the baboon walked by?* Say *feed the birds* and elicit *He was feeding the birds when the baboon walked by.* Continue in the same way—using different pronouns, animals, and activities—for three to four minutes.

Practice the Patterns

B. Listen and repeat.

1. Write the text from the pattern boxes on the board. Then play the recording, pointing to each word. Students listen.

   A: *What were you doing when the baboon walked by?*
   B: *We were washing the car when the baboon walked by.*

   A: *What was he doing when the baboon walked by?*
   B: *He was washing the car when the baboon walked by.*

2. Play the recording again. Students look at the pattern boxes in their books and repeat, pointing to each word.

3. Students work with partners to ask and answer the questions, while looking at the pattern boxes in their books.

C. Look at page 44. Listen and point.

Play the recording. Students look at page 44 and listen to the words, pointing to each person being talked about. Play the recording as many times as necessary for students to complete the task.

A: *What were they doing when the leopard walked by?*
B: *They were feeding the birds when the leopard walked by.*

A: *What was he doing when the parrot flew by?*
B: *He was reading a newspaper when the parrot flew by.*

A: *What was she doing when the camel walked by?*
B: *She was putting on makeup when the camel walked by.*

Games and Activities

1. **Drill.** Say *walk*. Students say its simple past form, *walked*. Do the same with *run, hop,* and *fly*. Then do the activity again, having a contest to see who can first correctly say and spell the simple past tense. Repeat the entire activity, this time having students say and spell the *-ing* form of the verbs in the box on page 45.

2. **Animal Show.** Divide the class into two groups. One group is the audience and the other pretends to be animals in a show. Each animal makes a big nametag for himself/herself (for example: *bear*). Say *wash the car*. Members of the audience pantomime washing a car as one of the animals walks, runs, flies, or hops by the audience. After the animal passes by, ask *What were you doing when the (bear) (walked) by?* Audience members say *We were washing the car when the (bear) (walked) by.* Continue in the same way, having the audience members pantomime different actions as the different animals move by them. Then have groups change roles and do the entire activity again.

3. **Make the Sentences.** (See Game 17, pages 155–156.) Do the activity using *I, He, She, We, They, you, he, she,* and *they* grammar cards and Unit 7 Word Time Word Cards, Focus Time Word Cards, and Grammar Cards.

Finish the Lesson

1. **Freeze.** Divide the class into Groups A and B and have a volunteer from each group come to the front of the classroom. Give the Group A volunteer (S1) a Unit 5 Word Time Picture Card. Give the Group B volunteer (S2) a Unit 7 Word Time Picture Card. S1 pantomimes the action on his/her card, and S2 walks, runs, flies, or hops by S1, acting like the animal on his/her card. Say *Freeze!* Students in Group A point to S1, and ask Group B *What was (Ken) doing when the (camel) (walked) by?* Group B students say *(He) was (taking medicine) when the (camel) (walked) by.* Continue in the same way with different volunteers for three to four minutes. Groups take turns asking and answering the questions.

2. Explain and assign Workbook page 45. (For instructions, see Teacher's Book page 170.)

Practice Time

Language Focus: Simple past tense of movement verbs; past tense continuous; *when* clauses [*What (were) (you) doing when the (bear) (walked) by? (I) (was) (chopping vegetables) when the (bear) (walked) by.*]

Function: Expressing actions that were in progress in the past

Materials Needed: CD/cassette and player

For general information on Practice Time, see pages 14–15.

Warm-Up and Review

1. **Pattern Review: Ask and Answer.** Write *What was she doing when the panda ran by? She was chopping vegetables when the panda ran by.* on the board. Point to each sentence and have students read it. Then say *they, parrot, fly* and have students ask the target question. Say *watch TV* and elicit the target answer. Continue in the same way—using different pronouns, animals, and activities—for three to four minutes.

2. Check Workbook page 45. (For instructions and answer key, see Teacher's Book page 170.)

Practice the Patterns

Students open their Student Books to page 46.

A. Listen and repeat. Then practice with a partner.

1. Play the recording. Students listen and repeat, pointing to each picture in their books.

   A: *What were you doing when the bear walked by?*
   B: *I was chopping vegetables when the bear walked by.*

   1. What were you doing when the moose ran by?
      I was talking on the phone when the moose ran by.
   2. What was he doing when the panda walked by?
      He was taking a nap when the panda walked by.
   3. What were you doing when the tiger ran by?
      We were watching TV when the tiger ran by.
   4. What was she doing when the kangaroo hopped by?
      She was taking out the garbage when the kangaroo hopped by.
   5. What were they doing when the leopard walked by?
      They were feeding the birds when the leopard walked by.
   6. What was he doing when the parrot flew by?
      He was reading a newspaper when the parrot flew by.
   7. What was it doing when the eagle flew by?
      It was climbing a tree when the eagle flew by.
   8. What was she doing when the camel walked by?
      She was putting on makeup when the camel walked by.

2. Students practice numbers 1–8 in pairs. (S1 in each pair asks the question, S2 answers.) Students then change roles and repeat the activity.

B. Look at page 44. Practice with a partner.

Students remain in pairs and look at page 44. They then take turns asking and answering questions about the large scene using the target patterns and vocabulary items. For example: S1 (pointing to the woman chopping vegetables): *What was she doing when the bear walked by?* S2: *She was chopping vegetables when the bear walked by.*

C. Listen and chant.

1. Students turn to the *What Were You Doing?* chant on page 76. They cover up the text, look at the pictures, and talk about what they see. Read the lyrics line by line. Students repeat each line. Play the recording. Students listen and follow along in their books.

What Were You Doing?

What was she doing when the tiger ran by?
  She was talking on the phone when the tiger ran by.
What was he doing when the tiger ran by?
  He was taking out the garbage when the tiger ran by.

What were you doing when the parrot flew by?
  We were climbing a tree when the parrot flew by.
What was it doing when the parrot flew by?
  It was taking a nap when the parrot flew by.

What were they doing when the panda walked by?
  They were doing laundry when the panda walked by.
What were you doing when the panda walked by?
  I was watching TV when the panda walked by.

2. Play the recording again. Students listen and chant along, using their books for reference. Play the recording as many times as necessary for students to become familiar with the chant.

3. Divide the class into Groups A and B. Play the karaoke version. Group A chants the questions, pantomiming the action of each animal. Group B chants the answers, pantomiming each activity.

Games and Activities

1. **Spelling Contest.** Divide the class into Teams A and B. Students open their Student Books to page 45 and look at the spelling of the –*ing* words in the box for 10–15 seconds. They then close their books. A student from each team comes to the board. Say a verb in the base form (for example: *put*). The two students write the –*ing* form (for example: *putting*). The first student to correctly spell the word receives two points. The other student also gets a point if he/she has correctly spelled the verb. Then choose a different volunteer from each team to use the –*ing* word in a sentence. Continue in the same way until most students have taken a turn. The team with the most points at the end wins.

2. **Your Schedule.** Give students three to four minutes to quickly jot down their schedule from yesterday. Then say *Yesterday, at 9:15 A.M., an elephant ran by you. What were you doing when the elephant ran by?* Students look at their schedules to see what they were doing yesterday morning at 9:15. Choose three to four different volunteers to answer *I was (studying English) when the elephant ran by.* Continue in the same way, asking questions about different times and animals, for five to six minutes.

3. **Listen Carefully.** Read the following paragraph to students, having them take notes as necessary.

   Last week, on Wednesday, my friend Jim was at home. He was studying English, when all of a sudden he looked out the window and saw a kangaroo hopping by! He thought, "Why is a kangaroo hopping by my window?" Then, around six o'clock, Jim was chopping vegetables with his father. They heard a noise and looked out the window. What did they see? There was a monkey running by! Jim asked, "Dad, what are these animals doing here?" Jim's father said, "Hmm…I don't know!" Then, when Jim was washing the pots and pans after dinner, he saw a parrot flying by. "Wow!" thought Jim. "There are a lot of animals here today!"

   Ask the following questions about the above paragraph, having students refer to their notes for reference. If necessary, read the paragraph several times.

   What was Jim doing when the parrot flew by?
   What were Jim and his father doing when the monkey ran by?
   What was Jim doing when the kangaroo hopped by?

Extra Practice
Explain and assign Worksheet 13, What Were You Doing?, page 200. (For instructions and answer key, see page 186.)

Finish the Lesson

1. **What Were You Doing?** Have students pantomime washing a car. Then, as they are pantomiming, pretend to be a ringing telephone. Have students stop pantomiming. Ask *What were you doing when the phone rang?* Students respond *We were washing the car when the phone rang.* Then have students pantomime watching TV. Drop a book. Students stop pantomiming. Ask *What were you doing when the book fell?* Elicit *We were watching TV when the book fell.* Ask *What were you doing at 4:00 yesterday afternoon?* Then ask *What were you doing at 1:00 last Saturday?*

2. Explain and assign Workbook page 46. (For instructions, see Teacher's Book page 170.)

Reading Time

Language Focus: Reading an informational sign

Materials Needed: CD/cassette and player; copies of reading, 1 per 6–8 students

For general information on Reading Time, see pages 16–17.

Warm-Up and Review

1. **Pattern Review: Chant.** Play the Unit 7 chant, *What Were You Doing?* Students listen. Play the chant again and have students chant along.
2. Check Workbook page 46. (For instructions and answer key, see Teacher's Book page 170.)

Introduce the Reading

Note: Students may learn the new vocabulary within the context of the reading, or each new word can be taught before students encounter it in the reading. Follow the steps below to introduce the new vocabulary and/or introduce the reading content.

1. Write the new words in a column on the board. Point to and read each word before explaining its meaning.

   giant: Say *Today's reading is about very, very big pandas. They're called giant pandas.*

   fact: Say *A fact is a true thing we know. Here are some facts: You are in English class. I am your teacher.*

   about: Say *I'm going to tell you about myself. I am a (woman). I teach English. I am your teacher. I like to (snorkel).*

   born: Say *I was born in (1964).* Then prompt several students to tell you what year they were born.

   weigh: Pick up a book and pretend to be determining its weight. Say *I think this book weighs (two) (kilograms).*

   bamboo: Say *Bamboo is a kind of tall grass.*

   hibernate: Say *Some animals sleep all winter. This is called hibernating.*

   endangered: Say *One hundred years ago, there were a lot of pandas in the world. Now there are only about 1,000. They are endangered.*

   around: Say *There are around (twenty) students in this class.*

   alive: Explain that *alive* means living.

2. Students open their Student Books to page 47. They look at the reading and picture and talk about what they see. For example: *These are pandas. There are many facts.* Ask students what they think the reading will be about.

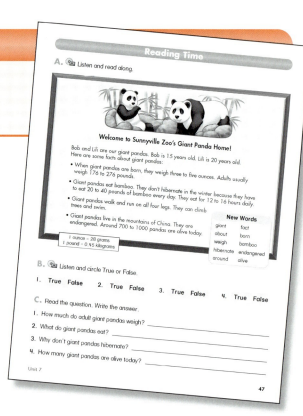

Practice the Reading

Students read the informational sign silently to themselves.

A. Listen and read along.

1. Play the recording. Students listen and read along in their Student Books.

   Welcome to Sunnyville Zoo's Giant Panda Home!

   Bob and Lili are our giant pandas. Bob is 15 years old. Lili is 20 years old. Here are some facts about giant pandas:

   - *When giant pandas are born, they weigh three to five ounces. Adults usually weigh 176 to 276 pounds.*
   - *Giant pandas eat bamboo. They don't hibernate in the winter because they have to eat 20 to 40 pounds of bamboo every day. They eat for 12 to 16 hours daily.*
   - *Giant pandas walk and run on all four legs. They can climb trees and swim.*
   - *Giant pandas live in the mountains of China. They are endangered. Around 700 to 1000 pandas are alive today.*

New Words
giant
fact
about
born
weigh
bamboo
hibernate
endangered
around
alive

2. Play the recording again, stopping it after each sentence. Students listen and repeat each sentence.

3. Divide the class into pairs. Students in each pair take turns reading the story aloud to their partner.

B. Listen and circle True or False.

1. Play the recording. For each number, students listen and circle *True* if the statement is true, and *False* if it is not.

   1. *When giant pandas are born, they weigh 176 pounds.*
   2. *Giant pandas walk and run on two legs.*
   3. *Giant pandas live in the mountains in China.*
   4. *Giant pandas can climb trees, but they can't swim.*

2. Check answers by saying *Number 1. When giant pandas are born, they weigh 176 pounds.* Students say *True* if they circled *True*, and *False* if they circled *False*. If the statement is false, choose a volunteer to make it true. Do the same for numbers 2–4.

   Answer Key:
   1. False   2. False   3. True   4. False

C. Read the question. Write the answer.

1. Students read each question and answer it based on the reading in exercise A.

2. Check answers by reading each question and having students read the answer they wrote.

   Answer Key:
   1. How much do adult giant pandas weigh? <u>Adults usually weigh 176 to 276 pounds.</u>
   2. What do giant pandas eat? <u>They eat bamboo.</u>
   3. Why don't giant pandas hibernate? <u>They don't hibernate because they have to eat 20 to 40 pounds of bamboo every day.</u>
   4. How many giant pandas are alive today? <u>Around 700 to 1000 pandas are alive today.</u>

Games and Activities

Note: For all Reading Time activities, students may use their Student Books for reference.

1. **Sentence Strips.** Divide the class into groups of six to eight and give each group a copy of the reading. Students in each group cut the reading so that each sentence is on a separate strip of paper. They then shuffle the strips. Play the recording. Students in each group work together to put the strips in order. Play the recording as many times as necessary for students to complete the task. Then have each group read a paragraph to the class.

   OPTION: Give students enlarged photocopies of the reading.

2. **Finish the Sentence.** Say *Giant pandas eat for _____.* A volunteer says *12 to 16 hours daily.* Do the same with three to four facts from the story (see Suggested Facts below).

   Suggested Facts:
   Giant pandas live in <u>the mountains of China.</u>
   When giant pandas are born, they weigh <u>three to five ounces.</u>
   Giant pandas have to eat <u>20 to 40 pounds of bamboo every day.</u>
   Bob and Lili are <u>Sunnyville Zoo's giant pandas.</u>

3. **Draw It.** Divide the class into pairs. Give students seven to nine minutes to work with their partners to illustrate each fact about pandas from the reading. When pairs are done, have them take turns telling the class about their illustrations.

Extra Practice
Explain and assign Worksheet 14, Animal Facts, page 201. (For instructions and answer key, see page 186.)

Finish the Lesson

1. **Discussion.** Spend four to five minutes discussing with students possible reasons why giant pandas are endangered.

2. Explain and assign Workbook page 47. (For instructions, see Teacher's Book page 170.)

Your Time

Language Focus: Personalizing animal, movement, and past activity language

Materials Needed: CD/cassette and player; 1 small ball or beanbag per 4–5 students

For general information on Your Time, see pages 18–19.

Warm-Up and Review

1. **Reading Review: Facts About Pandas.** Students open their Student Books to page 47 and quickly read the facts silently to themselves. Then have volunteers take turns saying facts about giant pandas.

2. Check Workbook page 47. (For instructions and answer key, see Teacher's Book page 170.)

Introduce the Lesson

Ask students five to six questions relating to animals, movement, and past actions (see Suggested Questions below).

Suggested Questions:
What's your favorite animal?
Did a parrot fly by you yesterday?
Did you see a leopard running by last week?
Do you like kangaroos?
What were you doing at 9:00 last night?
What were you doing at 9:00 this morning?

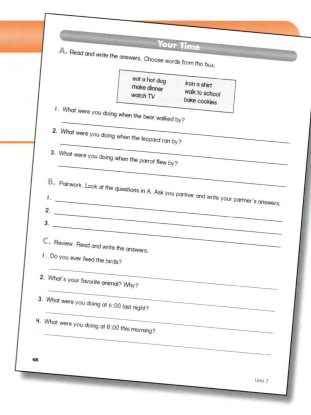

Practice the Lesson

Students open their Student Books to page 48.

A. Read and write the answers. Choose words from the box.

1. Students read the questions and write the answers, using the words in the boxes for their answers.

2. Check answers by dividing the class into pairs and having students in each pair read one question and answer to the class.

Answer Key:
Note: Words in parentheses may vary.
1. What were you doing when the bear walked by? <u>I was (ironing a shirt) when the bear walked by.</u>
2. What were you doing when the leopard ran by? <u>I was (baking cookies) when the leopard ran by.</u>
3. What were you doing when the parrot flew by? <u>I was (making dinner) when the parrot flew by.</u>

B. Pairwork. Look at the questions in A. Ask your partner and write your partner's answers.

Divide the class into pairs. Each student in the pair asks his/her partner the three questions from exercise A and writes his/her partner's answers in the space provided. Next, each student tells the class about his/her partner. For example: *(Ken) was eating a hot dog when the bear walked by.*

C. Review. Read and write the answers.

1. Students read each question and write an answer based on their own knowledge and experience.

2. Check answers by dividing the class into pairs and having students in each pair read one question and answer to the class.

Answer Key:
Answers will vary.

Games and Activities

1. **Memory Chain.** (See Game 18, page 156.) Play the game using *I was (taking a nap) when the (kangaroo) (hopped) by.*

2. **Toss the Ball.** Divide the class into groups of four to five. Students in each group form a circle. Give a group member (S1) a small ball or beanbag. S1 begins by asking *What were you doing at seven o'clock last night?* and tossing the ball to another group member (S2). S2 replies, then asks the same or a similar question and tosses the ball to another group member (S3). Groups continue in the same way for four to five minutes.

3. **Animal Facts.** Divide the class into groups of four to six. Each group chooses its favorite animal and writes down facts about it. For example: *It's brown. It has two legs. It can fly. It can't swim.* Then each group reads its facts to the class and other students try to guess the animal.

    OPTION: Students also draw their animal.

Finish the Lesson

1. **Class Interview.** Ask the class questions about the activities they did last Sunday (see Suggested Questions below). Volunteers answer, and the rest of the students take notes. Then point to various volunteers and ask the class about their Sunday activities. Seated students look at their notes and answer.

    Suggested Questions:
    What were you doing at eight o'clock on Sunday morning?
    What were you doing when your mother called you to breakfast?
    What were you doing at noon?
    What were you doing when the sun rose?

2. Explain and assign Workbook page 48. (For instructions, see Teacher's Book pages 170–171.)

3. Do Chapter 4 of Storybook 5, *Digger and the Thief*. (For instructions and answer key, see Teacher's Book pages 180 and 182.)

> **Assessment**
> Explain and assign the Unit 7 Test, page 226. (For instructions and answer key, see page 212.)

8 In Kindergarten

Conversation Time

Language Focus: Encouraging someone to try again

Materials Needed: CD/cassette and player; Wall Chart 15; Unit 5 Word Time Picture Cards, 1 card per student (see Picture and Word Card Book page 17)

For general information on Conversation Time, see pages 8–9.

Warm-Up and Review

1. **Review.** Give each student a Unit 5 Word Time Picture Card and have them pantomime the action on the card. Choose a volunteer (S1) to hop to the front of the classroom. As soon as S1 reaches the front of the classroom, students stop pantomiming. Ask *What were you doing when (Kate) hopped by?* Choose three to four volunteers to answer. Continue in the same way for three to four minutes, with different volunteers walking, running, and hopping to the front of the classroom.

2. Check Workbook page 48. (For instructions and answer key, see Teacher's Book pages 170–171.)

Introduce the Conversation

1. Set the scene and clarify meaning by saying *Today we will learn about Annie and Ted in the classroom when they were five years old.*

2. Bring a student to the front of the classroom (three other students sitting near the front of the classroom will also be involved in the conversation). Stand behind each student and model his/her lines of the conversation with the following actions:

   A: *Annie, please come to the front. Write the letter "d" on the board.*
   Smile and gesture for a student to come to the board. Hand him/her a marker or piece of chalk.

   B: *I don't know how. I'm sorry, Ms. Smart.*
   Go to the board, accept the marker/chalk from Student A, and write "b" on the board. Frown and sound sad.

   A: *That's okay. Let me show you how. It's easy.*
   Speak reassuringly. Prompt Student B to watch as you write "d" on the board.

   B: *No, I can't. It's too hard.*
   Take a small step away from the board. Shake your head and sound sad.

   A: *Come on, Annie. Don't give up.*
   Sound encouraging. Gesture for Student B to try again.

   B: *Hey! I can do it!*
   Smile bravely, walk to the board, and write "d." Sound happy and excited.

   A: *Good work, Annie. Please sit down.*
   Smile broadly. Gesture for Student B to sit.

   A: *Judy, please help me pass out the homework. Stan, erase the board, please.*
   Turn to a student sitting in the first row and pretend to hand him/her a stack of papers. Pretend to hand another student in the first row an eraser. The two students take the paper and eraser.

   C: *What did you get?*
   Pretend to be holding and looking at a homework paper.

   D: *I got a hundred!*
   Pretend to look down at a homework paper. Speak happily.

   B: *Yay! So did I!*
   Pretend to look down at a homework paper. Speak very happily.

3. Divide the class into Groups A, B, C, and D. Model the conversation again using facial expressions and body language. Group A repeats the teacher's lines, Group B repeats Annie's lines, and Group C and D repeat the other children's lines. Encourage students to copy your facial expressions and body language. Groups change roles and say the conversation again in the same way. Continue until each group has taken on each role.

4. Attach Wall Chart 15 to the board or open a Student Book to page 49. Students then open their Student Books to page 49. Ask the following questions:

> Who asks Annie to come to the front of the classroom?
> What does the teacher want Annie to do?
> Why is Annie unhappy?
> What is Judy going to do?
> Is someone going to erase the board?
> What did Annie get on the homework?

Practice the Conversation

A. Listen and repeat. Point to the speakers. Then listen again.

1. Play the recording (first version of the conversation). Students listen and repeat, pointing to each speaker.

   1. Teacher: *Annie, please come to the front. Write the letter "d" on the board.*
      Annie: *I don't know how.*
   2. Annie: *I'm sorry, Ms. Smart.*
      Teacher: *That's okay. Let me show you how. It's easy.*
   3. Annie: *No, I can't. It's too hard.*
      Teacher: *Come on, Annie. Don't give up.*
   4. Annie: *Hey! I can do it!*
      Teacher: *Good work, Annie. Please sit down.*
   5. Teacher: *Judy, please help me pass out the homework. Stan, erase the board, please.*
   6. Girl: *What did you get?*
      Boy: *I got a hundred!*
      Annie: *Yay! So did I!*

2. Play the recording (second version of the conversation). Students listen.

B. Role-play the conversation.

Divide the class into groups of four. Using their Student Books for reference, students in each group role-play the conversation. They then change roles and role-play the conversation again. Groups continue until each student has taken on each role.

Games and Activities

Note: For all Conversation Time activities, students may use their Student Books for reference.

1. **Match the Halves.** Divide the class into pairs. Students in each pair write each line of the target conversation on a separate piece of paper and then cut the sentences into halves. Pairs shuffle the pieces of paper and place them facedown. Say *Go!* Pairs try to be the first to turn over the pieces of paper, match the sentence halves, and put the complete sentences in the correct order. The first pair to do so raises their hands and says the conversation they have put together. If it is correct, they come to the front of the classroom and role-play the conversation for the rest of the class. If it is not correct, all pairs continue to work until one pair has put together the correct conversation. Students then change partners and do the activity again.

2. **Charades.** Divide the class into groups of three to four. Write the following on the board: *do laundry, chop vegetables, iron a shirt, slice fruit, buy groceries, bake bread*. A student in each group (S1) begins by saying to the other students in the group *Please (chop vegetables)*. The other students in the group say *We don't know how*. S1 says *Let me show you how* and shows them how to do it. The other students copy S1's actions and say *Hey! We can do it!* Groups continue in the same way, using different actions from the board, until each student has taken on the role of S1.

3. **Make It Your Own.** Write the following on the board:

   A: *What did you get?*
   B: *I got a hundred!*

   Students read the dialogue on the board. Then divide the class into pairs and write the following on the board:

   1. I'd rather not talk about it.
   2. Well, I did better than last time.
   3. I only got a ninety. I wanted to get a hundred.

   Students read each new response. Quickly clarify meaning if necessary. Then students in each pair role-play the dialogue on the board, substituting the new responses into the underlined part of the target conversation.

Finish the Lesson

1. **Happy Parrots.** (See Game 1, page 154.) Students play the game using the target conversation.
2. Explain and assign Workbook page 49. (For instructions, see Teacher's Book page 171.)

Word Time

Language Focus: Activities (*say the alphabet, throw a ball, blow a bubble, count to ten, build a sand castle, spell a word, catch a frog, cut out a heart, peel an orange, speak English*)

Materials Needed (excluding materials for optional activities):
CD/cassette and player; Wall Chart 16; Unit 8 Word Time Picture Cards, 1 set; Unit 8 Word Time Word Cards, 1 card per 2 students (see Picture and Word Card Book pages 29 and 30)

For general information on Word Time, see pages 10–11.

Warm-Up and Review

1. **Conversation Review: Listen, Please.** Play the recording of the Unit 8 conversation. Students listen and take notes if necessary to remember the information they hear. Then ask students three to four questions about the conversation (see Suggested Questions below).

   Suggested Questions:
   Who shows Annie how to write the letter "d"?
   Who will help Ms. Smart pass out the homework?
   Who will erase the board?
   Did anyone get a hundred on their test?

2. Check Workbook page 49. (For instructions and answer key, see Teacher's Book page 171.)

Introduce the Words

1. Hold up and name each of the Unit 8 Word Time Picture Cards. Students listen. Hold up and name the cards again, and have students repeat. Hold up the cards in random order and have students name them.

2. Attach the Unit 8 Word Time Picture Cards in a row to the board. Stand the Unit 8 Word Time Word Cards on the chalktray under the corresponding picture cards. Point to each picture/word card pair and read the word. Students repeat. Then reposition the word cards so they are no longer directly below the corresponding picture cards. Volunteers come to the board one by one and place a word card under its corresponding picture card, then point to and read the word. Seated students repeat.

3. Hold up each Unit 8 Word Time Picture Card and have students name the card and pantomime the action.

Talk About the Picture

1. Students open their Student Books to page 50. They look at the large scene and use complete sentences to identify anything they can.

2. Attach Wall Chart 16 to the board or open a Student Book to page 50. Read the following "story" while pointing to or touching the pictures (**bold** words) and pantomiming the actions (*italicized* words).

   This is a kindergarten class. The children are only around five years old. Some of the children can spell, count, and play nicely. And some can't. **Mike** is counting happily. And **Mandy** can speak English. But **this girl** can't *cut out a heart*. It's too hard for her. **Bob** can say **the alphabet** and **she** can *blow a bubble*. **Ivy** can *throw a ball*. **The girl** is *watching* **the boy** *peel an orange*. But **this boy** can't *catch a frog* and **Bill** can't *build a sand castle*.

3. Ask the following questions while pointing to or touching the pictures (**bold** words) and pantomiming the actions (*italicized* words).

   How many kids are on this **playground**?
   (**girl throwing ball**) Can Ivy *throw* a ball?
   Who can speak English?
   (**girl blowing bubble**) What is she doing?
   What are the kids *building* with **sand**?
   (**boy reaching for frog**) What is this boy trying to *catch*?
   What do you see on the **easel**?
   (**picture of dog**) What's this? Can you spell "dog"?

Practice the Words

A. Listen and repeat.

1. Play the recording. Students listen and repeat, pointing to each word in the vocabulary box.

   1. say the alphabet
   2. throw a ball
   3. blow a bubble
   4. count to ten
   5. build a sand castle
   6. spell a word
   7. catch a frog
   8. cut out a heart
   9. peel an orange
   10. speak English

2. Say the words in random order. Students point to them in the vocabulary box.

B. Point and say the words.

Students point to each of the target vocabulary items in the large scene and name them.

C. Listen and point.

Play the recording. Students listen to the words. For the vocabulary, they point to the person/people doing the named action; for the conversations, they point to the speakers. (References are shown in parentheses.) Play the recording as many times as necessary for students to complete the task.

Say the alphabet.
Cut out a heart.
Throw a ball.
Catch a frog.
Blow a bubble.
Speak English.
Count to ten.
Build a sand castle.
Peel an orange.
Spell a word.

Now listen and point to the speakers.

A: *What are you eating?* (boy peeling orange and girl)
B: *A cookie. Do you want some?*
A: *No, thanks. I'm going to eat this orange.*

A: *Look out! There's a bee behind you!* (children in sandbox)
B: *A bee? Where?*
A: *It's behind you.*

A: *How often do you get a haircut?* (Ted and girl cutting out heart)
B: *I get a haircut once a year. How about you?*
A: *I get a haircut once a month.*

Games and Activities

1. **Cut and Match.** Cut the Unit 8 Word Time Word Cards in half after the verb (for example: *build/a sand castle, throw/a ball*). Then give each student one of the card halves. Students walk around the classroom, looking for the other half of their card. Once they find a student with the other half of their card, the two students work together to write two different sentences using their verb phrase. For example: *I like building sand castles. I was building a sand castle when the eagle flew by.* Pairs then take turns reading their sentences to the class.

2. **Draw the Picture.** (See Game 13, page 155.) Play the game using the target vocabulary.

3. **Categorizing.** Divide the class into groups of two to three. Students in each group work together to make two lists. One list should contain the target actions that people generally do by themselves. The other list should contain the target actions that people generally do not do by themselves. Once each group has made their lists, have students share their lists with the class. Work with the class as a whole to come to a consensus about what should be on each list. Write the final lists on the board.

3. **Option: Personalize the Vocabulary.** Divide the class into pairs and give them three to four minutes to talk with their partners about things they liked and did not like to do when they were five years old (students can take notes if necessary to remember what their partner says). Then each pair joins with another pair and each student tells the others about his/her partner's activities.

   OPTION: Do the activity as above, also having students draw pictures to illustrate their partner's activities.

Finish the Lesson

1. **Pantomime Chain.** A volunteer (S1) comes to the front of the classroom and pantomimes one of the target actions. Students try to identify the action, saying *You're (catching a frog)*. If students guess correctly, S1 says *Yes, I'm (catching a frog)*. If students guess incorrectly, S1 says *No, I'm not (blowing a bubble)* and students continue guessing until they correctly name the action. The first student to correctly name the action is next to come to the front of the classroom and pantomime. Continue in the same way with six to eight students.

2. Explain and assign Workbook page 50. (For instructions, see Teacher's Book page 171.)

Focus Time

Language Focus: The verb *be*, present and past tense (*is, was*); *can*, present and past tense (*can, could*)

When clauses; affirmative and negative statements with *could* [*When (I) (was) little, (I) could/couldn't (peel an orange).*]

Function: Expressing past ability and inability

Materials Needed: CD/cassette and player; Unit 8 Word Time Picture Cards, 1 card per student; Unit 8 Word Time Word Cards, 1 set per 2 students; Unit 8 Focus Time Picture Cards, 1 set; *I, you, he, she, we,* and *they* grammar cards, 2 sets per 2 students; Unit 8 Grammar Cards, 1 set per 2 students (see Picture and Word Card Book pages 29, 30, 31, 43, and 51)

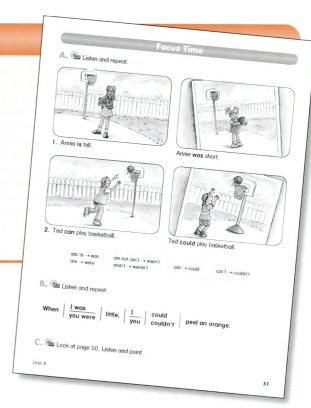

For general information on Focus Time, see pages 12–13.

Warm-Up and Review

1. **Vocabulary Review: Ability.** Stand the Unit 8 Word Time Picture Cards on the chalktray. Randomly point to the cards and have students name the actions. Volunteers then make true sentences using the action words and *can/can't*. For example: *I can speak English. I can't catch a frog.*

2. Check Workbook page 50. (For instructions and answer key, see Teacher's Book page 171.)

This lesson is in two parts.

Part 1: Introduce the Words

1. **(Annie) is tall. (Annie) was short.** Bring a tall volunteer to the board. Point to him/her and say *(Annie) is tall.* Students repeat. Write *Annie is tall.* on the board. Point to and read each word. Students repeat. Then indicate a shorter (Annie) with your hand and say *In (1997) (Annie) was five years old. (Annie) was short.* Students repeat. Write *Annie was short.* on the board. Point to and read each word. Students repeat.

2. **(Ted) can play basketball. (Ted) could play basketball.** Bring a volunteer to the front of the classroom and have him/her pantomime playing basketball. Point to him/her and say *(Ted) can play basketball.* Students repeat. Write *Ted can play basketball.* on the board. Point to and read each word. Students repeat. Then say *In (1997) (Ted) was five years old. In 1997, (Ted) could play basketball.* Students repeat. Write *Ted could play basketball.* on the board. Point to and read each word. Students repeat.

3. **Practice for Fluency.** Hold up each Unit 8 Focus Time Picture Card and have students say the corresponding sentence.

Practice the Words

Students open their Student Books to page 51.

A. Listen and repeat.

1. Play the recording. Students listen and repeat each word.

   1. *Annie is tall.*
      Annie was short.
   2. *Ted can play basketball.*
      Ted could play basketball.

2. Students study the verb changes in the box for 30 seconds. Then say *I am tall* and have students change the sentence into the past tense, *I was tall.* Do the same with *I am not tall, They are tall, They aren't tall, I can play basketball,* and *I can't play basketball.*

Part 2: Introduce the Patterns

1. **When (I) was little, (I) could (count to ten).** Say *In (1965) I was five years old.* Write *(1965)* on the board. Point to the date on the board, count to ten, and happily say *When I was little, I could count to ten.* Students point to themselves and repeat. Write *When I was little, I could count to ten.* on the board. Point to and read each word. Students point to themselves and repeat. Do the same with *throw a ball, blow a bubble,* and *spell a word.*

116   Unit 8

2. **When (I) was little, (I) couldn't (count to ten).** Point to the date on the board and then try to count to ten, struggling and missing some of the numbers as you do so. Look sad, shake your head, and say *When I was little, I couldn't count to ten.* Students point to themselves and repeat. Write *When I was little, I couldn't count to ten.* on the board. Point to and read each word. Students point to themselves and repeat. Do the same with *throw a ball*, *blow a bubble*, and *spell a word*.

3. **When (you) were little, (you) could (count to ten).** Do the same as in Step 1 above, having a volunteer do the activities to demonstrate *you*.

4. **When (you) were little, (you) couldn't (count to ten).** Do the same as in Step 2 above, having a volunteer do the activities to demonstrate *you*.

5. **Practice for Fluency.** Say *he*, then happily nod your head while saying *catch a frog*. Students say the corresponding target statement, *When he was little, he could catch a frog.* Then say *we* and sadly shake your head while saying *throw a ball*. Students say *When we were little, we couldn't throw a ball.* Continue in the same way for three to four minutes with different pronouns and actions, eliciting both positive and negative statements.

Practice the Patterns

B. Listen and repeat.

1. Write the text from the pattern boxes on the board. Then play the recording, pointing to each word. Students listen.

   When I was little, I could peel an orange.
   When I was little, I couldn't peel an orange.

   When you were little, you could peel an orange.
   When you were little, you couldn't peel an orange.

2. Play the recording again. Students look at the pattern boxes in their books and repeat, pointing to each word.

3. Students work with partners to say the sentences, while looking at the pattern boxes in their books.

C. Look at page 50. Listen and point.

Play the recording. Students look at page 50 and listen to the words, pointing to each person being talked about. Play the recording as many times as necessary for students to complete the task.

When he was little, he could cut out a heart.
When she was little, she could blow a bubble.
When he was little, he could say the alphabet.

Games and Activities

1. **Dictation.** Students make two columns on a piece of paper. They label one column *1995* and one column *Now*. Say *He can ride a bike.* Students repeat and write the sentence in the *Now* column. Then say *They were short.* Students repeat and write the sentence in the *1995* column. Do the same with five to six different sentences (see Suggested Sentences below). Check answers by having volunteers read the sentences they wrote in each column.

   Suggested Sentences:
   I can speak English.
   They couldn't build a sand castle.
   We are short.
   We were short.
   She could bake bread.
   He is tall.

2. **Act It Out.** Divide the class into groups of four to five and give each student a Unit 8 Word Time Picture Card. A student in each group begins by acting out—either well or badly—the action on his/her card and saying the corresponding target sentence. For example: A student has the *speak English* picture card. He/She pretends to be a little kid speaking English badly. He/She then says *When I was little, I couldn't speak English.* The other students in the group then say *When you were little, you couldn't speak English.* Groups continue until each student has taken a turn. They then exchange cards and do the activity again.

3. **Make the Sentences.** (See Game 17, pages 155–156.) Do the activity using *I, you, he, she, we,* and *they* grammar cards and Unit 8 Word Time Word Cards and Grammar Cards.

Finish the Lesson

1. **True Sentences.** Students use the target pattern to make true sentences about themselves. Allow students to use any verbs they know. Continue until most students have taken a turn.

2. Explain and assign Workbook page 51. (For instructions, see Teacher's Book pages 171–172.)

Practice Time

Language Focus: The verb *be,* present and past tense; *can,* present and past tense; *When* clauses; affirmative and negative statements with *could* [*When (I) (was) little, (I) (could) (say the alphabet).*]

Function: Expressing past ability and inability

Materials Needed: CD/cassette and player

For general information on Practice Time, see pages 14–15.

Warm-Up and Review

1. **Pattern Review: True Sentences.** Write *When my brother was little, he could spell a word.* on the board. Point to the sentence and have students read it. Then have students use this pattern to make positive true statements about people in their family. Allow students to use any verbs they know. Continue until most students have taken a turn.

2. Check Workbook page 51. (For instructions and answer key, see Teacher's Book pages 171–172.)

Practice the Patterns

Students open their Student Books to page 52.

A. Listen and repeat. Then practice with a partner.

1. Play the recording. Students listen and repeat, pointing to each picture in their books.

   When I was little, I could say the alphabet.

   1. *When we were little, we could throw a ball.*
   2. *When you were little, you couldn't cut out a heart.*
   3. *When he was little, he couldn't spell a word.*
   4. *When she was little, she could speak English.*
   5. *When I was little, I could blow a bubble.*
   6. *When he was little, he couldn't catch a frog.*
   7. *When he was little, he couldn't build a sand castle.*
   8. *When I was little, I could count to ten.*

2. Students practice numbers 1–8 in pairs. Students then change partners and repeat the activity.

B. Look at page 50. Practice with a partner.

Students remain in pairs and look at page 50. They then take turns making statements about the large scene using the target patterns and vocabulary items. For example: S1 (pointing to the girl in the sandbox): *When she was little, she could build a sand castle.* S2 (pointing to the girl trying to cut out a heart): *When she was little, she couldn't cut out a heart.*

C. Listen and sing along.

1. Students turn to the *When They Were Little* song on page 76. They cover up the text, look at the pictures, and talk about what they see. Read the lyrics line by line. Students repeat each line. Play the recording. Students listen and follow along in their books.

   When They Were Little
   (Melody: *Auld Lang Syne*)

   When I was little,
   I couldn't spell.
   I couldn't spell a word.
   When I was little,
   I couldn't spell.
   I couldn't spell a word.

   When I was little,
   I couldn't count.
   I couldn't count to ten.
   When I was little,
   I couldn't count.
   I couldn't count to ten.

   He couldn't spell a word.
   She couldn't count to ten.
   He couldn't spell, she couldn't count,
   but they could catch a frog.

2. Play the recording again. Students listen and sing along, using their books for reference. Play the recording as many times as necessary for students to become familiar with the song.

118   Unit 8

3. Divide the class into groups of three to four. Students in each group work together to write each line of the song on a separate piece of paper. They then shuffle the pieces of paper. Play the song again. Students in each group place their pieces of paper in the correct order. Play the song as many times as necessary for students to complete the task.

Games and Activities

1. **Draw and Tell.** Give students three to four minutes to illustrate two sentences made using the target pattern. They then write the corresponding sentence below each illustration. Divide the class into pairs and have each student tell their partner about the illustrations they drew.

2. **Act Out the Sentence.** Divide the class into groups of three to four. A volunteer in each group (S1) begins by saying *When you were little, you (couldn't) (blow a bubble)*. The other students in the group act the sentence out. Groups continue in the same way until each student has said two to three sentences for the others to act out.

    OPTION: Students act out the target patterns and their groupmates say the corresponding sentences.

3. **Write a Story.** Give students seven to ten minutes to write a short story about when they were little. Students then take turns reading their stories to the class. Offer support by writing the following on the board:

    When I was little, I could _____. I couldn't _____. My friends and I always _____. We liked to _____. We didn't like to _____. My friend _____ could _____!

    OPTION: Students illustrate their story.

> **Extra Practice**
> Explain and assign Worksheet 15, When I Was Little, page 202. (For instructions and answer key, see page 186.)

Finish the Lesson

1. **Favorite Heroes.** Elicit names of familiar book and/or movie heroes and write them on the board. Students make sentences about actions these heroes could or couldn't do when they were little. For example: *When Wonderboy was little, he couldn't catch a frog.* Allow students to use other names and verbs as well. Continue for three to four minutes.

2. Explain and assign Workbook page 52. (For instructions, see Teacher's Book page 172.)

Reading Time

Language Focus: Reading a letter
Materials Needed: CD/cassette and player

For general information on Reading Time, see pages 16–17.

Warm-Up and Review

1. **Pattern Review: Could/Couldn't.** Write *When my mother was little, she could _____.* and *When my mother was little, she couldn't _____.* on the board. Volunteers take turns reading the sentences and filling in the blanks with different verb phrases. Allow students to replace *mother* with other nouns (for example: *father, grandfather, sister, brother, friend*). Continue until most students have taken a turn.

2. Check Workbook page 52. (For instructions and answer key, see Teacher's Book page 172.)

Introduce the Reading

Note: Students may learn the new vocabulary within the context of the reading, or each new word can be taught before students encounter it in the reading. Follow the steps below to introduce the new vocabulary and/or introduce the reading content.

1. Write the new words in a column on the board. Point to and read each word before explaining its meaning.

   move away: Say *In 1998 my friend Jane lived here, in (Sunnyville). Then she moved away. Now she lives in New York.*

   miss: Say *My friend Jane lives in New York now. I can't see her every day. I miss her!*

   kindergarten: Explain that kindergarten is a class for young children, before they go to first grade. Children in kindergarten are usually between four and six years old.

   show: Say *Please show me your hands* and prompt students to show you their hands. Then say *Please show me your books* and prompt students to show you their books.

   funny: Say *People who tell jokes are funny.*

   enormous: Say *Enormous means the same as giant, or very big.*

   recess: Explain that recess is a break time at school to have fun between two classes.

   make friends: Say *When you move to a new city, you don't know anybody. All your friends are in your old city. You need to make friends in your new city.*

   soon: Write today's date on the board, and say *Today.* Then write a date three days in the future and say *soon.* Write a date a year from now and say *not soon.*

2. Ask students about their own experiences with moving and making new friends (see Suggested Questions below).

   Suggested Questions:
   Do you like to make new friends?
   When you were in kindergarten, did any of your friends move away?
   Did you miss them?

3. Students open their Student Books to page 53. They look at the reading and picture and talk about what they see. For example: *This is a letter. Here are Annie, Ted, and their friends.* Ask students what they think the reading will be about.

Practice the Reading

Students read the letter silently to themselves.

A. Listen and read along.

1. Play the recording. Students listen and read along in their Student Books.

   Dear Stan,

   How are you? When you moved away, we were sad. We miss you very much. Do you miss us?

   Last Saturday, we saw Ms. Smart. She was our kindergarten teacher. Do you remember her? Annie and I went to her house for lunch. She showed us old photos of our kindergarten class. She told some funny stories, too. She said when you were little, you could

120 Unit 8

build enormous sand castles. When you were in the sandbox at recess, you never wanted to get out. Remember?

Do you like Washington? How's your new school? Are you making a lot of friends? Please write soon!

Your friend,
Ted Lee

New Words
move away
miss
kindergarten
show
funny
enormous
recess
make friends
soon

2. Play the recording again, stopping it after each sentence. Students listen and repeat each sentence.

3. Divide the class into pairs. Students in each pair take turns reading the letter aloud to their partner.

B. Listen and circle True or False.

1. Play the recording. For each number, students listen and circle *True* if the statement is true, and *False* if it is not.

   1. *Ted and Annie saw Ms. Smart on Sunday.*
   2. *Ms. Smart showed them funny pictures.*
   3. *Stan could build enormous sand castles when he was little.*
   4. *Stan lives in California.*

2. Check answers by saying *Number 1. Ted and Annie saw Ms. Smart on Sunday.* Students say *True* if they circled *True*, and *False* if they circled *False*. If the statement is false, choose a volunteer to make it true. Do the same for numbers 2–4.

   Answer Key:
   1. False   2. False   3. True   4. False

C. Read the question. Write the answer.

1. Students read each question and answer it based on the reading in exercise A.

2. Check answers by reading each question and having students read the answer they wrote.

   Answer Key:
   1. Who is Stan? <u>Stan is Ted's friend from kindergarten.</u>
   2. Was Ms. Smart Ted and Annie's first-grade teacher? <u>No, she was their kindergarten teacher.</u>
   3. What did Ted do at Ms. Smart's house? <u>He and Annie ate lunch, looked at old photographs, and listened to stories.</u>
   4. What could Stan do when he was little? <u>When Stan was little, he could build enormous sand castles.</u>

Games and Activities

Note: For all Reading Time activities, students may use their Student Books for reference.

1. **Complete the Sentences.** Read Ted's letter, sentence by sentence, leaving each sentence incomplete. Students repeat and complete each sentence with information from their Student Books.

2. **Sequencing.** Divide the class into groups of two to three. Write the sentences below on the board, and have each group of students work together to write the sentences on their papers in the order that they happened. Check answers by having a group read its list of sentences to the class.

   Stan could build enormous sand castles.
   Annie and Ted went to Ms. Smart's house for lunch.
   Stan moved to Washington.
   Ted wrote Stan a letter.

   Answer Key:
   1. Stan could build enormous sand castles.
   2. Stan moved to Washington.
   3. Annie and Ted went to Ms. Smart's house for lunch.
   4. Ted wrote Stan a letter.

3. **Letter Writing.** Write the following outline of a letter on the board for reference:

   Dear _____,

   How are you?
   Last Saturday we _____.
   Do you remember when _____?
   Please write soon.

   Your friends,

   _____

   Divide the class into groups of three to four. Each group works together to write a letter to a friend about things they did together when they were in kindergarten. Each group reads its letter to the class.

   Extra Practice
   Explain and assign Worksheet 16, New Friends, page 203. (For instructions and answer key, see page 186.)

Finish the Lesson

1. **Use It in a Sentence.** Say *enormous*. A volunteer says a sentence using *enormous* (this can be either an original sentence or a sentence from the reading). Do the same with the remaining New Words from the lesson.

2. Explain and assign Workbook page 53. (For instructions, see Teacher's Book page 172.)

Your Time

Language Focus: Personalizing actions in the past and ability/inability language

Materials Needed: CD/cassette and player

For general information on Your Time, see pages 18–19.

Warm-Up and Review

1. **Reading Review: Listen and Read.** Play the recording of Ted's letter. Students listen. Then volunteers read the letter, one sentence per student.

2. Check Workbook page 53. (For instructions and answer key, see Teacher's Book page 172.)

Introduce the Lesson

Ask students four to five questions about their past actions (see Suggested Questions below).

Suggested Questions:
When you were seven, did you like to plant flowers?
Did you like climbing trees when you were five?
When you were little, could you ride a bike?
Where did you live when you were eight?
When you were little, did you ever take the bus?

Practice the Lesson

Students open their Student Books to page 54.

A. Listen and answer the questions.

1. Play the recording. For each number, students listen to the question and answer it based on their own knowledge and experience.

   1. *When you were four, could you say the alphabet?*
   2. *When you were seven, could you throw a ball?*
   3. *When you were six, could you speak English?*
   4. *When you were three, could you spell a word?*
   5. *When you were two, could you build a sand castle?*

2. Check answers by dividing the class into pairs and having students in each pair read one question and answer to the class.

   Answer Key:
   Answers will vary.

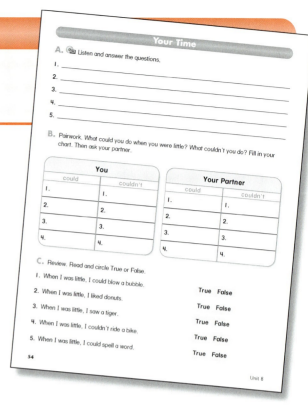

B. Pairwork. What could you do when you were little? What couldn't you do? Fill in your chart. Then ask your partner.

Divide the class into pairs. Each student fills in the *You* chart about what they could and couldn't do when they were little. Then each student asks his/her partner *What could you do when you were little? What couldn't you do?* and fills in the *Your Partner* chart. When they have finished, each student tells the class about his/her partner. For example: *When (Ken) was little, (he) could (swim well).*

C. Review. Read and circle True or False.

1. Students read each statement and circle *True* or *False* based on their own knowledge and experience.

2. Check answers by having volunteers say whether they circled *True* or *False* for each sentence.

   Answer Key:
   Answers will vary.

Games and Activities

1. **Survey.** Students create a survey on a sheet of paper by writing *Name, Could,* and *Couldn't* in a row at the top of the paper. Students then go around the classroom and ask six classmates *What could you do when you were little? What couldn't you do?* Students respond *I could/couldn't (count to ten) when I was little.* Students record their classmates' names and answers on their surveys, then sit down. Ask students questions about the survey, for example: *What could (Mari) do when (she) was little?* Students who know this information respond *When (she) was little, (she) could (blow bubbles).*

2. **When I Was Eight.** Divide students into pairs. Students draw for two to three minutes and make sentences about things they did or did not do when they were certain ages: four, six, eight, etc. They then show their pictures and tell their partners what they did and did not do.

3. **Talking.** Divide the class into pairs and give students three to four minutes to talk with their partners about what they could and could not do when they were little (students can take notes if necessary to remember what their partner says). Then each pair joins with another pair and each student tells the others about his/her partner's activities.

Finish the Lesson

1. **Around the Class.** Write *What could you do when you were little?* on the board. Point to each word and have students say the sentence. Ask a volunteer (S1) *What could you do when you were little?* S1 answers *I could (feed the birds).* Then S1 turns to the student on his/her right (S2) and asks *What could you do when you were little?* S2 says *I could (talk on the phone).* S2 then asks S3 the question in the same way. Continue in the same way until most students have taken a turn.

2. Explain and assign Workbook page 54. (For instructions, see Teacher's Book page 172.)

> **Assessment**
> Explain and assign the Unit 8 Test, page 227. (For instructions and answer key, see page 212.)

9 Cities Around the World

Conversation Time

Language Focus: Interviewing an airline pilot
Materials Needed: CD/cassette and player; Wall Chart 17

For general information on Conversation Time, see pages 8–9.

Warm-Up and Review

1. **Review: When You Were Little…** Write *When I was little, I could ride a bike.* on the board. Point to the sentence and have students read it. Then say *climb a tree* and have a volunteer say a true *could* or *couldn't* sentence using *climb a tree*. Continue in the same way for three to four minutes.

2. Check Workbook page 54. (For instructions and answer key, see Teacher's Book page 172.)

Introduce the Conversation

1. Set the scene and clarify meaning by saying *Jan and Joe are writing for the school newspaper. They are talking with a pilot about her job. She flies all over the world.* Then introduce the new words by writing each word on the board. Point to and read each word before explaining its meaning. Students repeat each word.

   interview: Pretend to hold a microphone. Say to a student, *Could I interview you? I'd like to ask you some questions about this class.*

   female: Say *(Jan) is female. Your mother is female. (Tom) is not female. Your father is not female.*

   pilot: Say *A pilot is a person who flies an airplane.*

   airline: Say the name of an airline in your country. Then say *This is an airline. Can you name any other airlines?*

   one third: On the board write *1/3 = 33%*. Then draw a pie with one third colored in.

   abroad: Explain that going abroad means travelling outside one's country.

2. Bring three students to the front of the classroom. Students A and C should pretend to hold pencils and pads of paper. Stand behind each student and model his/her lines of the conversation with the following actions:

   A: *Captain West, we'd like to interview you for our school newspaper. Could we ask you a few questions?*
   Walk with Student C up to Student A. Speak politely.

   B: *Sure. Go ahead.*
   Smile and speak in a lively voice.

A: *How many female pilots work for your airline?*
Ask in a friendly, questioning tone.

B: *I think one third of the pilots are female.*
Speak in a friendly tone.

A: *Do you ever fly abroad?*
Pretend to write down Student B's answer from above. Then ask the question in a friendly, questioning tone.

B: *Yes. I have an overseas flight once a month.*
Nod your head and hold up one finger.

C: *Do you fly the plane by yourself?*
Pretend to write down Student B's answer from above. Then ask the question in a friendly, questioning tone.

B: *No. I always have a copilot.*
Shake your head and gesture to an imaginary person beside you.

C: *Do you like being a pilot?*
Pretend to write down Student B's answer from above. Then ask the question in a friendly, questioning tone.

B: *Yes, very much!*
Speak enthusiastically.

A: *Thanks for your time, Captain West.*
Put your paper and pencil away. Sound friendly and turn to walk away.

B: *My pleasure.*
Nod. Speak in a friendly voice.

3. Divide the class into Groups A, B, and C. Model the conversation again using facial expressions and body language. Group A repeats Jan's lines, Group B repeats the pilot's lines, and Group C repeats Joe's lines. Encourage students to copy your facial expressions and body language. Groups change roles and say the conversation again in the same way.

4. Attach Wall Chart 17 to the board or open a Student Book to page 55. Students then open their Student Books to page 55. Ask the following questions:

   Who are Jan and Joe interviewing?
   Where can students read Jan and Joe's interview?
   Does the pilot fly to other countries?
   How many female pilots work for Captain West's airline?
   How many times a month does the pilot fly overseas?
   Who flies the airplane with the pilot?
   Does Captain West like her job?

Practice the Conversation

A. Listen and repeat. Point to the speakers. Then listen again.

1. Play the recording (first version of the conversation). Students listen and repeat, pointing to each speaker.

   1. Jan: *Captain West, we'd like to interview you for our school newspaper. Could we ask you a few questions?*
      Pilot: *Sure. Go ahead.*
   2. Jan: *How many female pilots work for your airline?*
      Pilot: *I think one third of the pilots are female.*
   3. Jan: *Do you ever fly abroad?*
      Pilot: *Yes. I have an overseas flight once a month.*
   4. Joe: *Do you fly the plane by yourself?*
      Pilot: *No. I always have a copilot.*
   5. Joe: *Do you like being a pilot?*
      Pilot: *Yes, very much!*
   6. Jan: *Thanks for your time, Captain West.*
      Pilot: *My pleasure.*

2. Play the recording (second version of the conversation). Students listen.

B. Role-play the conversation.

Divide the class into groups of three. Using their Student Books for reference, students in each group role-play the conversation. They then change roles and role-play the conversation again. Groups continue until each student has taken on each role.

Games and Activities

Note: For all Conversation Time activities, students may use their Student Books for reference.

1. **True/False/I Don't Know.** Say five to six statements about the conversation (see Suggested Statements below). Students say *True* if the statement is true, and *False* if it is false. If a statement is false, choose a volunteer to make it true. If students don't have enough information to determine if the statement is true or false, they say *I don't know.*

   Suggested Statements:
   Captain West drives a train.
   Captain West flies a plane three times a week.
   Jan and Joe like Captain West.
   Captain West likes being a pilot.
   Jan and Joe are writing an article for their school newspaper.
   Captain West flies by herself every day.

2. **Your Turn.** Ask students which jobs they would want to learn about if they were writing an article for a newspaper. List the jobs on the board. Then divide the class into groups of three to four. Each group chooses a job from the board and writes four to five questions that they would ask about that job. Groups then share the questions with the class.

   OPTION: Students find people with interesting jobs and interview them about their work. They then report back to the class about what they have found out.

3. **Make It Your Own.** Write the following on the board:

   A: *Do you fly the plane by yourself?*
   B: *No. I always have a copilot.*

   A: *Do you like being a pilot?*
   B: *Yes, very much!*

   Students read the dialogue on the board. Then divide the class into pairs and write the following on the board:

   1. bake bread
      Yes, I usually bake bread by myself.
      baker
   2. fight fires
      No, I always have other firefighters with me.
      firefighter

   Students read each new component. Quickly clarify meaning if necessary. Then students in each pair role-play the dialogue on the board, substituting the new components into the underlined parts of the target conversation.

Finish the Lesson

1. **Discussion.** Have a short discussion (for about three to four minutes) with the class, talking about what jobs they would like to do when they are older.

2. Explain and assign Workbook page 55. (For instructions, see Teacher's Book page 173.)

Word Time

Language Focus: Cities (*Rome, Taipei, Tokyo, London, Seoul, New York City, Paris, Honolulu, San Francisco, Hong Kong*)

Materials Needed (excluding materials for optional activities):
CD/cassette and player; Wall Chart 18

For general information on Word Time, see pages 10–11.

Warm-Up and Review

1. **Conversation Review: Say Alternate Lines.** Play the recording of the Unit 9 conversation. Then, using their Student Books for reference if necessary, students on the right and left sides of the classroom say alternate lines of the conversation (one side asks the questions and the other answers). They then switch roles and say the conversation again.

2. Check Workbook page 55. (For instructions and answer key, see Teacher's Book page 173.)

Introduce the Words

1. Attach Wall Chart 18 to the board or open a Student Book to page 56. Ask a volunteer to point on the map to the country where students live. Elicit the names of other countries on the map.

2. Point to each city on the Wall Chart and name it. Students repeat. Then point to each city and have students name it.

   OPTION: Show students a traditional world map or globe and point out each of the target cities.

Talk About the Picture

1. Students open their Student Books to page 56. They look at the large scene and use complete sentences to identify anything they can.

2. Attach Wall Chart 18 to the board or open a Student Book to page 56. Read the following "story" while pointing to or touching the pictures (**bold** words).

   Two **pilots** are visiting **the classroom**. There is a **big map** on the wall. Do you know the names of the cities? Here's **Rome**. It's in Italy. Here's **Tokyo**, and here's **Taipei**. Can you see **Seoul**? **New York City**, **San Francisco**, and **Honolulu** are all in the U.S.

3. Ask the following questions while pointing to or touching the pictures (**bold** words).

   (**Seoul**) What's this?
   (**Hong Kong**) Is this Hong Kong?
   Is **London** near **Honolulu**?
   Is **Tokyo** near **Taipei**?
   Did you go to **San Francisco** last year?
   Do you live in **Rome**?
   Is **Paris** a big city?
   Do you live in **New York City**?

Practice the Words

A. **Listen and repeat.**

1. Play the recording. Students listen and repeat, pointing to each word in the vocabulary box.

   1. *Rome*
   2. *Taipei*
   3. *Tokyo*
   4. *London*
   5. *Seoul*
   6. *New York City*
   7. *Paris*
   8. *Honolulu*
   9. *San Francisco*
   10. *Hong Kong*

B. Point and say the words.

Students point to each of the target cities in the large scene and name them.

C. 🔊 **Listen and point.**

Play the recording. Students listen to the words. For the vocabulary, they point to the named city; for the conversations, they point to the speakers. (References are shown in parentheses.) Play the recording as many times as necessary for students to complete the task.

Tokyo.
San Francisco.
Taipei.
Paris.
Hong Kong.
Honolulu.
London.
New York City.
Seoul.
Rome.

Now listen and point to the speakers.

A: *What a cool plane!* (boy holding plane and friend)
B: *I want to see it.*
A: *No.*
B: *Come on! Let me see it.*
A: *I can't lift this by myself. It's so heavy.* (Ted and girl)
B: *Here, let me help you.*
A: *Thanks.*
A: *Do you ever fly at night?* (Annie and male pilot)
B: *Yes, I often fly at night. I need a lot of coffee.*
A: *How much coffee do you have?*
B: *I usually drink four cups of coffee.*

Games and Activities

1. **Draw a Map.** Divide the class into pairs. Each student in the pair takes three to four minutes to trace the map of the world from Student Book page 56, placing dots where the cities are (but not writing the city names). Each student then gives his/her partner the map he/she drew. Students then fill in the city names. Partners check each other's work.

2. **How Will You Get There?** Say *You want to go to Rome. How will you get there?* A volunteer says the different forms of transportation that he/she would take to get to Rome. For example: *I will drive to the airport in my car. Then I will fly on an airplane to Rome.* Do the same with the remaining target cities.

3. **Tell Me About It.** As a class, choose two of the target cities that students have visited or know something about. Write each of the city names on the board. Then bring a volunteer to the board. Seated students call out things they know about the two cities, and the volunteer writes the information on the board below the corresponding city name. Then divide the class into groups of three to four and have each group write a mini-description of one of the cities on the board. Groups share their descriptions with the class.

4. **Option: Personalize the Vocabulary.** Each student chooses a target city that he/she would like to visit. Then, for five to seven minutes, students draw pictures of themselves visiting the city they have chosen. Students then take turns telling the class about their pictures and what they would like to do when they visit the city.

Finish the Lesson

1. **Questions.** Ask students questions about cities of the world (see Suggested Questions below). Continue for three to four minutes.

   Suggested Questions:
   What two cities do you really want to visit?
   Can you go skiing in Honolulu?
   Can you climb a mountain in Rome?
   Can you take a train to Paris?
   Can you take a train to New York City?

2. Explain and assign Workbook page 56. (For instructions, see Teacher's Book page 173.)

Focus Time

Language Focus: Months (*January, February, March, April, May, June, July, August, September, October, November, December*)

Wh- questions with *when* and *how long* [*When did (he) go to (Hong Kong)? (He) went in (April). How long (was) (he) there? (He) (was) there for (one week).*]

Function: Inquiring about the time and duration of activities in the past

Materials Needed: CD/cassette and player; Unit 9 Word Time Picture Cards, 1 set; Unit 9 Word Time Word Cards, 1 set per 2 students; Unit 9 Focus Time Picture Cards, 1 set; Unit 9 Focus Time Word Cards, 1 set per 2 students; *I, He, She, We, They, you, he, she,* and *they* grammar cards, 2 sets per 2 students; Unit 9 Grammar Cards (see Picture and Word Card Book pages 33, 34, 35, 36, 37, 38, 43, 46, 51, and 52)

For general information on Focus Time, see pages 12–13.

Warm-Up and Review

1. **Vocabulary Review: I Went to (Rome) on Friday.** Students open their Student Books to page 56 and take 30 seconds to study the map. Then say *I went to Rome on Friday. Where did you go?* A volunteer begins by saying *I didn't go to Rome. I went to (Hong Kong).* Students continue around the room in the same way until most students have taken a turn.
2. Check Workbook page 56. (For instructions and answer key, see Teacher's Book page 173.)

This lesson is in two parts.

Part 1: Introduce the Words

1. Write today's date on the board (for example: *March 12, 2003*). Say *Today is (March 12, 2003). This month is March. Last month was February. Every year has twelve months. They are January, February, March, April, May, June, July, August, September, October, November, and December.* Then name each month again and have students repeat.
2. Draw twelve vertical columns on the board to make a calendar. Number the columns from 1 to 12 and attach a Unit 9 Focus Time Word Card at the top of each column. Point to each card and elicit its name.

Practice the Words

Students open their Student Books to page 57.

A. Listen and repeat.

Play the recording. Students listen and repeat each word.

1. *January*
2. *February*
3. *March*
4. *April*
5. *May*
6. *June*
7. *July*
8. *August*
9. *September*
10. *October*
11. *November*
12. *December*

Part 2: Introduce the Patterns

1. **When did (he) go to (Rome)? (He) went in (April).** Bring a volunteer to the front of the classroom and give him or her the *Rome* and *April* picture cards. Point to the volunteer and say *(He) went to Rome in April. (He) went in April.* Students repeat. Write *He went in April.* on the board. Point to and read each word. Students repeat. Then ask the class *When did he go to Rome?* Students repeat. Then ask the question again and elicit *He went in April.* Write *When did he go to Rome?* on the board to the left of *He went in April.* Point to and read each word. Students repeat. Do the same with *London/March, Tokyo/October,* and *Paris/July.*

2. **How long was (he) there? (He) was there for (one week).** Draw an April calendar on the board and write *Joe to Rome* on a Sunday, then draw a line through that week. Say *Joe went to Rome in April. He was there for one week.* Students repeat. Write *He was*

there for one week. on the board. Point to and read each word. Students repeat. Then ask the class *How long was he there?* Students repeat. Ask the question again and elicit *He was there for one week.* Write *How long was he there?* on the board to the left of *He was there for one week.* Point to and read each word. Students repeat. Do the same with *London/March/one day, Tokyo/October/two weeks,* and *Paris/July/five days.*

3. **How long were (they) there? (They) were there for (one week).** Do the same as in Step 2 above, writing two names on the calendar to demonstrate *they.*

4. **Practice for Fluency.** Say *they, London* and elicit *When did they go to London?* Say *May.* Elicit *They went in May.* Then say *one week* and elicit both the target question and answer, *How long were they there? They were there for one week.* Do the same with *he/Seoul/July/one day, you/Taipei/August/eight weeks,* and *she/Tokyo/December/three days.*

Practice the Patterns

B. Listen and repeat.

1. Write the text from the pattern boxes on the board. Then play the recording, pointing to each word. Students listen.

    A: *When did he go to Hong Kong?*
    B: *He went in April.*
    A: *How long was he there?*
    B: *He was there for one week.*

    A: *When did they go to Hong Kong?*
    B: *They went in April.*
    A: *How long were they there?*
    B: *They were there for one week.*

2. Play the recording again. Students look at the pattern boxes in their books and repeat, pointing to each word.

3. Students work with partners to ask and answer the questions, while looking at the pattern boxes in their books.

C. Look at page 56. Listen and point.

Play the recording. Students look at page 56 and listen to the words, pointing to the person being talked about. Play the recording as many times as necessary for students to complete the task.

    A: *When did she go to Paris?*
    B: *She went in October.*
    A: *How long was she there?*
    B: *She was there for four days.*

Games and Activities

1. **Months: Please Stand Up.** Say *If your birthday is in January, please stand up.* Any student whose birthday is in January stands up and says *My birthday is in January!* Do the same with four other months. Then ask students about different events during the year (see Suggested Questions below).

    Suggested Questions:
    When does school start?
    When is our (winter) vacation?
    When does the New Year start?
    When is (Independence Day)?
    When is your mother's birthday?

2. **Ask Them Questions.** Bring five volunteers to the front of the classroom and give each of them a Unit 9 Word Time Picture Card and a Unit 9 Focus Time Picture Card. One of the volunteers begins by saying *I went to (Honolulu).* Seated students say *When did you go to (Honolulu)?* The volunteer says *I went in (August).* Seated students ask *How long were you there?* The volunteer responds using any length of time he/she desires, *I was there for (one year).* Continue in the same way with the remaining volunteers.

3. **Make the Sentences.** (See Game 17, pages 155–156.) Do the activity using *I, He, She, We, They, you, he, she,* and *they* grammar cards and Unit 9 Word Time Word Cards, Focus Time Word Cards, and Grammar Cards.

Finish the Lesson

1. **When Did You Go to Mars?** Walk around the classroom asking students questions about interplanetary travel. For example: *When did you go to Mars? I went in June. How long were you there? I was there for ten minutes.* Continue for four to five minutes using other planets.

2. Explain and assign Workbook page 57. (For instructions, see Teacher's Book pages 173–174.)

Practice Time

Language Focus: Months; *Wh-* questions with *when* and *how long*
[*When did (you) go to (San Francisco)? (I) went in (March). How long (were) (you) there? (I) (was) there for (two days).*]

Function: Inquiring about the time and duration of activities in the past

Materials Needed: CD/cassette and player; Unit 9 Word Time Word Cards, 1 set; Unit 9 Focus Time Word Cards, 1 set (see Picture and Word Card Book pages 34, 36, and 38)

For general information on Practice Time, see pages 14–15.

Warm-Up and Review

1. **Pattern Review: The Vanishing Dialogue.** Write the following on the board:

   When did you go to Rome?
   I went in April.
   How long were you there?
   I was there for one week.

   Point to each line and elicit the sentence, with half of the class asking the questions and the other half answering. Erase a word from each sentence. The two halves of the class say the sentences, trying to fill in the missing words. Continue in the same way, erasing more words each time, until students can say the sentences from memory.

2. Check Workbook page 57. (For instructions and answer key, see Teacher's Book pages 173–174.)

Practice the Patterns

Students open their Student Books to page 58.

A. Listen and repeat. Then practice with a partner.

1. Play the recording. Students listen and repeat, pointing to each picture in their books.

   A: *When did you go to San Francisco?*
   B: *I went in March.*
   A: *How long were you there?*
   B: *I was there for two days.*

   1. *When did you go to Taipei?*
      I went in April.
      How long were you there?
      I was there for one week.

   2. *When did he go to Paris?*
      He went in December.
      How long was he there?
      He was there for three days.

   3. *When did she go to Tokyo?*
      She went in June.
      How long was she there?
      She was there for two weeks.

   4. *When did you go to London?*
      I went in January.
      How long were you there?
      I was there for one day.

   5. *When did you go to Seoul?*
      We went in August.
      How long were you there?
      We were there for four days.

   6. *When did he go to New York City?*
      He went in May.
      How long was he there?
      He was there for two days.

   7. *When did she go to Honolulu?*
      She went in September.
      How long was she there?
      She was there for one day.

   8. *When did they go to Rome?*
      They went in July.
      How long were they there?
      They were there for five days.

2. Students practice numbers 1–8 in pairs. (S1 in each pair asks the question, S2 answers.) Students then change roles and repeat the activity.

B. Look at page 56. Practice with a partner.

Students remain in pairs and look at page 56. S1 points to a city on the map and says *I went to (Taipei)*. S2 then uses the target patterns to ask S1 about his/her trip. S1 responds using the target patterns. For example: S2: *When did you go to Taipei?* S1: *I went in September.* S2: *How long were you there?* S1: *I was there for three days.*

C. Listen and chant.

1. Students turn to the *When Did You Go to Paris?* chant on page 77. They cover up the text, look at the pictures, and talk about what they see. Read the lyrics line by line. Students repeat each line. Play the recording. Students listen and follow along in their books.

When Did You Go to Paris?

When did you go to Paris?
  I went to Paris in September.
How long were you there?
  I was there for eight days.
  I played tennis in Paris.

When did you go to London?
  I went to London in October.
How long were you there?
  I was there for a week.
  I played soccer in London.

When did you go to Tokyo?
  I went to Tokyo in May.
How long were you there?
  I was there for two weeks.
  I bought a yo-yo in Tokyo.

When did you go to Honolulu?
  I went to Honolulu in April.
How long were you there?
  I was there for a day.
  I bought some shoes in Honolulu.

2. Play the recording again. Students listen and chant along, using their books for reference. Play the recording as many times as necessary for students to become familiar with the chant.

3. Divide the class into Groups A and B. Play the karaoke version. Group A sings the questions while pointing to Group B. Group B sings the answers, pantomiming the action in the last line of each verse. Groups changes roles and chant again.

Games and Activities

1. **Complete the Dialogue.** Attach the Unit 9 Word Time Word Cards and the Unit 9 Focus Time Word Cards in two rows to the board for reference. Then write the following on the board:

   A: When did you go to _____?
   B: I went in _____.
   A: How long were you there?
   B: I was there for _____.

Ask two volunteers to read the sentences on the board, filling in any words from the target patterns. Then divide the class into groups of four. Each group practices substituting names of places, months, and time periods into the sentences on the board. After four to five minutes, each group writes down one of the substitutions that they practiced and reads it to the class.

2. **Listen Carefully.** Read the following paragraph to students, having them take notes as necessary.

   My friend Ed loves going to the beach. He likes swimming and snorkeling. Once when he was at the beach he even saw a whale and a dolphin! In January, Ed went to Honolulu, because the best beaches are there. He was there for two weeks, and every day he swam all day long. Once or twice he went snorkeling with his friends, too.

   Ask the following questions about the above reading, having students refer to their notes for reference. If necessary, read the paragraph several times.

   Where did Ed go?
   Why did he go there?
   When did Ed go to Honolulu?
   How long was he there?
   Did he go sailing?
   Did he snorkel?

3. **Students' Trips.** Divide the class into pairs. Each student writes about a true or imaginary trip he/she took recently. Each student then tells his/her partner *I went to (Rome)*. Give students five to seven minutes to ask their partners questions about the recent trips. If necessary, students can take notes to remember what their partners say. Then each pair joins with another pair and each student tells the others about his/her partner's recent trip.

   OPTION: Do the activity as above, also having students draw pictures to illustrate important sights and happenings on their trips.

   Extra Practice
   Explain and assign Worksheet 17, Cities of the World, page 204. (For instructions and answer key, see page 187.)

Finish the Lesson

1. **When Did You…?** Ask students questions about past activities. For example: *When did you go to your friend's house? When did you go to the movie theater? When did you visit your grandmother?* Continue for four to five minutes.

2. Explain and assign Workbook page 58. (For instructions, see Teacher's Book page 174.)

Reading Time

Language Focus: Reading a tourist brochure
Materials Needed: CD/cassette and player

For general information on Reading Time, see pages 16–17.

Warm-Up and Review

1. **Pattern Review: Dictation.** Students open their Student Books to page 58 and look at the pattern boxes for about 30 seconds. They then close their books. Say *When did you go to San Francisco?* Students write the question on a piece of paper, using correct capitalization and punctuation. The first student to correctly write the question reads it to the class. Do the same with the remaining three sentences at the top of page 58.

2. Check Workbook page 58. (For instructions and answer key, see Teacher's Book page 174.)

Introduce the Reading

Note: Students may learn the new vocabulary within the context of the reading, or each new word can be taught before students encounter it in the reading. Follow the steps below to introduce the new vocabulary and/or introduce the reading content.

1. Write the new words in a column on the board. Point to and read each word before explaining its meaning.

million: Write *a million = 1,000,000* on the board. Point to and read each word.

world: Explain that *world* refers to all the towns, cities, and countries on Earth.

most exciting: Write the names of three popular, exciting adventure movies on the board. Point to each of the first two movies and enthusiastically say *That's an exciting movie.* Then point to the third movie and, with even more enthusiasm in your voice, say *That's the most exciting movie.*

thousand: Write *a thousand = 1,000* on the board. Point to and read each word.

opera: Say *Opera is a show where actors sing a story.* If possible, play students a small portion of a recorded opera.

jazz: Explain that jazz is a type of music pioneered by African Americans. If possible, play students a jazz song.

available: Say *The bakery has cherry pies. Cherry pies are available.*

information: Say *You want to go to a movie. You need to know what movies you can see and what time they're on. You can call the movie theater for that information.*

rent: Say *When you rent something, someone else owns it, but they let you use it for a little while if you give them money.*

2. Students open their Student Books to page 59. They look at the pictures and talk about what they see. For example: *This is New York City. Here's the Statue of Liberty. Here's the Empire State Building.* Ask students what they think the reading will be about.

Practice the Reading

Students read the brochure silently to themselves.

A. Listen and read along.

1. Play the recording. Students listen and read along in their Student Books.

Welcome to New York City, the Big Apple!

Over 30 million people visit New York City every year. Why? Because it's one of the world's most exciting places. There are 18 thousand restaurants, 10 thousand shops, and 150 museums. Basketball, opera, theater, jazz…New York City has it all!

Visit the Statue of Liberty and the Empire State Building. Get tickets for a show at a Broadway theater. Have a sandwich at Carnegie Deli. Don't forget to shop at Macy's! It's the world's biggest department store.

Walking tours, boat tours, and bus tours are available daily. For information, call us at 1 (800) 555-2112. We can help you find a hotel room, buy plane tickets, or rent a car.

New Words
million
world
most exciting
thousand
opera
jazz
available
information
rent

2. Play the recording again, stopping it after each sentence. Students listen and repeat each sentence.

3. Divide the class into pairs. Students in each pair take turns reading the brochure aloud to their partner.

B. **Listen and circle True or False.**

1. Play the recording. For each number, students listen and circle *True* if the statement is true, and *False* if it is not.

   1. *People visit New York City because it's one of the world's most exciting places.*
   2. *There are 80 thousand restaurants in New York City.*
   3. *Carnegie Deli is the world's largest department store.*
   4. *When you're in New York City, you can take a boat tour.*

2. Check answers by saying *Number 1. Three thousand people visit New York City every year.* Students say *True* if they circled *True*, and *False* if they circled *False*. If the statement is false, choose a volunteer to make it true. Do the same for numbers 2–4.

   Answer Key:
   1. True   2. False   3. False   4. True

C. Read the question. Write the answer.

1. Students read each question and answer it based on the reading in exercise A.

2. Check answers by reading each question and having students read the answer they wrote.

   Answer Key:
   1. How many museums are in New York City? <u>There are 150 museums in New York City.</u>

   2. Why do people visit New York City? <u>People visit New York City because it's one of the world's most exciting places.</u>

   3. What kinds of tours are available? <u>Walking tours, boat tours, and bus tours are available daily.</u>

   4. What is the "Big Apple"? <u>New York City is the "Big Apple."</u>

Games and Activities

Note: For all Reading Time activities, students may use their Student Books for reference.

1. **Name the Place.** Describe four to five places discussed in the reading (see Suggested Descriptions below). Students look in their books and name those places.

   Suggested Descriptions:
   An exciting city in America (New York City)
   A tall statue in New York (the Statue of Liberty)
   A place to see shows in New York (a Broadway theater)
   The world's largest department store (Macy's)
   A place to eat in New York City (Carnegie Deli)

2. **Radio Advertisement.** Volunteers take turns pretending to be radio announcers recording an advertisement for New York City. They read the reading with as much enthusiasm and drama as possible.

3. **Posters.** Divide the class into groups of three to four. Using the information from the reading, each group works together to create a travel poster encouraging people to visit New York City. The poster should contain both pictures and words.

   OPTION: Students create a travel poster for their own town.

Extra Practice
Explain and assign Worksheet 18, Ted's Trip to London, page 205. (For instructions and answer key, see page 187.)

Finish the Lesson

1. **Discussion.** Ask students to tell about cities they have toured. Continue the discussion for four to five minutes.

2. Explain and assign Workbook page 59. (For instructions, see Teacher's Book page 174.)

Your Time

Language Focus: Personalizing travel and time language
Materials Needed: CD/cassette and player

For general information on Your Time, see pages 18–19.

Warm-Up and Review

1. **Reading Review: Complete the Sentence.** Read the Unit 9 reading slowly, pausing before different words. Students say the missing words. For example: Say *Over 30 million people visit _____ every year.* Students say *New York City*. Students may use their Student Books for reference if necessary.

2. Check Workbook page 59. (For instructions and answer key, see Teacher's Book page 174.)

Introduce the Lesson

Ask students five to six questions relating to time (see Suggested Questions below).

Suggested Questions:
What time did you eat breakfast today?
Did you visit your grandparents on Saturday?
Did you go on a trip last August?
Do you ever go to the beach in December?
Do you ever go skiing in January?

Practice the Lesson

Students open their Student Books to page 60.

A. Listen and answer the questions.

1. Play the recording. For each number, students listen to the question and answer it based on their own knowledge and experience.

   1. *What time did you eat lunch yesterday?*
   2. *What time did you do your homework yesterday?*
   3. *Did you go to the beach in July?*
   4. *Did you go to Honolulu in August?*

2. Check answers by dividing the class into pairs and having students in each pair read one question and answer to the class.

   Answer Key:
   Answers will vary.

B. Pairwork. Read the questions. Write the answers. Then ask your partner.

Divide the class into pairs. Each student fills in the information in the *You* column, then asks his/her partner the questions and fills in the *Your Partner* column. At the end, each student tells the class about his/her partner, using the sentence cues and information from his/her chart. For example: *(Ken) went to Honolulu on his favorite trip. He went in September. He was there for two weeks.*

C. Review. Read and write.

1. Students read each sentence and complete it based on their own knowledge and experience.

2. Check answers by having four volunteers read one sentence to the class.

   Answer Key:
   Answers will vary.

Games and Activities

1. **Memory Chain.** (See Game 18, page 156.) Play the game using *I went to (Tokyo) in (March)*.

2. **What Did You Do?** Write *What did you do on your last trip?* on the board. Then divide the class into pairs. Each student asks his or her partner the question and writes down the answer. Then the students tell the class what their partners did on their last trip.

3. **Draw and Tell.** Each student takes five to six minutes to draw a picture of himself/herself doing three actions that he/she likes to do. When students have finished drawing go around the classroom, look at each student's picture, and ask them *When did you (listen to music)?* Students show their picture to the class and say *I (listened to music) (on Tuesday)*.

Finish the Lesson

1. **From Words to Sentences.** Write *always, sometimes, hardly ever, never* on the board. Point to each word and have students read it. Then write *I never get a sunburn in December.* on the board. Point to the sentence and have students read it. Then have students take turns substituting words for the underlined words in the sentence in order to make true sentences about themselves or someone they know. Continue until most students have taken a turn.

2. Explain and assign Workbook page 60. (For instructions, see Teacher's Book page 174.)

3. Do Chapter 5 of Storybook 5, *Digger and the Thief*. (For instructions and answer key, see Teacher's Book pages 180 and 182.)

> **Assessment**
> Explain and assign the Unit 9 Test, page 228. (For instructions and answer key, see page 213.)

10 At School

Conversation Time

Language Focus: Discussing yesterday's TV programs
Materials Needed: CD/cassette and player; Wall Chart 19

For general information on Conversation Time, see pages 8–9.

Warm-Up and Review

1. **Review: When?** Ask *What time did you go home yesterday?* and have several students respond. Then ask *What time did you talk on the phone yesterday?* and have several students respond. Do the same with *When do you do your homework?*
2. Check Workbook page 60. (For instructions and answer key, see Teacher's Book page 174.)

Introduce the Conversation

1. Set the scene and clarify the meaning. Say *Emily and Matt are talking about TV programs. Matt saw one about animals in Africa.* Then introduce the new phrase by writing it on the board. Point to and read the words before explaining their meaning. Students repeat the phrase.

   come over: Say *When a friend wants you to visit, she'll say "Do you want to come over?"*

2. Bring two students to the front of the classroom. Stand behind each student and model his/her lines of the conversation with the following actions:

   A: *Where were you yesterday afternoon?*
   Speak in a friendly tone.

   B: *At Annie's house. We were watching TV.*
   Speak in a friendly tone.

   A: *What was on?*
   Sound interested.

   B: *A program about animals in Africa.*
   Sound excited. Open your eyes wide.

   A: *Aw, I missed it. Was it good?*
   When saying *Aw,* sound a little disappointed.

   B: *Yeah, it was. The gorillas were really cool.*
   Speak in a happy, excited tone.

   A: *Did you watch the soccer game last night?*
   Speak in a questioning, friendly voice.

   B: *No, my mom was watching the news. Besides, I don't like watching soccer on TV.*
   Frown and shake your head.

   A: *Me, neither. It's not as fun as watching a real game.*
   Frown and shake your head.

   B: *Hey! There's a good movie on tonight. Do you want to come over?*
   Use a bright, inviting voice.

   A: *I can't. My mom won't let me watch TV on a school night.*
   Frown and shake your head. Sound a little disappointed.

   B: *Too bad. Oh! There's the bell. Time for class!*
   Pretend to hear a bell and turn to walk away.

3. Divide the class into Groups A and B. Model the conversation again using facial expressions and body language. Group A repeats the first line of the conversation, Group B repeats line two, and so on. Encourage students to copy your facial expressions and body language. Groups change roles and say the conversation again in the same way.

4. Attach Wall Chart 19 to the board or open a Student Book to page 61. Students then open their Student Books to page 61. Ask the following questions:

   Where are Emily and Matt talking?
   Who watched a program about animals on TV?
   Did both Emily and Matt see the program about animals?
   Does Emily like soccer on TV?
   Why can't Emily watch TV on a school night?
   How do Matt and Emily know it's time for class?

Practice the Conversation

A. 🔊 **Listen and repeat. Point to the speakers. Then listen again.**

Play the recording (first version of the conversation). Students listen and repeat, pointing to each speaker. Play the recording (second version of the conversation). Students listen and point to each speaker.

1. Emily: *Where were you yesterday afternoon?*
   Matt: *At Annie's house. We were watching TV.*
2. Emily: *What was on?*
   Matt: *A program about animals in Africa.*
3. Emily: *Aw, I missed it. Was it good?*
   Matt: *Yeah, it was. The gorillas were really cool.*
4. Emily: *Did you watch the soccer game last night?*
   Matt: *No, my mom was watching the news. Besides, I don't like watching soccer on TV.*
5. Emily: *Me, neither. It's not as fun as watching a real game.*
   Matt: *Hey! There's a good movie on tonight. Do you want to come over?*
6. Emily: *I can't. My mom won't let me watch TV on a school night.*
   Matt: *Too bad. Oh! There's the bell. Time for class!*

B. Role-play the conversation.

Students choose a partner and, using their Student Books for reference, role-play the conversation. They then change roles and role-play the conversation again.

Games and Activities

Note: For all Conversation Time activities, students may use their Student Books for reference.

1. **Say It Together.** (See Game 4, page 154.) Play the game using the target conversation.
2. **Back-to-Back.** Divide the class into pairs. Students sit with their backs to their partners and role-play the conversation without looking at each other. Partners then change roles and repeat the activity.
3. **Make It Your Own.** Write the following on the board:

   A: *Where were you yesterday afternoon?*
   B: <u>*At Annie's house. We were watching TV.*</u>

   Students read the dialogue on the board. Then divide the class into pairs and write the following on the board:

   1. *I was at my grandparents' house. We had lunch and then played a game.*
   2. *I went swimming with my brother.*
   3. *I was taking care of my little sister.*

Students read each new response. Quickly clarify meaning if necessary. Then students in each pair role-play the dialogue on the board, substituting the new responses into the underlined part of the target conversation.

Finish the Lesson

1. **Discussion.** Ask students five to six questions about their TV viewing (see Suggested Questions below).

   Suggested Questions:
   Who watched TV last night?
   What was on?
   What are your favorite TV programs?
   What programs do you usually watch?
   How many of you usually watch that program?
   Do you like to watch sports like soccer on TV?
   Do you watch TV on school nights?
   When do you usually go to bed?

2. Explain and assign Workbook page 61. (For instructions, see Teacher's Book page 175.)

Word Time

Language Focus: Actions (*skip lunch, forget my homework, go to bed late, fall off my chair, get a good grade, lose my favorite pencil, make a mistake, take off my jacket, win a prize, turn off the fan*)

Materials Needed (excluding materials for optional activities):
CD/cassette and player; Wall Chart 20; Unit 5 Word Time Picture Cards, 1 set per 3–4 students; Unit 10 Word Time Picture Cards, 1 set per 3–4 students, Unit 10 Word Time Word Cards, 1 set (see Picture and Word Card Book pages 17, 39, and 40)

For general information on Word Time, see pages 10–11.

Warm-Up and Review

1. **Conversation Review: True/False/I Don't Know.** Play the recording of the Unit 10 conversation, having students take notes if necessary to remember the information they hear. Say four to five statements about the conversation (see Suggested Statements below). Students say *True* if the statement is true, and *False* if it is false. If a statement is false, choose a volunteer to make it true. If students don't have enough information to determine if the statement is true or false, they say *I don't know*.

   Suggested Statements:
   Emily, the girl, watched TV with Annie yesterday.
   Matt, the boy, watched a program about animals.
   The boy thought the tigers were cool.
   The boy's mom watched the news last night.
   The girl likes playing soccer.

2. Check Workbook page 61. (For instructions and answer key, see Teacher's Book page 175.)

Introduce the Words

1. Hold up and name each of the Unit 10 Word Time Picture Cards. Students listen. Hold up and name the cards again, and have students repeat. Hold up the cards in random order and have students name them.

2. Attach the Unit 10 Word Time Picture Cards in a row to the board. Stand the Unit 10 Word Time Word Cards on the chalktray under the corresponding picture cards. Point to each picture/word card pair and read the word. Students repeat. Then reposition the word cards so they are no longer directly below the corresponding picture cards. Volunteers come to the board one by one and place a word card under its corresponding picture card, then point to and read the word. Seated students repeat.

Talk About the Picture

1. Students open their Student Books to page 62. They look at the large scene and use complete sentences to identify anything they can.

2. Attach Wall Chart 20 to the board or open a Student Book to page 62. Read the following "story" while pointing to or touching the pictures (**bold** words) and pantomiming the actions (*italicized* words).

   In Annie's classroom the students and teacher are *thinking* about many things. The **teacher** is *thinking* about skipping lunch. **Ted** is looking at **the board** and thinking, "Am I going to make a mistake?" **This girl** went to bed late. **This boy** is thinking about his test. **Jan** is dreaming about winning a **prize**. **Annie** is asking herself, "Did I forget my homework?"

3. Ask the following questions while pointing to or touching the pictures (**bold** words).

   Is **Annie** thinking about forgetting her homework?
   Who is thinking about falling off his **chair**?
   Who is thinking about taking off her jacket?
   Who is thinking about turning off the **fan**?
   Who is thinking about losing her favorite pencil?
   Who is thinking about winning a prize?

Practice the Words

A. 🔊 **Listen and repeat.**

Play the recording. Students listen and repeat, pointing to each word in the vocabulary box.

1. skip lunch
2. forget my homework
3. go to bed late
4. fall off my chair
5. get a good grade
6. lose my favorite pencil
7. make a mistake
8. take off my jacket
9. win a prize
10. turn off the fan

B. Point and say the words.

Students point to each of the target vocabulary items in the large scene and name them.

C. 🔊 **Listen and point.**

Play the recording. Students listen to the words. For the vocabulary, they point to the person/people doing the named action; for the conversations, they point to the speakers. (References are shown in parentheses.) Play the recording as many times as necessary for students to complete the task.

Fall off my chair.
Forget my homework.
Take off my jacket.
Lose my favorite pencil.
Make a mistake.
Get a good grade.
Skip lunch.
Win a prize.
Turn off the fan.
Go to bed late.

Now listen and point to the speakers.

A: *Excuse me. May I borrow a pencil?* (Annie and boy)
B: *Sure. Here you are.*
A: *Thanks.*

A: *When did you go to Paris?* (boys by fan)
B: *I went in June.*
A: *How long were you there?*
B: *I was there for three days.*

A: *Here you are. Today's special is ham and potatoes.*
B: *No, thank you. I'm not in the mood for ham.*
A: *Are you sure?*
B: *Positive. I'm not hungry today.*

Games and Activities

1. **Charades.** Divide the class into groups of five to six and give each group a set of Unit 10 Word Time Picture Cards. A student in each group begins by looking at a picture card and then pantomiming the action. The first student to correctly name the action, saying *You're (going to bed late)*, is next to pantomime an action. Groups continue in this way for five to seven minutes.

2. **Categorizing.** Divide the class into groups of two to three. Students in each group work together to make two lists. One list should contain the target actions that generally make people happy. The other list should contain the target actions that generally make people sad or upset. Once each group has made its lists, have students share their lists with the class. Work with the class as a whole to come to a consensus about what should be on each list. Write the final lists on the board.

3. **Ask and Answer.** Write *always, usually, often, sometimes, hardly ever,* and *never* on the board. Point to each word and have students read it. Then quickly review the *Do you ever (go to bed late)?* pattern. Divide the class into groups of three to four and give each group a set of Units 5 and 10 Word Time Picture Cards. Groups place the cards faceup in front of them. A student in each group begins by asking *Does (Kim) ever (skip lunch)?* The first student to touch the named card asks (Kim) *Do you ever skip lunch?* (Kim) answers truthfully and then takes a turn asking a *Does (Tom) ever…* question. Groups continue in the same way for five to seven minutes.

   Note: Remind students to change *my* to *your* or *his/her* as necessary.

4. **Option: Personalize the Vocabulary.** Divide the class into pairs and give each pair a set of Units 8 and 10 Word Time Picture Cards. Choosing from the activities listed on the cards, students write a list of five things they want to do and five things they do not want to do. Students then read their lists to each other and say why they want and do not want to do the activities.

Finish the Lesson

1. **How often…?** Write *once a day, three times a week, twice a month,* and *four times a year* on the board. Point to each word and have students read it. Then ask *How often do you make a mistake?* and have several students respond. Then ask *How often do you win a prize?* and have several students respond. Do the same with *How often do you lose your favorite pencil?*

   Note: Students can also use the pattern *I (never) (lose my favorite pencil)* to respond to the questions.

2. Explain and assign Workbook page 62. (For instructions, see Teacher's Book page 175.)

Focus Time

Language Focus: Adjectives (*hungry, nervous, tired, embarrassed, happy, sad, disappointed, cold, hot, proud*)

If clauses [*If (I) (skip lunch), (I'll) be (hungry).*]

Function: Expressing conditions and emotions/attitudes; expressing consequences

Materials Needed: CD/cassette and player; Unit 4 Focus Time Word Cards, 1 set; Unit 10 Word Time Word Cards, 1 set per 2 students; Unit 10 Focus Time Picture Cards, 1 set; Unit 10 Focus Time Word Cards, 1 set per 2 students; *I, you, she, he, we,* and *they* grammar cards, 1 set per 2 students; Unit 10 Grammar Cards, 1 set per 2 students (see Picture and Word Card Book pages 16, 40, 41, 42, 43, 44, 52, and 59)

For general information on Focus Time, see pages 12–13.

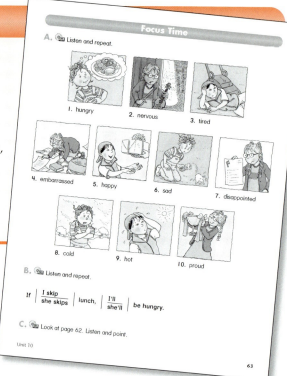

Warm-Up and Review

1. **Vocabulary Review: True Sentences.** Attach the Unit 10 Word Time Word Cards in a column to the board. Point to each card and elicit the verb phrases. Next, attach the Unit 4 Focus Time Word Cards to the board in a column to the left of the first. For three to four minutes volunteers make true sentences about themselves or people they know, using the prompts on the board. For example: *I never go to bed late. My father often skips lunch.*

2. Check Workbook page 62. (For instructions and answer key, see Teacher's Book page 175.)

This lesson is in two parts.

Part 1: Introduce the Words

1. Hold up and name each Unit 10 Focus Time Picture Card. Students listen. Hold up and name each card again. Students repeat. Hold up the cards in random order and have students name them.

2. Attach the Unit 10 Focus Time Picture Cards in a row to the board. Stand the Unit 10 Focus Time Word Cards on the chalktray under the corresponding picture cards. Point to each picture/word card pair and read the word. Students repeat. Then reposition the word cards so they are no longer directly below the corresponding picture cards. Volunteers come to the board one by one and place a word card under its corresponding picture card, then point to and read the word. Seated students repeat.

3. Hold up each Unit 10 Focus Time Picture Card and have students name the card and pantomime the emotion.

Practice the Words

Students open their Student Books to page 63.

A. Listen and repeat.

Play the recording. Students listen and repeat each word.

1. *hungry*
2. *nervous*
3. *tired*
4. *embarrassed*
5. *happy*
6. *sad*
7. *disappointed*
8. *cold*
9. *hot*
10. *proud*

Part 2: Introduce the Patterns

1. **If (I) (fall off my chair), (I'll) be (embarrassed).** Say *I fell off my chair yesterday. I was embarrassed. Maybe I'll fall off my chair tomorrow. If I fall off my chair tomorrow, I'll be embarrassed.* Students repeat each sentence. If necessary, quickly review the meaning of *maybe*. Write *If I fall off my chair, I'll be embarrassed.* on the board. Point to and read each word. Do the same with *go to bed late/tired, turn off the fan/hot,* and *skip lunch/hungry.*

2. **If (she) (falls off her chair), (she'll) be (embarrassed).**
Do the same as in Step 1 with a girl to demonstrate *she*.

3. **Practice for Fluency.** Say *he, turn off the fan, hot* and have students say the corresponding target sentence. Do the same with different pronouns, actions, and adjectives for three to four minutes.

Practice the Patterns

B. **Listen and repeat.**

1. Write the text from the pattern boxes on the board. Then play the recording, pointing to each word. Students listen.

    A: *If I skip lunch, I'll be hungry.*
    B: *If she skips lunch, she'll be hungry.*

2. Play the recording again. Students look at the pattern boxes in their books and repeat, pointing to each word.

3. Students work with partners to say the sentences, while looking at the pattern boxes in their books.

C. **Look at page 62. Listen and point.**

Students look at page 62. Play the recording. Students listen to the patterns and point to the person doing each activity they hear named. Play the recording as many times as necessary for students to complete the task.

If she takes off her jacket, she'll be cold.
If he falls off his chair, he'll be embarrassed.
If she forgets her homework, she'll be nervous.

Games and Activities

1. **Upside Down.** Hold up a Unit 10 Focus Time Picture Card upside down. Elicit the word. Do the same with the remaining Unit 10 Focus Time Picture Cards. Then attach the cards to the board right side up. Volunteers attach the corresponding word cards to the board below the pictures, pantomime the adjectives, and use each adjective in a sentence.

2. **If I Skip Lunch…** Say *Maybe I'll take off my jacket.* Then hold up the *cold* picture card. Elicit *If you take off your jacket, you'll be cold.* Do the same with *fall off my chair/embarrassed, go to bed late/tired, win a prize/proud,* and *lose my favorite pencil/sad.* Then have a volunteer take on the teacher's role and elicit the target sentences in the same way.

3. **Make the Sentences.** (See Game 17, pages 155–156.) Do the activity using *I, you, she, he, we,* and *they* grammar cards and Unit 10 Word Time Word Cards, Focus Time Word Cards, and Grammar Cards.

Finish the Lesson

1. **What Might Happen?** Point to a girl and say *If she skips lunch…* The girl pantomimes an adjective and the rest of the class completes the sentence, saying *…she'll be (hungry).* Do the same with different volunteers and actions for three to four minutes.

2. Explain and assign Workbook page 63. (For instructions, see Teacher's Book page 175.)

Practice Time

Language Focus: Adjectives; *If* clauses [*If (you) (take off your jacket), (you'll) be (cold).*]

Function: Expressing conditions and emotions/attitudes; expressing consequences

Materials Needed: CD/cassette and player; Unit 10 Word Time Picture Cards, 2 sets; Unit 10 Word Time Word Cards, 1 card per 2 students; Unit 10 Focus Time Word Cards, 1 card per 2 students; *I, you, we, he, she,* and *they* grammar cards, 1 set (see Picture and Word Card Book pages 39, 40, 42, and 43)

For general information on Practice Time, see pages 14–15.

Warm-Up and Review

1. **Pattern Review: Consequences.** Write *If you take off your jacket, you'll be cold.* on the board. Point to the sentence and have students read it. Next, give each student on the right side of the classroom a Unit 10 Word Time Word Card. Give each student on the left side of the classroom a Unit 10 Focus Time Word Card. A volunteer (S1) on the right side holds up his/her card and says *Maybe I'll (skip lunch)*. A student on the left side with an appropriate adjective on his/her card holds it up and says *If you (skip lunch), you'll be (hungry)*. Students continue until most have taken a turn.

2. Check Workbook page 63. (For instructions and answer key, see Teacher's Book page 175.)

Practice the Patterns

Students open their Student Books to page 64.

A. Listen and repeat. Then practice with a partner.

1. Play the recording. Students listen and repeat, pointing to each picture in their books.

   If you take off your jacket, you'll be cold.

   1. If I forget my homework, I'll be nervous.
   2. If she loses her favorite pencil, she'll be sad.
   3. If he gets a good grade, he'll be happy.
   4. If you fall off your chair, you'll be embarrassed.
   5. If she goes to bed late, she'll be tired.
   6. If they win a prize, they'll be proud.
   7. If I make a mistake, I'll be disappointed.
   8. If we turn off the fan, we'll be hot.

2. Students practice numbers 1–8 in pairs. Students then change partners and repeat the activity.

B. Look at page 62. Practice with a partner.

Students remain in pairs and look at page 62. They then take turns making statements about the large scene using the target patterns and vocabulary items. For example: S1 (pointing to the teacher): *If she skips lunch, she'll be hungry.* S2 (pointing to Ted): *If Ted makes a mistake, he'll be embarrassed.*

C. Listen and sing along.

1. Students turn to the *H-A-P-P-Y* song on page 77. They cover up the text, look at the pictures, and talk about what they see. Read the lyrics line by line. Students repeat each line. Play the recording. Students listen and follow along in their books.

   H-A-P-P-Y
   (Melody: *B-I-N-G-O*)

   If he gets a good grade, he'll be very happy.
   H-A-P-P-Y, H-A-P-P-Y, H-A-P-P-Y.
   He'll be very happy.

   If she goes to bed late, she'll be very tired.
   T-I-R-E-D, T-I-R-E-D, T-I-R-E-D.
   She'll be very tired.

   If he takes off his jacket, he'll be very cold.
   C-O-L-D, C-O-L-D, C-O-L-D.
   He'll be very cold.

   If she wins a prize, she'll be very proud.
   P-R-O-U-D, P-R-O-U-D, P-R-O-U-D.
   She'll be very proud.

2. Play the recording again. Students listen and sing along, using their books for reference. Play the recording as many times as necessary for students to become familiar with the song.

3. Play the karaoke version. Students sing along, pantomiming each adjective as they sing it.

Games and Activities

1. **Round-Up.** Attach the Unit 10 Word Time Word Cards in a row to the board for reference. Then place the *I, you, we, he, she,* and *they* grammar cards in one pile, and the Unit 10 Focus Time Word Cards in another pile. Hold up one card from each pile and point to a verb phrase on the board. Students say the corresponding target pattern. Continue in the same way with the remaining cards.

2. **Find Your Partner(s).** In pairs, students write a target sentence on a strip of paper, then cut the strip in the middle. Spread out the strips of paper face down on a desk and shuffle them. Students pick out a strip each. Then they look around the classroom for the students who have the other half of the sentence. When students have found their partner(s), they come to the front of the classroom and read their sentences to the class.

3. **Chain of Events.** Write *If I go to bed late, I'll be tired.* on the board. Next, elicit a number of *If* sentences derived from the first. For example: *If I'm tired, I'll make a mistake. If I make a mistake, I'll be embarrassed.* Write the sentences on the board for reference. Then divide the class into groups of six to eight. Give students four to six minutes to write their own sequences of *If* sentences. Students may use action vocabulary from other lessons in addition to the Unit 10 vocabulary. When most groups have finished writing, have volunteers take turns reading their group's sentences aloud to the class.

Extra Practice
Explain and assign Worksheet 19, If..., page 206. (For instructions and answer key, see page 187.)

Finish the Lesson

1. **True Sentences.** Students take turns making target sentences about family members or friends for three to four minutes.

2. Explain and assign Workbook page 64. (For instructions, see Teacher's Book page 175.)

Reading Time

Language Focus: Reading information on a web site

Materials Needed (excluding materials for optional activities):
CD/cassette and player

For general information on Reading Time, see pages 16–17.

Warm-Up and Review

1. **Pattern Review: Sing Along.** Play the Unit 10 song, *H-A-P-P-Y*. Students listen. Play the song again and have students sing along.
2. Check Workbook page 64. (For instructions and answer key, see Teacher's Book page 175.)

Introduce the Reading

Note: Students may learn the new vocabulary within the context of the reading, or each new word can be taught before students encounter it in the reading. Follow the steps below to introduce the new vocabulary and/or introduce the reading content.

1. Write the new words in a column on the board. Point to and read each word before explaining its meaning.

   web site: Write a few common web site addresses on the board. Point to them and say *These are web sites.*

   fan: Explain that *fan* has two meanings. Say *You already know about the kind of fan you can turn on to cool a room. Another kind of fan is someone who likes something very much.* For example: a famous person, a sport, or a kind of music can have fans.

   find out: Say *Please find out if (Mari) had breakfast this morning.* Prompt students to ask (Mari) if she had breakfast. Then say *Please find out if (Ken) won a prize yesterday.* Prompt students to ask (Ken) if he won a prize.

   go on sale: Explain that, in this context, to go on sale means that something is now available to be bought.

   public: Say *If something is public, it is for everybody.*

   broadcasting: Explain that broadcasting refers to sound and picture being transmitted over the air to be seen on a TV.

   begin: Say *Please begin writing* and prompt students to begin writing. Then say *Please begin talking* and prompt students to talk quietly with a classmate nearby.

   baseball: Draw a baseball bat and ball on the board. Pantomime hitting a baseball with a bat. Say *I'm playing baseball!*

   percent: Draw a few circles with different percentages of the circle colored in. Then point to each one and say, for example, *fifty percent, twenty-five percent.*

   remote control: Walk to the back of the classroom, point

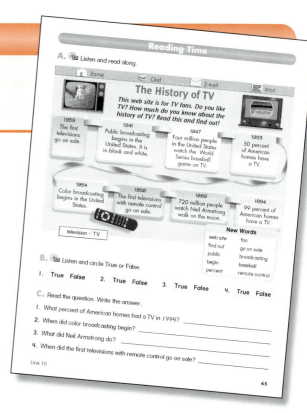

to a pretend TV, and say *A TV is here.* Then return to the front of the classroom, pretend to be using a remote control, and say *I'm using a remote control to turn off the TV.*

2. Students open their Student Books to page 65. They look at the pictures and talk about what they see. For example: *This is a web site. Here is a remote control.* Ask students what they think the reading will be about.

Practice the Reading

Students read the story silently to themselves.

A. Listen and read along.

1. Play the recording. Students listen and read along in their Student Books.

   The History of TV

   This web site is for TV fans. Do you like TV? How much do you know about the history of TV? Read this and find out!

   1939 The first televisions go on sale.

   1941 Public broadcasting begins in the United States. It is in black and white.

   1947 Four million people in the United States watch the World Series baseball game on TV.

   1953 50 percent of American homes have a TV.

   1954 Color broadcasting begins in the United States.

   1956 The first televisions with remote control go on sale.

1969 720 million people watch Neil Armstrong walk on the moon.

1994 99 percent of American homes have a TV.

New Words
web site
fan
find out
go on sale
public
broadcasting
begin
baseball
percent
remote control

2. Play the recording again, stopping it after each sentence. Students listen and repeat each sentence.

3. Divide the class into pairs. Students in each pair take turns reading the story aloud to their partner.

B. **Listen and circle True or False.**

1. Play the recording. For each number, students listen and circle *True* if the statement is true, and *False* if it is not.

   1. *720 million people watched Neil Armstrong walk on the moon in 1969.*
   2. *50 percent of American homes had a TV in 1953.*
   3. *Public broadcasting was in color in 1941.*
   4. *The World Series has never been on TV.*

2. Check answers by saying *Number 1. 720 million people watched Neil Armstrong walk on the moon in 1969.* Students say *True* if they circled *True*, and *False* if they circled *False*. If the statement is false, choose a volunteer to make it true. Do the same for numbers 2–4.

   Answer Key:
   1. True   2. True   3. False   4. False

C. Read the question. Write the answer.

1. Students read each question and answer it based on the reading in exercise A.

2. Check answers by reading each question and having students read the answer they wrote.

   Answer Key:
   1. What percent of American homes had a TV in 1994? <u>99 percent of American homes had a TV in 1994.</u>
   2. When did color broadcasting begin? <u>Color broadcasting began in the United States in 1954.</u>
   3. What did Neil Armstrong do? <u>Neil Armstrong walked on the moon in 1969.</u>
   4. When did the first televisions with remote control go on sale? <u>The first televisions with remote control went on sale in 1956.</u>

Games and Activities

Note: For all Reading Time activities, students may use their Student Books for reference.

1. **Complete the Information.** Divide the class into groups of four to six. Each group sits in a circle. A student in each group (S1) begins by saying the first half of a sentence from the reading. The next student in the circle (S2) repeats S1's words and then adds the second half of that sentence. The next student (S3) begins the following sentence from the reading. Groups continue around the circle until they have said the entire reading.

2. **Make a Narrative.** Work with students to turn the information on Student Book page 65 into a narrative. For example: *Here is some information about the history of TV. In 1939, the first televisions went on sale. Then in 1941, public broadcasting began in the United States. It was in black and white. By 1947, many people liked to watch TV.*

   OPTIONS:
   1. Students illustrate the narrative with drawings or pictures cut from magazines.

   2. Students go to the library or use the internet to do further research on TV. They then include the new information in the narrative.

3. **Questionnaire.** Write these questions on the board:

   1. *Do you have a TV at home? How many TVs do you have?*
   2. *Do you have a black and white or a color TV?*
   3. *Do you watch TV in the morning, afternoon, or evening?*
   4. *What's your favorite show?*
   5. *Do you like American TV shows? Why or why not?*

   Divide the class into pairs. Partners ask each other these questions and write the answers in their notebooks. Then they tell the class about their partners' answers.

   Extra Practice
   Explain and assign Worksheet 20, My Grandmother, page 207. (For instructions and answer key, see page 187.)

Finish the Lesson

1. **What Happened in That Year?** Say *1954*. Students look in their Student Books, find the information corresponding to that year, and then say what happened in 1954 (in their own words if possible). Do the same with the other years from the reading.

2. Explain and assign Workbook page 65. (For instructions, see Teacher's Book pages 175–176.)

Your Time

Language Focus: Personalizing consequence language
Materials Needed: CD/cassette and player

For general information on Your Time, see pages 18–19.

Warm-Up and Review

1. **Reading Review: Find the Facts.** Say *color broadcasting*. Students look at Student Book page 65 to find those words. When they do, they read or say aloud the sentence containing the words as well as the corresponding year. For example: *1954. Color broadcasting begins in the United States.* Do the same with *public broadcasting, the first televisions, Neil Armstrong, 99 percent, 50 percent, the World Series.*

2. Check Workbook page 65. (For instructions and answer key, see Teacher's Book pages 175–176.)

Introduce the Lesson

Ask students five to six questions relating to students' actions (see Suggested Questions below).

Suggested Questions:
How often do you fall off your chair?
How often do you get a good grade?
Do you ever make a mistake?
Do you ever lose your favorite pencil?
Do you like winning a prize?
Do you like forgetting your homework?

Practice the Lesson

Students open their Student Books to page 66.

A. Listen and answer the questions.

1. Play the recording. For each number, students listen to the question and answer it based on their own knowledge and experience.

   1. *If you skip breakfast tomorrow, will you be hungry?*
   2. *If you forget your homework tomorrow, will you be proud?*
   3. *If you go to bed at 11:00 tonight, will you be tired tomorrow?*
   4. *If you get a good grade today, will you be disappointed?*

2. Check answers by dividing the class into pairs and having students in each pair read one question and answer to the class.

   Answer Key:
   Answers will vary.

B. Write four feelings. Ask your classmates. Write their names and circle Yes or No.

Students write four different feelings in the *Feeling* column of their chart. They then circulate around the classroom and ask their classmates the target questions, circling *Yes* or *No* to indicate the answers they hear. Then ask students questions about the survey. For example: Ask *If Bob wins a prize, will he be happy?* Students who know this information respond either *Yes, he will* or *No, he won't*.

C. Review. Read and write the answers.

1. Students read each question and answer it based on their own knowledge and experience.

2. Check answers by having volunteers read one question and answer to the class.

   Answer Key:
   Answers will vary.

Games and Activities

1. **Memory Chain.** (See Game 18, page 156.) Play the game using *If I (win a prize), I'll be (sad)*.

2. **Yesterday's Actions.** Divide the class into pairs. A student in each pair (S1) begins by pantomiming different actions he/she did yesterday. His/Her partner (S2) writes down the actions he/she thinks S1 is pantomiming. Once S1 has finished pantomiming, S2 checks his/her list, asking *Did you (make a mistake) yesterday?* S1 says either *Yes, I did* or *No, I didn't*. Pairs continue until S2 has an accurate list of S1's activities. Pairs then change roles and do the activity again.

3. **Drawing.** Give students five to six minutes to draw pictures of themselves doing both activities that make them happy and activities that make them sad or upset. Once students have finished drawing, divide the class into pairs and write *When I (visit a friend), I'm happy.* on the board. Students tell their partners about their drawings. For example: *This is me. When I get a good grade, I'm happy.*

Finish the Lesson

1. **How About You?** Write *If I get a good grade, I'll be happy.* on the board. Then say *embarrassed* and have a volunteer substitute *embarrassed* and an appropriate verb/verb phrase into the sentence on the board. Do the same with five to six different adjectives.

2. Explain and assign Workbook page 66. (For instructions, see Teacher's Book page 176.)

3. Do Chapter 6 of Storybook 5, *Digger and the Thief*. (For instructions and answer key, see Teacher's Book pages 180 and 182.)

> **Assessment**
> Explain and assign the Unit 10 Test, page 229. (For instructions and answer key, see page 213.)

Review 2

Conversation Time Review

Review Focus: Units 6–10 conversations
Materials Needed: CD/cassette and player

Warm-Up

1. **Review Units 6–10 Conversations.** Students turn to each Conversation Time page (pages 37, 43, 49, 55, and 61). Elicit each conversation.
2. Check Workbook page 66. (For instructions and answer key, see Teacher's Book page 176.)

Practice the Language

Students open their Student Books to page 67.

A. Listen and circle the correct picture.

1. Play the recording. Students listen and, for each number, they circle the picture that corresponds to the conversation they hear.

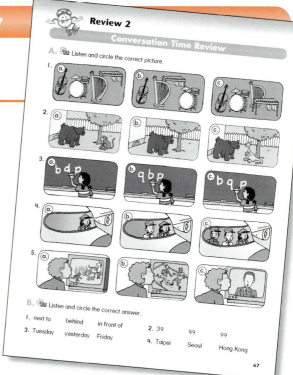

1. Annie: Hi, Ted. Do you want some help?
   Ted: Sure! You can move the cello. Put it over there.
   Annie: Beside the harp?
   Ted: No. Don't put it by the harp. Put it beside the drums.
   Annie: Okay.
   Ted: Now put the harp behind the xylophone.

2. Woman: 911. What's the emergency?
   Boy: There's a wild animal in my backyard! I think it's a bear.
   Woman: A bear?
   Boy: No, it isn't a bear. I think it's a baboon!
   Woman: A kangaroo?
   Boy: No, a baboon. Oh! There are two animals! A baboon and a bear!
   Woman: Okay. I'm sending a police officer now.

3. Teacher: Kim, please come to the board. Write the letter "p."
   Kim: Okay.
   Teacher: No, that's not a "p." That's a "b." No, that's a "q."
   Kim: I can't. It's too hard.
   Teacher: Come on, Kim. Don't give up!
   Kim: Okay. Hey! I can do it.
   Teacher: Good work, Kim!

4. Boy: Captain Jones, could I interview you for my school newspaper?
   Pilot: Sure! Go ahead.
   Boy: Do you fly the plane by yourself?
   Pilot: No. I always have a copilot.
   Boy: Do you enjoy being a pilot?
   Pilot: Yes, I do.
   Boy: Thanks for your time, Captain Jones.
   Pilot: My pleasure!

5. Girl: Where were you last night?
   Boy: I was at home watching TV.
   Girl: What was on?
   Boy: A program about animals in Africa. It was great!
   Girl: Aw…I missed it. Did you watch the soccer game last night?
   Boy: No. My mom was watching the news. I went to bed.

2. Check answers by having students listen to the conversations again. Stop the recording after each conversation and have students say the letter of the picture they have circled.

Answer Key:
1. c
2. a
3. c
4. b
5. a

B. Listen and circle the correct answer.

1. Play the recording. Students listen and, for each number, they circle the number or words that they hear discussed in the conversation.

    1. Ted: *Put the bass over there, Annie.*
       Annie: *Okay. Wow! This is heavy.*
       Ted: *Look out for the box!*
       Annie: *Where? Behind me?*
       Ted: *No, by the window, in front of you!*
       Annie: *Oh, there it is. Thanks, Ted.*

    2. Woman: *What's your name and address?*
       Dan: *Dan Day. 49 Maple Lane.*
       Woman: *Okay. Dan Day at 99 Maple Lane. Oh! Sorry, you said 39 Maple Lane.*
       Dan: *No, it's 49 Maple Lane.*
       Woman: *Got it.*

    3. Teacher: *Jenny, please help me pass out the homework.*
       Girl: *Is it homework from Tuesday?*
       Teacher: *No, it's homework from yesterday.*
       Girl: *But yesterday was Sunday.*
       Teacher: *Oh yes, you're right. It's homework from Friday.*

    4. Boy: *Captain West, do you ever fly abroad?*
       Pilot: *Yes, I have an overseas flight once a month.*
       Boy: *So you fly to Hong Kong once a month?*
       Pilot: *Oh, I never fly to Hong Kong. I fly to Taipei once a month.*

2. Check answers by having students listen to the conversations again. Stop the recording after each conversation and have students say the number or words they have circled.

    Answer Key:
    1. in front of
    2. 49
    3. Friday
    4. Taipei

Games and Activities

1. **Role Play.** Write the third conversation from exercise A on the board. Point to each line and have students read it. Then divide the class into pairs and have students in each pair role-play the conversation. Students change roles and role-play the conversation again.

2. **Act It Out.** Divide the class into pairs. Students in each pair work together to write out a mini-dialogue (approximately four to five lines long) between two friends discussing what they did last night. Once students have created their dialogues, choose volunteers to role-play their dialogues for the class.

3. **Illustrators.** Read the first conversation from exercise B. Students listen and then draw pictures to illustrate the conversation. Volunteers then take turns showing their pictures to the class and explaining them.

Finish the Lesson

1. **Who Says It?** Read the second conversation from exercise B. Discuss with students where they think the conversation is being held, and who the speakers might be.

2. Explain and assign Workbook page 67. (For instructions, see Teacher's Book page 176.)

Digger and Max

Review Focus: Units 6–10 conversations, vocabulary, and patterns

Materials Needed: CD/cassette and player

Warm-Up

1. **Review Units 6–10 Vocabulary and Patterns.** Turn to each Word Time page (pages 38, 44, 50, 56, and 62), and Focus Time page (pages 39, 45, 51, 57, and 63). Elicit each vocabulary item and pattern.
2. Check Workbook page 67. (For instructions and answer key, see Teacher's Book page 176.)

Work with the Pictures

Students open their Student Books to pages 68 and 69.

1. Divide the class into groups of three. Groups find and name any items or characters they recognize in the pictures.
2. Ask each group how many items they found. Encourage groups to name as many items or characters as they can, using complete sentences when possible.
3. When groups have finished, have each group name one item, and write a sentence with that item on the board. Once all the sentences have been written, point to and read each sentence. Students repeat, pointing to those items in their books.
4. Ask students what they think the readings will be about.

Practice the Reading

A. 🎧 Listen and read along. Then number the pictures.

1. Play the recording. Students listen and read along.

   Dogs' Daily
   January Music Special

   1. Reporter: *You play the flute very well, Digger.*
      Digger: *Thank you. When I was little, I couldn't play well. But practice makes perfect!*
      Reporter: *You went to New York City, right?*
      Digger: *Yes, I did. I went in December.*
      Reporter: *How long were you there?*
      Digger: *I was there for two weeks. New York is the most exciting city in the world! I had a good time.*

   2. Reporter: *Did you go to New York by yourself?*
      Digger: *No, I went with Max and our orchestra. We gave our winter performance.*
      Reporter: *Oh! Were there any soloists?*
      Digger: *I was the soloist on the flute. Max was the soloist on the cymbals.*
      Reporter: *How did he play the cymbals?*
      Digger: *He played the cymbals very loudly! It was funny.*

   3. Reporter: *How many dogs are in your orchestra?*
      Digger: *Five.*
      Reporter: *How often do you rehearse?*
      Digger: *We rehearse three times a week.*

   4. Reporter: *Do you ever play the cello, Digger?*
      Digger: *No, I can't play the cello. It's too big.*
      Reporter: *Do you ever play the trumpet?*
      Digger: *Yes! I love playing the trumpet.*
      Reporter: *What's your favorite kind of music?*
      Digger: *I like jazz. We're going to give a jazz performance on television in March.*
      Reporter: *Sounds great! Thanks for your time, Digger.*
      Digger: *My pleasure.*

2. Play the recording again, stopping after each paragraph. For each number, students find the corresponding picture and write the number in the space provided.

   Answer Key:
   4, 3, 1, 2

150   Review 2

B. 🎧 **Listen and read along. Then number the pictures.**

1. Play the recording. Students listen and read along.

   Dogs' Daily
   March Music Special

   1. Reporter: *Max, I'd like to interview you for* Dogs' Daily *Newspaper.*
      Max: *Wow! Okay.*
      Reporter: *How often do you and Digger play abroad?*
      Max: *Our orchestra plays abroad about six times a year. We went to Rome in February!*
      Reporter: *How long were you there?*
      Max: *I think we were there for one week. I don't remember. But the food was delicious!*

   2. Reporter: *Did you give a performance in Rome?*
      Max: *Well, yes. I was nervous and fell off my chair. I was so embarrassed!*
      Reporter: *What was Digger doing when you fell off your chair?*
      Max: *He was playing the flute. He was the soloist. The performance was a hit.*

   3. Reporter: *That's great! Let's talk about the cymbals now. You play the cymbals. Is it hard?*
      Max: *No, it's easy. I'll show you.*
      Reporter: *You play the cymbals loudly, Max!*
      Max: *Are you okay?*
      Reporter: *My ears hurt.*
      Max: *I'm sorry!*

   4. Reporter: *It's okay. So, are you going to perform in Sunnyville soon?*
      Max: *Yes! We're going to give a performance at the Sunnyville Theater. It will be on TV, too!*
      Reporter: *Oh, yes, I remember now. I'm going to buy a ticket.*
      Max: *It's free!*
      Reporter: *Great! Thanks for your time, Max.*
      Max: *You're welcome.*

2. Play the recording again, stopping after each paragraph. For each number, students find the corresponding picture and write the number in the space provided.

   Answer Key:
   2, 4, 3, 1

Games and Activities

1. **Listen Carefully.** Play the recording of Digger's interview again. Students listen and write down Digger's favorite kind of music and how many dogs are in his orchestra. Then play the recording of Max's interview. Students listen and write how long Max was in Rome, and what happened to Max at the concert in Rome.

2. **Tell the Story.** Divide the class into pairs. Students in each pair cover the text on each interview page. They then take turns looking at the pictures and telling the events to their partners.

3. **Make a New Story.** Each student divides a piece of paper in four equal parts. He/She then creates a new story about *either* Digger or Max by drawing original scenes. Students then take turns standing up and describing their story to the rest of the class.

Finish the Lesson

1. **Questions.** Ask students five to six questions about Max's and Digger's interviews (see Suggested Questions below).

   Suggested Questions:
   When did Digger go to New York City?
   When did Max go to Rome?
   Does Digger ever play the cello?
   Does Max like Italian food?
   How often does Digger's orchestra rehearse?
   How does Max play the cymbals?

2. Explain and assign Workbook pages 68–69. (For instructions, see Teacher's Book pages 176–177.)

Word Time and Focus Time Review

Review Focus: Units 6–10 vocabulary and patterns
Materials Needed: CD/cassette and player

Warm-Up

1. **Questions.** Ask students *When you were little, could you catch a frog?* Several students answer. Do the same with *When did you do your homework?* and *How long were you at school on Tuesday?*
2. Check Workbook pages 68–69. (For instructions and answer key, see Teacher's Book pages 176–177.)

Review

Students open their Student Books to page 70.

A. Look and write.

Divide the class into pairs. Students in each pair work together to label the cities on the world map. Then check answers by asking volunteers to say the names of the cities, going from west to east.

Answer Key:

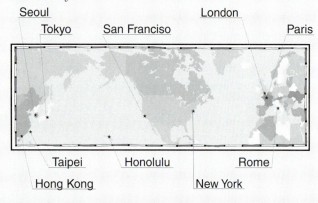

Seoul, Tokyo, San Franciso, London, Paris, Taipei, Honolulu, Rome, Hong Kong, New York

B. Read and complete the puzzle.

Divide the class into pairs. Students in each pair work together to fill in the crossword puzzle. Check the answers by having volunteers read the completed sentences.

Answer Key:
Across
1. I'm not hungry. I'm going to <u>skip</u> lunch.
2. They played the <u>cymbals</u> loudly.
3. When he was little, he could <u>throw</u> a ball.
4. If I <u>lose</u> my favorite pencil, I'll be sad.

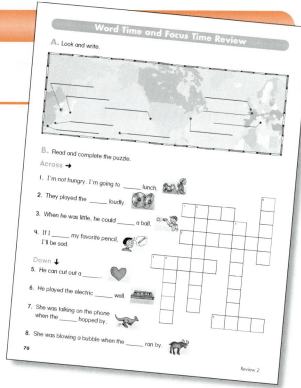

Down
5. He can cut out a <u>heart</u>.
6. He played the electric <u>keyboard</u> well.
7. She was talking on the phone when the <u>kangaroo</u> hopped by.
8. She was blowing a bubble when the <u>moose</u> ran by.

Finish the Lesson

1. **Word Relay.** Write the name of a musical instrument on the board (for example: *tuba*). A student (S1) begins by making a sentence containing that word. Continue with different instruments in the same way for two to three minutes. Then write a verb phrase on the board and repeat the procedure.

2. Explain and assign Workbook page 70. (For instructions and answer key, see Teacher's Book page 177.)

Pairwork

Review Focus: Personalizing Units 6–10 language
Materials Needed: CD/cassette and player

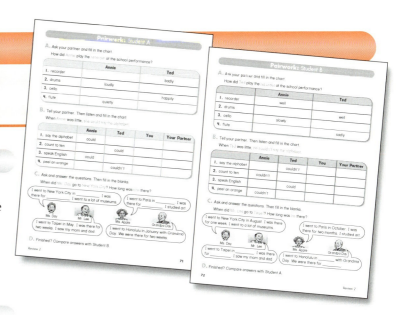

Warm-Up

1. **Questions.** Ask students *When you were little, could you say the alphabet?* Several students answer. Do the same with *When do you study math?* and *Do you ever go to Rome?*

2. Check Workbook page 70. (For instructions and answer key, see Teacher's Book page 177.)

Review

Divide the class into pairs. One student in each pair opens his/her Student Book to page 71. The other student in each pair opens his/her Student Book to page 72.

A. Ask your partner and fill in the chart.

1. Students in each pair ask their partner the target questions in order to get the information necessary to fill in the blanks.

2. Check answers by having pairs of students read the questions and answers to the class.

Answer Key:

	Annie	Ted
1. recorder	well	badly
2. drums	loudly	well
3. cello	slowly	happily
4. flute	quietly	sadly

B. Tell your partner. Then listen and fill in the chart.

1. Each student fills in the *You* column of the chart. Then students in each pair tell their partner about what they have written in the *You* column in order to get the information necessary to fill in the blanks.

2. Check answers by having each student tell the class about his/her partner.

Answer Key:

	Annie	Ted	You	Your Partner
1. say the alphabet	could	couldn't		Answers will vary.
2. count to ten	couldn't	could		
3. speak English	could	could		
4. peel an orange	couldn't	couldn't		

C. Ask and answer the questions. Then fill in the blanks.

1. Students ask and answer the target questions in order to get the information necessary to fill in the blanks.

2. Check answers by having pairs of students read the statements to the class.

Answer Key:
Ms. Day: I went to New York City in <u>August</u>. I was there for <u>one week</u>. I went to a lot of museums.

Ms. Apple: I went to Paris in <u>October</u>. I was there for <u>two months</u>. I studied art.

Mr. Lee: I went to Taipei in <u>May</u>. I was there for <u>two weeks</u>. I saw my mom and dad.

Grandpa Day: I went to Honolulu in <u>January</u> with Grandma Day. We were there for <u>two weeks</u>.

D. Finished? Compare answers with Student A/Student B.

Students compare answers with their partner.

Games and Activities

Option: Project. For a week, students keep a list of animals and musical instruments that they see on television. Then have students share their lists in class.

Finish the Lesson

1. Explain and assign Checklist 2 (see Student Book pages 82–85) for students to do at home or in class.

2. Explain and assign Workbook pages 71–72. (For instructions and answer key, see Teacher's Book pages 177–178.) Students can complete the four remaining Workbook review pages (pages 73–76) in class or at home. (For instructions and answer key, see Teacher's Book pages 178–179.)

Assessment
Explain and assign the Final Test, pages 230–235. (For instructions and answer key, see pages 214–215.)

Games and Activities

Games and Activities for Conversation Practice

1. Happy Parrots.
Bring two pairs of volunteers (Pair 1 and Pair 2) to the front of the classroom. The students in Pair 1 say alternate lines of the conversation with proper intonation. Pair 2, the "parrots," acts out each conversation line as Pair 1 says it, using the proper intonation and body language. Pair 1 and Pair 2 then change roles and do the activity again. Then divide the class into groups of four and have each group do the activity as above.

2. Missing Words.
Divide the class into Groups A and B. Write the conversation on the board. Elicit alternate lines from Groups A and B. Erase two to three key words from each line. Groups then change roles and say alternate lines of the conversation, trying to fill in the missing words. Continue in the same way, erasing more words from the conversation each time, until students can say the conversation from memory.

3. Puppet Show.
Each student makes a puppet (see puppet-making ideas below). Then students form pairs or groups (in each group there should be one student for each speaker in the conversation) and role-play the conversation using their puppets as speakers. Make sure students give puppets appropriate gestures and facial expressions. Students in each pair/group then change roles and role-play the conversation again.

> VARIATION: Turn a table on its side and have pairs/groups take turns sitting behind the table and performing the conversation for their classmates. Make sure students give puppets appropriate gestures and facial expressions when performing.
>
> PUPPET-MAKING IDEAS:
> 1. Students draw pictures of the characters on paper or cardboard. They then cut out the pictures and glue them onto popsicle sticks or pencils.
>
> 2. Students use markers to draw a face on a sock, and glue yarn on the sock for hair. Students put their hands in the sock with the thumb in the heel and fingers in the toe. They then bring the tips of the thumb and fingers together to manipulate the puppet's mouth.

4. Say It Together.
Divide the class into Groups A and B, and have the two groups stand in two lines facing each other. The two groups take turns saying alternate lines of the conversation in unison, speaking and responding to the student directly across from them. Groups then change roles and practice the conversation again.

5. Toss the Ball.
Toss a ball to a student and say the first line of the conversation. That student responds with the second line of the conversation, then tosses the ball to another student who says the third line of the conversation, and so on around the class. Students continue until everyone has said a line of the conversation.

6. Unscramble.
Write the conversation on the board in scrambled order. Students try to be the first to unscramble and write down the conversation. The first two students to do so raise their hands and read alternate lines of the conversation.

7. Which Line Doesn't Belong?
Write each line of three to four different conversations on a piece of paper, then copy it. Cut up both sheets to make two identical sets of strips of paper, each with one line of a conversation on it. Divide the class into Teams A and B. A volunteer from each team comes to the front of the classroom. Give each volunteer a set of identical strips of paper that includes a complete conversation plus one strip from a different conversation. Say *Go!* The volunteers look at their pieces of paper and place the line of conversation that does not belong on the chalktray. The first volunteer to place the correct piece of paper on the chalktray wins a point for his/her team. The team wins another point for each line of the conversation that the members of the team can correctly say. Continue in the same way 3–4 more times. The team with the most points at the end wins.

Games and Activities for Vocabulary Practice

8. Beanbags.
Divide the class into groups of three to four and give each group a beanbag (or other soft object) and a set of picture cards. Each group lays its cards out on the floor. Students in each group take turns tossing their beanbag onto one of the cards. The other students ask *What's that?* The student who tossed the beanbag responds *It's (apple pie)*, naming the item on which the beanbag has landed. Continue in the same way for five to seven minutes.

9. Bingo!
Give each student 16 picture cards. Students place their picture cards faceup in a 4×4 grid. One by one, call out the items illustrated on the picture cards. When a named item is in a student's grid, he/she places a marker on the card. If a student marks four items in a row (horizontal, vertical, or diagonal), he/she calls out *Bingo!*, then names the cards making up the row and wins a point. Students reposition the cards on their grids and play again.

VARIATIONS:

1. Give students blank grids. On the board, write a list of words to be practiced. Students choose words from this list and write the words or draw pictures of the items in the grid squares.

2. Before beginning play, students take turns naming the cards or pictures on their grids, then using these words in sentences.

3. Instead of calling out the names of items, give only hints about the items. The first student to say the correct word puts his/her marker on that picture.

10. Concentration.

Shuffle ten pairs of matching picture cards and lay them facedown on a desk. Students take turns turning over two cards and naming them. If a student cannot name the cards, he/she turns the cards facedown again and the next student takes a turn. If the student names the cards correctly but they do not match, the cards must also be turned facedown, and play moves to the next student. If the student does correctly name the cards and they do match, that student keeps the pair and takes another turn. The student who has the most pairs once all cards are taken wins the game.

VARIATION: Shuffle ten picture cards and the corresponding word cards. Students play Concentration as above, matching the picture card to the corresponding word card.

11. Dance of the Ostriches.

Divide the class into Teams A and B, and have a student from each team come to the front of the classroom. Tape a picture card to the back of each of these two students, and have them put their hands behind their backs. Say *Go!* and have the two students try to name the card on the other student's back, while at the same time trying to make it so the other student cannot name the card on his/her back. The student who correctly names the other student's card first wins a point for his/her team. Bring two new students to the front of the classroom and continue in the same way until all students have come to the front of the classroom. The team with the most points at the end wins.

VARIATION: Give each pair just 30 seconds to correctly name their partner's card. If the time limit expires before a correct identification is made, a new pair comes to the front of the classroom to play.

12. Do It!

Give each student a picture card. Name one of the cards twice and then give a command. For example: *Camel, camel, do a jumping jack!* Student(s) with that card name the card and do the action. For added challenge, name two cards at once so that more students are doing the actions. Students then take on the teacher's role. Continue in the same way for four to five minutes.

13. Draw the Picture.

Divide the class into Teams A and B. Place word cards into a hat, large envelope, or small bag. Bring a volunteer from each team to the front of the classroom and ask each volunteer to choose a different card from the hat. The volunteers then draw a picture of their word on the board and their teams try to be the first to identify the picture. The first team to correctly identify the picture wins a point. The volunteers return to their seats and a new volunteer from each team comes to the board and repeats the procedure. Continue until all words have been chosen from the hat. The team with the most points at the end wins.

VARIATIONS:

1. Both volunteers draw a picture of the same word.

2. Limit the drawing time to one minute. For extra challenge, shorten the amount of time even more.

14. Read and Write.

Divide the class into pairs. Give each pair a set of word cards and corresponding picture cards. A student in each pair (S1) begins by holding up a word card and reading it. S2 repeats the word, holds up the corresponding picture card, and uses the word in a sentence. Both students write the sentence down in their notebooks. Partners then change roles and continue in the same way until they have written down a sentence using each of the words.

15. Slow Reveal.

Hold up a picture card with another card or piece of paper covering it so that only a small portion of the picture is showing. Students try to name the picture. Each time a student incorrectly names the picture, slide the covering card down to gradually reveal more of the picture. Continue sliding the cover down until a student is able to name the picture. Continue in the same way with five to seven different cards.

16. What's in the Bag?

Place realia of vocabulary items in a bag. A volunteer reaches into the bag and tries to identify an item without looking at it. Ask him/her *What's that?* The volunteer says *It's (a flute)* and removes it from the bag. If the student correctly identified the item, he/she keeps it and another volunteer takes a turn. If he/she did not correctly identify the item, he/she puts the item back in the bag and another volunteer takes a turn. Continue in the same way until no items are left in the bag.

Games and Activities for Grammar Practice

17. Make the Sentences.

Divide the class into pairs. Give each pair a set of grammar cards and the related Word Time and Focus Time Word Cards. Students use these cards to make statements or questions and answers following the target pattern. For statements: pairs make statements with their cards, then read them aloud. For questions and answers: one student in each pair creates a question with their cards, then reads it aloud. His/Her partner then makes the answer and reads it aloud.

> VARIATION: Prepare six to eight sentences (or questions and answers) using the target patterns. Dictate each sentence (or question and answer). Students repeat and write each complete sentence on a piece of paper. When finished, have a volunteer come to the front of the classroom, write the first sentence on the board, and read it aloud. If the sentence is incorrect, have volunteers make corrections. Students then check their own sentence and correct it if necessary. Continue in the same way until all the sentences have been written correctly on the board.

18. Memory Chain.
A student (S1) makes a statement using the pattern. For example: *I had one bottle of root beer.* The student sitting next to or behind S1 (S2) says S1's name, repeats his/her statement, and then adds his/her own statement. For example: *(Ken), you had one bottle of root beer. I had three slices of ham.* The student sitting next to or behind S2 (S3) then repeats S1 and S2's statements, and adds his/her own. Students continue in the same way until someone is unable to repeat all the previous statements. The activity then begins again starting with this student.

19. Move Your Marker!
Write an example question and answer of the pattern you are practicing on the board. Divide the class into groups of six or eight, and then divide each group into pairs. Each group lays 16 Word Time Picture Cards faceup in a circle. Give each pair a pile of eight to ten *you, they, he, she,* and *it* grammar cards, and a die. Specify how many times pairs must go around the circle to win the game. A pair in each group (P1) begins by placing a marker such as a pen cap or coin on a card and rolling the die and moving their marker around the circle the number shown. Once they land on their card, they pick up a pronoun card. One student in the pair asks the question, and the other answers it. If the pair does this correctly, they remain on that card. If not, they return their marker to where it was at the start of their turn. Groups continue in the same way until one pair in each group has made it around the circle the predetermined number of times.

Games and Activities for Reading and Writing Practice

20. Authentic Readings.
Students read an authentic piece of material (for example: an English-language newspaper, magazine, or web site). Ask students questions about what they read, or have them present a report about the material.

21. Class Stories.
Following the style or topic of the Reading Time reading they have just read, a student begins telling you a story. Another student then continues the story, and so on around the classroom. Write the story that the class tells you on the board. Choose volunteers to read the story to the class. Then divide the class into groups of three to four and have students in each group draw pictures to illustrate the story.

22. Grammar Work.
Give each student a copy of the Reading Time reading. Students underline all the nouns in red and all the verbs in blue. Then read the story slowly to the class. Each time they hear a noun, students raise their hands. Each time they hear a verb, students stand up.

23. What Do You Think?
Before students see the Reading Time reading, write two to three questions on the board relating to the reading's topic. Students spend five to six minutes writing responses to the questions. Then divide the class into groups of three to four and have students in each group discuss the questions and their answers for four to five minutes.

24. Word Maps.
Before students see the Reading Time reading, write a word related to the reading's topic on the board. Then work with students to create a word map on the board, having students say words and phrases related to the topic. Write students' responses around the topic on the board. Then divide the class into groups of three to four. Students in each group spend four to five minutes discussing their own experiences with the topic, and then what they think the reading might be about. Students can also spend several minutes writing a few short paragraphs concerning their knowledge of the topic.

25. Write Your Own.
Students create their own original piece of writing following the style of the Reading Time reading they have just read. Work with students to create final, polished drafts of their writings. Then collect the writings together in a class book.

Workbook Instructions and Answer Key

Do You Remember?

Page iii

A. Read and check the best response.
For each number, students read the sentence in the left-hand column and then check the best response in the right-hand column.

Check answers by saying *Number 1. I'm really thirsty.* A volunteer reads the response he/she checked. Do the same for numbers 2–5.

Answer Key
1. I'm really thirsty./Me, too. Let's get some juice.
2. Come on. Just a little./Oh, all right. But not too much.
3. You're kidding!/No, it's true. I made it.
4. You dance really well./Thanks. I love dancing.
5. I don't have enough money./That's okay. It's my treat.

B. Find and circle the words. Then write.
Students find each illustrated word in the word search. Then they write each word under the corresponding picture.

Check answers by saying *Number 1* and having a volunteer say, spell, and point to the word in the puzzle. Do the same for numbers 2–10.

Answer Key

s	n	o	r	k	e	l	u	w	i	n	t	e	r	v	w	u	H	i	e	c
h	j	u	S	t	a	t	r	g	i	r	a	f	f	e	h	b	a	p	k	o
a	k	r	e	m	c	h	n	d	b	d	c	d	r	S	a	t	u	r	n	g
r	s	l	b	f	s	i	n	g	w	t	o	i	o	z	l	l	t	s	g	p
k	g	v	s	l	k	n	a	r	t	i	s	t	l	k	e	Z	u	k	d	v

1. whale   2. artist
3. giraffe   4. sing
5. snorkel   6. thin
7. winter   8. shark
9. Saturn   10. tacos

Page iv

C. Read the question. Write the answer.
Students read and answer each question.

Check answers by pointing to each picture, asking the corresponding question, and having a volunteer read his/her answer.

Answer Key
1. Which one is faster? <u>The cheetah is faster.</u>
2. What do they like to do? <u>They like to fish.</u>
3. Did he wash the pots and pans? <u>No, he didn't. He drank juice.</u>
4. Why does he want to be a musician? <u>Because he likes playing the violin.</u>
5. Is the shark bigger than the octopus? <u>No, it isn't.</u>

D. Fill in the blanks. Then number the pictures.
Students fill in the missing letters to complete each sentence. Then they find the picture that corresponds to each sentence and write the number of the sentence in the space provided.

Check answers by saying *Number 1* and having a volunteer say the sentence and point to the corresponding picture. Do the same for numbers 2–3.

Answer Key
1. Un<u>cle</u> John ate lob<u>ster</u> in a <u>sau</u>cer.
2. The <u>girl</u> with a <u>purse</u> <u>pointed</u> to the m<u>oo</u>n.
3. Joy chopp<u>ed</u> some w<u>oo</u>d and duste<u>d</u> the b<u>ar</u>n.

The pictures are numbered: 2, 3, 1

Unit 1

Conversation Time, Page 1

A. Read and circle.
Students circle the words that make up each line of the conversation.

Check answers by saying *Number 1* and having a volunteer say the line of conversation. Do the same for numbers 2–7.

Answer Key
1. Good <u>morning,</u> Sunnyville <u>Museum</u>. How <u>can</u> I <u>help</u> you?
2. Hi! <u>What</u> are <u>your</u> hours?
3. <u>We're</u> open <u>from</u> 9:00 <u>to</u> 6:00.
4. <u>Are</u> you open <u>on</u> Sundays?
5. Yes. We're open <u>daily,</u> except on <u>holidays.</u>
6. How <u>much</u> does it cost to <u>get in?</u>
7. It's <u>three</u> dollars for <u>adults</u> and two dollars for <u>children.</u>

B. Read the question. Write the answer.
Students answer each question based on the information on the movie theater's sign.

Check answers by saying *Number 1. How much does it cost for children?* and having a volunteer say the answer he/she wrote. Do the same for numbers 2–3.

Answer Key
(In this exercise, it is acceptable for students not to write complete sentences.)
1. How much does it cost for children? <u>It's two dollars for children.</u>
2. Is it open on Saturdays? <u>Yes, it is.</u>
3. How much does it cost for adults? <u>It's five dollars for adults.</u>

Word Time, Page 2

A. Look and write.
Students look at each numbered spot in the large scene. Then, for each number, they write the corresponding word below.

Check answers by saying *Number 1*. Students point to the corresponding building. A volunteer says and spells the corresponding word. Do the same for numbers 2–10.

Answer Key
1. barbershop
2. hotel
3. post office
4. theater
5. bank
6. school
7. sidewalk
8. bridge
9. train station
10. library

B. Where were they? Look at A and write.
For each number, students look at the small picture cue and find that person in the scene in exercise A. Then, following the example sentence, they write the location of that person.

Check answers by saying *Number 1* and having a volunteer point to that person in exercise A and say the corresponding sentence. Do the same for numbers 2–4.

Answer Key
1. He was at the bank.
2. She was at the hotel.
3. They were at the school.
4. He was at the theater.

Focus Time, Page 3

A. Look and write.
For each number, students look at the picture and write Digger's location in relation to the park bench.

Check answers by saying *Number 1* and having a volunteer say the corresponding word or phrase. Do the same for numbers 2–6.

Answer Key
1. beside
2. in front of
3. across from
4. behind
5. above
6. near

B. Read and circle True or False.
For each number, students read the sentence and look at the picture. Then they circle *True* if the sentence accurately describes the picture and *False* if it does not.

Check answers by having volunteers read each sentence and say if it is true or false.

Answer Key
1. True   2. True   3. False

C. Read the question. Write the answer.
Students read and answer each question based on the corresponding picture.

Check answers by saying *Number 1* and having a volunteer read both the question and answer. Do the same for numbers 2–3.

Answer Key
1. Was there a school across from the theater? No, there wasn't.
2. Was there a bridge above the barbershop? No, there wasn't.
3. Was there a sidewalk in front of the hotel? Yes, there was.

Practice Time, Page 4

A. Read and write.
For each number, students write the missing words to complete the target question and answer.

Check answers by pointing to each picture and having a volunteer read the question. A different volunteer reads the answer.

Answer Key
1. Was there a restaurant across from the bakery? Yes, there was.
2. Was there a library beside the hospital? Yes, there was.
3. Was there a barbershop above the museum? No, there wasn't.

B. Write the questions and answers.
For each number, students use the word cues to write the target question. Then they look at the scene to get the information to answer the question.

Check answers by saying *Number 1* and having a volunteer read the corresponding question and answer. Do the same for numbers 2–3.

Answer Key
1. Was there a bridge above the train station? No, there wasn't.
2. Was there a hotel near the post office? Yes, there was.
3. Was there a barbershop behind the hotel? No, there wasn't.

Reading Time, Page 5

A. Read.
Students read the informational sign.

B. Read the question. Write the answer.
Students read and answer each question based on the reading in exercise A.

Check answers by reading each question and having a volunteer read his/her answer.

Answer Key
1. When did John Montagu invent the sandwich? He invented the sandwich in 1750.
2. Where can you buy sandwiches in the United States? You can buy sandwiches at sandwich shops and at every grocery store.
3. Is the sandwich one of America's favorite foods? Yes, it is.
4. What did John Montagu use for the first sandwich? He used bread and meat.

C. Write and draw.
Students draw their favorite sandwich and write about it.

Check answers by having students take turns standing up and sharing their pictures and answers.

Answer Key
Answers will vary.

Your Time, Page 6
A. Look at the map. Answer the questions.
Students pretend that the map shows their town and answer each question.

Check answers by reading each question and having a volunteer read his/her answer.

Answer Key
1. Is the movie theater beside your house? No, it isn't.
2. How much does it cost for children? It's two dollars for children.
3. Is the museum near your house? Yes, it is.
4. What are its hours? It's open from 9:00 to 6:00.

B. Draw an old town. Include a school, library, barbershop, bank, hotel, post office, and sidewalk. Write six sentences.
Students draw an old town with a school, library, barbershop, bank, hotel, post office, and sidewalk. Then they write six sentences about the town they drew.

Check answers by having students take turns standing up, sharing their picture, and reading one or two of the sentences they wrote.

Answer Key
Answers will vary.

Unit 2

Conversation Time, Page 7
A. Unscramble and fill in the blanks. Then write.
For each number, students unscramble the sentence(s) and fill in the missing word. Then they write the sentence(s).

Check answers by saying *Number 1* and having a volunteer read the corresponding line of conversation. Do the same for the numbers 2–5.

Answer Key
1. Hello. Are you ready to order?
2. I think so. I'll have a steak.
3. How about a salad?
4. Sounds good. What's today's special?
5. Spaghetti and meatballs.

B. Look at A. Read and circle.
Students answer each question based on information from exercise A.

Check answers by reading each question and having students say the letter and word(s) they circled.

Answer Key
1. b   2. b   3. a

Word Time, Page 8
A. What did they eat and drink? Look and write.
For each number, students look at the small picture cue and find that person in the scene above. Then, following the example sentence, they write what that person ate and drank.

Check answers by saying *Number 1* and having a volunteer read the corresponding sentences. Do the same for numbers 2–4.

Answer Key
1. She ate roast beef. She drank lemonade.
2. She ate apple pie. She drank root beer.
3. He ate fruit salad. He drank iced tea.
4. He ate chicken soup. He drank coffee.

B. Look at the chart. Answer the questions.
Students answer each question based on information from the chart.

Check answers by reading each question and having a volunteer read the corresponding answer.

Answer Key
1. Did Ted drink coffee? No, he didn't.
2. Did Tim and Sue eat garlic bread? Yes, they did.
3. Did Annie eat apple pie? No, she didn't.
4. Did Ted eat ham and apple pie? Yes, he did.

Focus Time, Page 9
A. Read and write.
Students write the missing singular or plural form of the words.

Check answers by saying *Number 1* and having a volunteer read both the singular and plural forms. Do the same for numbers 2–8.

Answer Key
1. a bottle/two bottles
2. a can/four cans
3. a slice/three slices
4. a piece/two pieces
5. a bowl/six bowls
6. a cup/seven cups
7. a glass/two glasses
8. a loaf/three loaves

B. Read and write.
Students look at the scene and complete the sentences.

Check answers by saying *Number 1* and having a volunteer read the sentence. Do the same for numbers 2–4.

Answer Key
1. They're going to have <u>four glasses</u> of iced tea.
2. He's going to have <u>three bowls</u> of fruit salad.
3. It's going to have <u>four slices</u> of ham.
4. She's going to have <u>one bottle</u> of root beer.

C. Write the questions and answers.
Students complete the target question and answer about each person.

Check answers by saying *Number 1* and having a volunteer read the corresponding question and answer. Do the same for number 2.

Answer Key
1. How many <u>glasses of iced tea</u> did Jack have? He had <u>five glasses of iced tea.</u>
2. How much <u>chicken soup</u> did Kelly have? She had <u>three bowls of chicken soup.</u>

Practice Time, Page 10
A. Look at the chart. Answer the questions.
Students answer each question based on information from the chart.

Check answers by reading each question and having a volunteer read the answer.

Answer Key
1. How much root beer did Jill have? <u>She had five bottles of root beer.</u>
2. How much coffee did Jill have? <u>She had three cups of coffee.</u>
3. How much lemonade did Jay have? <u>He had two cans of lemonade.</u>
4. How much ham did Jay have? <u>He had six slices of ham.</u>
5. How much cake did Jill and Jay have? <u>They had six pieces of cake.</u>

B. Read and write.
Students look at the pictures, complete the questions, and write the answers.

Check answers by saying *Number 1* and having a volunteer read the corresponding question and answer. Do the same for numbers 2–4.

Answer Key
1. How much lemonade did he have? He had two cans of lemonade.
2. <u>How much</u> iced tea did they have? <u>They had one glass of iced tea.</u>
3. <u>How many</u> bowls of fruit salad did you have? <u>I had one bowl of fruit salad.</u>
4. <u>How many</u> bottles of root beer did you have? <u>We had two bottles of root beer.</u>

Reading Time, Page 11
A. Read.
Students read the restaurant review.

B. What did they say? Write.
Students look at the reading in exercise A and write the words that Tom and Jim said.

Check answers by having a volunteer read his/her answers.

Answer Key
1. Big Mama's meatballs are the best meatballs in town.
2. I'm going to bring my sister here tomorrow. Kids under six eat free!

C. Read the question. Write the answer.
Students read and answer each question based on the reading in exercise A.

Check answers by reading each question and having a volunteer read his/her answer.

Answer Key
1. Who is the chef at Big Mama's? <u>Big Mama is the chef.</u>
2. When did Big Mama's open? <u>It opened on Wednesday.</u>
3. Who eats free at Big Mama's? <u>Kids under six eat free.</u>

Your Time, Page 12
A. Read the question. Write the answer.
Students read and answer each question based on their personal experience.

Check answers by asking the questions and having students take turns reading their answers to the class.

Answer Key
Answers will vary.

B. What do you want for dinner? Write and draw.
Students write and draw what they want to eat and drink for dinner.

Check answers by having students take turns standing up and sharing their pictures and answers.

Answer Key
Answers will vary.

C. Read and check.
Students read each question and check their answer. If students check *Yes*, they also answer the question *How much?*

Check answers by asking each question and having several volunteers say their answers.

Answer Key
Answers will vary.

Unit 3

Conversation Time, Page 13
A. Number the sentences in the correct order.
Students number the lines of the conversation in the correct order.

Check answers by saying *Sorry. We're out of cherry.* and having a volunteer say the number he/she wrote. Do the same with the remaining lines of the conversation. Then have a volunteer read the entire conversation in the correct order.

Answer Key
4 Sorry. We're out of cherry.
6 They're five dollars each.
2 We have lemon and peach.
5 How much are the peach pies?
1 What kinds of pie do you have today?
8 Great! I'll get a fresh pie for you.
3 Do you have any cherry pies?
7 Okay. I'll take one.

B. Read the question. Write the answer.
Students read and answer each question.

Check answers by reading the questions and having a volunteer read his/her answers.

Answer Key
1. What kinds of cookies does Carly have? She has peanut butter, chocolate chip, lemon, and butter cookies.
2. Does she have any chocolate chip cookies? Yes, she does.
3. How much are the lemon cookies? They're 30¢ each.

Word Time, Page 14
A. Look and write.
Students look at the pictures and write what Sam is going to do.

Check answers by pointing to each picture and having a volunteer say the corresponding sentence.

Answer Key
1. He's going to wash his hair at 7:15.
2. He's going to iron a shirt at 8:10.
3. He's going to buy groceries at 9:20.
4. He's going to chop vegetables at 10:30.
5. He's going to slice fruit at 10:40.
6. He's going to do laundry at 11:25.

B. Look and write.
Following the model, students write two sentences about each picture.

Check answers by saying *Number 1* and having a volunteer read the corresponding sentences. Do the same for numbers 2–3.

Answer Key
1. She likes to do laundry. She doesn't like to iron a shirt.
2. They like to chop vegetables. They don't like to slice fruit.
3. She likes to stay home. She doesn't like to go to the dentist.

Focus Time, Page 15
A. Read and write.
For each number, students read the pronoun and write the corresponding reflexive pronoun.

Check answers by saying *Number 1. she* and having a volunteer say *she, herself.* Do the same for numbers 2–6.

Answer Key
1. she → herself
2. he → himself
3. I → myself
4. they → themselves
5. we → ourselves
6. you → yourself or yourselves

B. Read and write True or False.
For each number, students read the sentence and look at the picture. Then they write *True* if the sentence describes the picture and *False* if it does not.

Check answers by saying *Number 1* and having a volunteer read the sentence. Another volunteer then says if it is true or false. Do the same for numbers 2–4.

Answer Key
1. False
2. True
3. True
4. False

C. What did they do? Look and write.
For each number, students look at the small picture cue and find the person(s) in the scene above. Then they use the target pattern to write what the person(s) did.

Check answers by saying *Number 1* and having a volunteer say the corresponding sentence. Do the same for numbers 2–4.

Answer Key
1. I sliced fruit by myself.
2. We bought groceries by ourselves.
3. You ironed a shirt by yourself.
4. You took a bus by yourself.

Practice Time, Page 16
A. Read and write.
Students read each verb phrase and write its present or past tense form.

For each number, choose a volunteer to say *Today, I'm going to (buy groceries). On Sunday, I (bought groceries).*

Answer Key
1. buy groceries → bought groceries
2. take a bus → took a bus
3. go to the dentist → went to the dentist
4. chop vegetables → chopped vegetables
5. walk to school → walked to school
6. slice fruit → sliced fruit
7. iron a shirt → ironed a shirt
8. wash my hair → washed my hair

B. Look and write.
For each number, students look at the small picture cue and find the person/people in both scenes above. Then, following the example sentences, they write what the person/people did and did not do alone.

Check answers by saying *Number 1* and having a volunteer read the corresponding sentences. Do the same for numbers 2–3.

Answer Key
1. She did laundry by herself. She didn't stay home by herself.
2. He chopped vegetables by himself. He didn't take a bus by himself.
3. They washed their hair by themselves. They didn't stay home by themselves.

Reading Time, Page 17

A. Read. Then number the pictures in the correct order.
Quickly teach students that we can also put groceries in a *basket*, which is smaller than a cart. Students then read the story and number the pictures in chronological order.

Check answers by pointing to each picture and having volunteers say the number they wrote. Then they read the line(s) of the story that correspond(s) to the picture.

Answer Key
2, 1, 3, 6, 4, 5

B. Read the question. Write the answer.
Students read and answer each question based on the reading in exercise A.

Check answers by reading each question and having a volunteer read the answer.

Answer Key
1. What did Sally forget? Sally forgot the grocery list and the money.
2. Why did Sally run home? Sally ran home because she forgot the grocery list. *or* Sally ran home to get the grocery list.
3. Where did Sally put the groceries? Sally put the groceries in the basket.

Your Time, Page 18

A. Draw some pies. Write a price for each pie. Then answer the questions.
Students draw several pies and write a price for each pie. Then they answer the questions based on what they drew.

Check answers by having students take turns standing up, showing their picture, and sharing their answers.

Answer Key
Answers will vary.

B. Answer the questions.
Students read and answer each question based on their personal experience.

Check answers by asking each question and having a volunteer read his/her answer.

Answer Key
Answers will vary.

C. What can you do by yourself? Write.
Each student writes four different sentences answering the question *What can you do by yourself?*

Check answers by having students take turns standing up and sharing their answers.

Answer Key
Answers will vary.

Unit 4

Conversation Time, Page 19

A. Unscramble and write. Then number the sentences in the correct order.
Students unscramble and write each line of the conversation. Then they number the sections of the conversation in the correct order.

Check answers by pointing to the first line of the conversation and having a volunteer read it. Then point to the second line of the conversation and have a volunteer read it. A third volunteer then says the number he/she wrote for that section. Do the same for the remaining lines of the conversation. Then have a volunteer read the entire conversation in the correct order.

Answer Key
3 Can you take a message?
   Sure. Who's calling?

1 Hello. May I speak to Robert, please?
   He's not in right now.

4 This is Barbara. I'm going to be late for lunch today.
   Got it. I'll give him your message.

2 What time will he be back?
   I'm sorry. I don't know.

B. Look at A. Answer the questions.
Students answer each question based on the conversation in exercise A.

   Check answers by reading each question and having a volunteer read his/her answer.

   Answer Key
1. Who's calling? Barbara is calling.
2. Does Robert talk to Barbara? No, he doesn't.
3. Is Robert going to be late for lunch? No, he isn't. Barbara is going to be late for lunch.

Word Time, Page 20

A. Use the code to write the words. Then number the pictures.
For each number, students use the code to write the words. Then they find the corresponding picture and write the number in the space provided.

   Check answers by saying *Number 1* and having a volunteer say the phrase and point to the corresponding picture. Do the same for numbers 2–10.

   Answer Key
1. fall in love
2. wear a wig
3. drive a sports car
4. get a sunburn
5. take a nap
6. talk on the phone
7. have an accident
8. sign autographs
9. put on makeup
10. listen to pop music

The pictures are numbered: 7, 2, 8, 1, 6, 3, 9, 5, 4, 10

B. What do they like to do? Look and write.
Students look at the picture and write what the boy and girl like to do.

   Check answers by having a volunteer read what he/she wrote.

   Answer Key
He likes to talk on the phone. She likes to listen to pop music.

Focus Time, Page 21

A. Read and match.
For each number, students match the word(s) to the corresponding bar.

   Check answers by saying *Number 1. never* and having a volunteer point to the corresponding bar. Do the same for numbers 2–6.

   Answer Key
1. matches the second bar
2. matches the third bar
3. matches the first bar
4. matches the sixth bar
5. matches the fourth bar
6. matches the fifth bar

B. Look and write.
Students look at the pictures and the corresponding bars to complete each sentence.

   Check answers by saying *Number 1* and having a volunteer read the sentence. Do the same for numbers 2–5.

   Answer Key
1. He often takes a nap.
2. She always gets a sunburn.
3. I hardly ever wear a wig.
4. They sometimes talk on the phone.
5. He never signs autographs.

C. Look at Sally's schedule. Answer the questions.
Students answer the questions about Sally's schedule.

   Check answers by saying *Number 1* and having a volunteer read the question and answer. Do the same for number 2.

   Answer Key
1. Does she ever take a nap? Yes, she always takes a nap.
2. Does she ever put on makeup? Yes, she usually puts on makeup.

Practice Time, Page 22

Look at the chart. Write the questions and answers.
Using information from the chart, students complete each question and write the answer.

   Check answers by saying *Number 1* and having a volunteer say the corresponding question and answer. Do the same for numbers 2–6.

   Answer Key
1. Does he ever use a computer? Yes, he usually uses a computer.
2. Do they ever rent a video? No, they hardly ever rent a video.
3. Does he ever drive a sports car? Yes, he always drives a sports car.
4. Does she ever talk on the phone? Yes, she often talks on the phone.
5. Does he ever take a nap? Yes, he sometimes takes a nap.
6. Does he ever rent a video? No, he never rents a video.

Reading Time, Page 23

A. Read. Fill in the blanks with the correct verb forms.
Students read and fill in the blanks with the correct form of a verb from the help box.

   Check answers by choosing a volunteer to read each sentence.

Answer Key
Hi, Tommy!
I'm having a good time in Florida! I visited Disney World yesterday. Today I visited Universal Studios, a movie studio. They make all kinds of movies. Today they were making an adventure movie. I watched the actors rehearse a scene. Then I talked to Michael Stiles (the movie star).
I'm going to go to a water park tomorrow. I can't wait! See you on Monday!
Your friend,
Ted

B. Read and circle True or False.
Students read each sentence and circle *True* if the sentence is true and *False* if it is not, based on the reading in exercise A.

Check answers by saying *Number 1* and having a volunteer read the sentence. Another volunteer then says if it is true or false. Do the same for numbers 2–4.

Answer Key
1. False   2. True   3. False   4. True

C. Read the question. Write the answer.
Students read and answer each question based on the reading in exercise A.

Check answers by reading each question and having a volunteer read his/her answer.

Answer Key
1. Where is Disney World? Disney World is in Florida.
2. Who is Michael Stiles? Michael Stiles is a movie star.
3. Why did Ted say "I can't wait"? Because he's going to go to a water park tomorrow.
4. When will Ted see Tommy? Ted will see Tommy on Monday.

Your Time, Page 24
A. Read the question. Write the answer.
Students read and answer each question based on their personal experience.

Check answers by asking each question and having several volunteers read their answers.

Answer Key
Answers will vary.

B. Write a letter about a trip. Look at page 23 for help.
Students write a letter about a trip they took or would like to take. If necessary, they can look at the letter on page 23 of the Workbook for help.

Check answers by having students take turns standing up and sharing their answers.

Answer Key
Answers will vary.

Unit 5

Conversation Time, Page 25
Circle the mistakes and write.
Students circle the mistakes and rewrite the sentences with the correct words.

Check answers by saying *Number 1* and having a volunteer read the answer. Do the same for numbers 2–9.

Answer Key
1. Hello, Charlie. Have the sit.
   Hello, Charlie. Have a seat.
2. Thanks. Phew! It hot tonight.
   Thanks. Phew! It's hot today.
3. That's wrong. It's 92 degree!
   That's right. It's 92 degrees!
4. Wow! Do you know it's wants to rain?
   Wow! Do you think it's going to rain?
5. Maybe. It's going cloudy.
   Maybe. It's getting cloudy.
6. So, what's your family, Charlie?
   So, how's your family, Charlie?
7. They're five. But my sister have the flu.
   They're fine. But my sister has the flu.
8. I'm happy to hear that.
   I'm sorry to hear that.
9. It's no serious. She's doing better yesterday.
   It's not serious. She's doing better today.

Word Time, Page 26
A. Look and write.
Students look at each picture and write the corresponding verb phrase.

Check answers by pointing to each picture and having volunteers say the corresponding phrases.

Answer Key
1. read a newspaper   2. give a speech
3. visit a museum   4. go on a date
5. bake bread   6. take a math test

B. What are they going to do? Look and write.
Students look at each numbered spot in the large scene. Then, following the model, students write what each person is going to do.

Check answers by saying *Number 1* and having a volunteer read the sentence. Do the same for numbers 2–4.

Answer Key
1. She's going to feed the birds.
2. She's going to take medicine.
3. He's going to get a haircut.
4. They're going to take the subway.

Focus Time, Page 27

A. Use the code to write the words.
Students use the code to write the words.

Check answers by saying *Number 1* and having a volunteer say the phrase he/she wrote. Do the same for numbers 2–6.

Answer Key
1. once a day
2. three times a week
3. twice a month
4. three times a year
5. four times a day
6. twice a week

B. Look at Kelly's schedule. Write True or False.
For each number, students write *True* if the sentence accurately describes Kelly's schedule and *False* if it does not.

Check answers by saying *Number 1* and having a volunteer read the sentence. A different volunteer then says if it is true or false. Do the same for numbers 2–3.

Answer Key
1. True   2. False   3. True

C. Look at B. Read and write.
Students read and answer each question about Kelly's schedule from exercise B.

Check answers by reading each question and having a volunteer read the answer.

Answer Key
1. How often does she take medicine? She takes medicine twice a day.
2. How often does she take the subway? She takes the subway five times a week.

Practice Time, Page 28

Look and write.
Students write the questions and answers about the man's schedule.

Check answers by saying *Number 1* and having a volunteer read the question and answer. Do the same for numbers 2–6.

Answer Key
1. How often does he do laundry? He does laundry twice a month.
2. How often does he visit a museum? He visits a museum once a month.
3. How often does he get a haircut? He gets a haircut once a month.
4. How often does he read a newspaper? He reads a newspaper five times a week.
5. How often does he give a speech? He gives a speech once a week. *or* He gives a speech four times a month.
6. How often does he go on a date? He goes on a date three times a month.

Reading Time, Page 29

A. Read.
Students read the advice column.

B. Read the question. Write the answer.
Students read and answer each question based on the reading in exercise A.

Check answers by reading each question and having a volunteer read the answer.

Answer Key
1. Who's a pest? Peter is a pest.
2. Who told Debby and Kay to be patient? Their teacher told them to be patient.
3. Why does the pest bother Debby and Kay? Because he wants attention.

C. Read and match.
Based on the reading in exercise A, students match each name in the left-hand column with what the person(s) said or did in the right-hand column.

Check answers by saying *Number 1* and having a volunteer read the corresponding parts from each column. Do the same for numbers 2–6.

Answer Key
1. Peter/is in Debby and Kay's class. *or* Peter/takes their things without asking.
2. Gabby/told them to spend time with Peter. *or* Gabby/says, "Help him find some friends."
3. Debby and Kay/say, "It's not fair!"
4. Their teacher/told them to be patient.
5. Gabby/says, "Help him find some friends." *or* Gabby/told them to spend time with Peter.
6. Peter/takes their things without asking. *or* Peter/is in Debby and Kay's class.

Your Time, Page 30

A. Read and check.
Students check when they do each activity. They can check more than one box for each activity.

Check answers by asking *Do you (brush your teeth) in the (morning)?* Students raise their hands if they do. Do the same for *afternoon* and *night* and continue with each activity in the chart.

Answer Key
Answers will vary.

B. Read the question. Write the answer.
Students read and answer each question based on their personal experience.

Check answers by reading each question and having several volunteers read their answers.

Answer Key
Answers will vary.

Workbook Instructions and Answer Key

Review 1

Conversation Time, Page 31

A. Read and match.
Students match each question in the left-hand column with the most logical answer in the right-hand column.

Check answers by saying *Number 1* and having a volunteer read the corresponding question and answer. Do the same for numbers 2–5.

Answer Key
1. Do you have any lemon pies?/Sorry. We're out of lemon. But the cherry pies are very nice.
2. Are you ready to order?/I think so. I'll have the soup and salad.
3. Do you think it's going to rain?/Maybe. It's getting cloudy.
4. What's your number?/505-555-1212.
5. How much does it cost to get in?/It's five dollars for adults and three dollars for children.

B. Read the question. Write the answer.
Students read and answer each question.

Check answers by saying *Number 1* and reading the question. Then choose a volunteer to read the answer. Do the same for numbers 2–5.

Answer Key
1. What are its hours? It's open from 7:00 to 9:00.
2. What is today's special? Today's special is chicken soup.
3. How much are the blueberry pies? They're $4.50 each.
4. What time will she be back? She'll be back at 2:30.
5. How is Charlie's sister? She has the flu.

Word Time, Page 32

A. Look and write.
Students look each picture and write the corresponding word(s).

Check answers by saying *Number 1* and pointing to the picture. Have a volunteer say what he/she wrote. Do the same for numbers 2–12.

Answer Key
1. bridge
2. root beer
3. post office
4. fruit salad
5. chicken soup
6. hotel
7. lemonade
8. bank
9. sidewalk
10. coffee
11. library
12. apple pie

B. What were they doing? Look and write.
Students look at each numbered spot in the large scene. Then, for each number, they write a sentence about what the people were doing.

Check answers by saying *Number 1* and having a volunteer read the sentence he/she wrote. Do the same for numbers 2–6.

Answer Key
1. He was doing laundry.
2. She was ironing a shirt.
3. They were baking bread.
4. He was taking a nap.
5. She was putting on makeup.
6. He was taking medicine.

Focus Time, Page 33

A. How much food do you see? Write.
Students look at each picture and write the corresponding phrase for the amount of food pictured.

Check answers by saying *Number 1* and having a volunteer read what he/she wrote. Do the same for numbers 2–6.

Answer Key
1. five cans of lemonade
2. four loaves of garlic bread
3. six bowls of chicken soup
4. three slices of ham
5. two bottles of root beer
6. six slices of apple pie

B. Look and write.
Students look at the pictures and word cues and write the sentences.

Check answers by saying *Number 1* and having a volunteer read what he/she wrote. Do the same for numbers 2–4.

Answer Key
1. They sometimes feed the birds.
2. He listens to pop music six times a week.
3. He always walks to school (by himself).
4. She takes medicine three times a week.

Practice Time, Page 34

A. Read and write.
Students complete each question and answer.

Check answers by saying *Number 1* and having a volunteer read the question. A different volunteer reads the answer. Do the same for numbers 2–3.

Answer Key
1. How much iced tea did he have? He had one glass of iced tea.
2. Was there a theater next to the bank? No, there wasn't.
3. How often do they give a speech? They give a speech once a month.

B. Write the questions or answers.
Students look at each picture and write the corresponding question or answer.

Check answers by saying *Number 1* and having a volunteer read the question and answer. Do the same for numbers 2–4.

Answer Key
1. Was there a library near the bridge? Yes, there was.
2. Did he go to a restaurant by himself? No, he didn't.
3. How many bowls of chicken soup did she have? *or* How much chicken soup did she have? She had one bowl of chicken soup.
4. Does Ted ever talk on the phone? Yes, Ted often talks on the phone.

Reading Time, Page 35
A. Read and number the pictures.
Students find the picture that corresponds to each title and write the title's number in the space provided.

Check answers by saying *Number 1. Big Mama's Restaurant Opens* and having a volunteer point to the corresponding picture. Do the same for numbers 2–5.

Answer Key
3, 4, 1, 2, 5

B. Read and write the name. Use each name twice.
Students read each sentence and write the name of the person each sentence describes. Use each name twice. Students may look back at each unit's reading for reference, if necessary.

Check answers by reading each sentence and having a volunteer say the name he/she wrote.

Answer Key
1. John Montagu
2. Peter
3. Big Mama
4. Ted
5. Sally
6. John Montagu
7. Ted
8. Big Mama
9. Peter
10. Sally

Your Time, Page 36
A. Read the question. Write the answer.
Students read and answer each question based on their personal experience.

Check answers by reading each question and having several volunteers read their answers.

Answer Key
Answers will vary.

B. Read and circle True or False.
Students read the sentences and circle *True* or *False* based on their personal experience.

Check answers by saying *Number 1. I can eat ten slices of ham. True.* Have students raise their hands if they circled *True*. Then say *I can eat ten slices of ham. False.* Now have students raise their hands if they circled *False*. Do the same for numbers 2–6.

Answer Key
Answers will vary.

C. What do you like to do by yourself? Draw and write.
Students draw a picture showing what they like to do by themselves. Then they write about their drawing.

Check answers by having students take turns standing up, showing their picture, and reading what they wrote.

Answer Key
Answers will vary.

Unit 6

Conversation Time, Page 37
A. Fill in the blanks.
Students fill in the missing words to complete the lines of conversation.

Check answers by saying *Number 1* and having a volunteer read the corresponding lines of conversation. Do the same for numbers 2–4.

Answer Key
1. What are you doing?/I'm helping Mr. Tune clean up the music room.
2. Do you want some help?/Sure. You can move the bass.
3. Look out! There's a box behind you!/Ahhhh!
4. What's going on in here?/We're cleaning up.

B. Read and match.
Students match each line of conversation to the corresponding picture.

Check answers by pointing to each picture and having a volunteer read the corresponding line of conversation.

Answer Key
1. c   2. b   3. d   4. a

Word Time, Page 38
A. Look and write.
Students look at each picture and, following the example, write two sentences to describe it.

Check answers by saying *Number 1* and having a volunteer read the sentences. Do the same for numbers 2–5.

Answer Key
1. This is a tuba. That's a flute.
2. This is a cello. That's a recorder.
3. This is an electric keyboard. That's a xylophone.
4. This is a harp. That's a trumpet.
5. These are drums. Those are cymbals.

B. Look and write.

For each number, students look at the small picture cue and find that person in each scene above. Then they write two sentences, saying what instrument the person played last year and what instrument he/she plays now.

Check answers by saying *Number 1* and having a volunteer read both sentences. Do the same for numbers 2–3.

Answer Key
1. Last year she played the flute. Now she plays the xylophone.
2. Last year he played the trumpet. Now he plays the cymbals.
3. Last year he played the drums. Now he plays the tuba.

Focus Time, Page 39
A. Read and write.
For each number, students read the adjective and write the corresponding adverb.

Check answers by saying *Number 1. quiet* and having a volunteer say *quietly*. Do the same for numbers 2–8.

Answer Key
1. quiet → quietly
2. bad → badly
3. slow → slowly
4. loud → loudly
5. quick → quickly
6. sad → sadly
7. happy → happily
8. good → well

B. Look and circle the correct word.
Students look at each picture and circle the correct adverb to complete each sentence.

Check answers by saying *Number 1* and having a volunteer read the sentence. Do the same for numbers 2–4.

Answer Key
1. He plays the drums quickly.
2. She plays the harp sadly.
3. They play the tuba loudly.
4. I play the cello badly.

C. Read and write.
Students look at the scene. Then, following the example, students complete each question and answer.

Check answers by saying *Number 1* and having a volunteer read the question and answer. Do the same for numbers 2–4.

Answer Key
1. How did he play the tuba? He played the tuba well.
2. How did he play the harp? He played the harp happily.
3. How did they play the cymbals? They played the cymbals loudly.
4. How did she play the drums? She played the drums sadly.

Practice Time, Page 40
A. Read and check.
For each number, students read the question and answer. Then they check the corresponding picture.

Check answers by saying *Number 1* and having a volunteer read the question and answer and point to the picture he/she checked. Do the same for numbers 2–3.

Answer Key
1. second picture
2. second picture
3. first picture

B. Write the questions and answers. Then number the pictures.
Students write questions based on the word cues. Then, for each number, they find the corresponding picture and write the number in the space provided. Then they write an answer based on the word cues and picture.

Check answers by saying *Number 1* and having a volunteer read the question. A different volunteer reads the answer and points to the corresponding picture. Do the same for numbers 2–4.

Answer Key
1. How did she play the flute? She played the flute sadly.
2. How did you play the trumpet? I played the trumpet well.
3. How did he play the drums? He played the drums quickly.
4. How did you play the recorder? We played the recorder happily.

The pictures are numbered: 3, 2, 1, 4

Reading Time, Page 41
A. Read.
Students read the newspaper article.

B. Read and write.
Students complete each sentence based on the reading in exercise A.

Check answers by saying *Number 1* and having a volunteer read the sentence. Do the same for numbers 2–4.

Answer Key
1. The <u>teachers</u> at Lovetown Elementary School gave their fall <u>performance</u>.
2. Larry White sang with the teachers' <u>chorus</u>. He was the <u>soloist</u>.
3. The teachers' <u>orchestra</u> <u>performed</u> music by Mozart and Chopin.
4. There was a spaghetti <u>dinner</u> at Big Mama's after the <u>performance</u>.

C. Read the question. Write the answer.
Students read and answer each question based on the reading in exercise A.

Check answers by saying *Number 1. Who performed the play?* Then have a volunteer read his/her answer. Do the same for numbers 2–4.

Answer Key
1. Who performed the play? <u>The first grade teachers performed the play.</u>
2. How did Larry White sing? <u>He sang well.</u>
3. Where was the spaghetti dinner? <u>It was at Big Mama's Restaurant.</u>
4. When did the teachers give their fall performance? <u>The teachers gave their fall performance last night.</u>

Your Time, Page 42
A. Read and check Yes or No.
Students read each question and check *Yes* or *No* to answer it about themselves.

Check answers by saying *Do you play the flute well? Yes.* Have students raise their hands if they checked *Yes*. Then say *Do you play the flute well? No.* Have students raise their hands if they checked *No*. Do the same for the remaining questions in the chart.

Answer Key
Answers will vary.

B. Write and draw.
Students write and draw about an instrument they play or would like to play.

Check answers by having students take turns standing up, showing their picture, and sharing their answers.

Answer Key
Answers will vary.

Unit 7

Conversation Time, Page 43
A. Write and match.
Students write the missing words to complete each sentence. Then they match each question in the left-hand column with the most logical response in the right-hand column.

Check answers by saying *Number 1* and having a volunteer read the corresponding question and answer. Do the same for numbers 2–4.

Answer Key
1. 911. What's the <u>emergency</u>?/Help! There's something in my <u>backyard</u>!
2. <u>What</u> is it?/I think…I think it's a <u>wild</u> animal! I can see its <u>eyes</u>!
3. What's your name and <u>address</u>?/Dan Day. 49 Maple Lane.
4. What <u>should</u> I do?/Stay <u>calm</u>. I'm <u>sending</u> an officer now.

B. Look at A. Answer the questions.
Students answer the questions based on the conversation in exercise A.

Check answers by asking each question and having a volunteer read his/her answer.

Answer Key
1. Why did Dan call 911? <u>Because there was something in his backyard.</u>
2. Where does Dan live? <u>Dan lives at 49 Maple Lane.</u>
3. What did the woman tell Dan? <u>The woman told Dan to stay calm.</u>
4. Who did the woman send? <u>The woman sent an officer.</u>

Word Time, Page 44
A. Look and write.
Students complete each sentence based on the picture.

Check answers by saying *Number 1* and having a volunteer read the sentence. Do the same for numbers 2–4.

Answer Key
1. The <u>baboon</u> is climbing a tree.
2. The <u>bear</u> is eating a fish.
3. The <u>leopard</u> is taking a nap.
4. The <u>panda</u> is eating leaves.

B. Read and circle the correct words.
Students circle the correct words to complete the sentences based on the information from the scene.

Check answers by saying *Number 1* and having a volunteer read the sentence. Do the same for numbers 2–4.

Answer Key
1. The <u>eagle</u> is faster than the <u>parrot</u>.
2. The <u>kangaroo</u> is slower than the <u>moose</u>.
3. The <u>moose</u> is bigger than the <u>kangaroo</u>.
4. The <u>tiger</u> is smaller than the <u>moose</u>.

Focus Time, Page 45

A. Read and write.
Students read each verb and then write its past tense form.

Check answers by saying *Number 1. walk* and having a volunteer say and spell *walked*. Do the same for numbers 2–4.

Answer Key
1. walk → walked
2. fly → flew
3. run → ran
4. hop → hopped

B. Look and write.
Students look at each picture and, following the example, write a sentence about it.

Check answers by saying *Number 1* and pointing to the picture. Then have a volunteer say the sentence. Do the same for numbers 2–4.

Answer Key
1. The leopard walked and the tiger ran.
2. The kangaroo hopped and the moose walked.
3. The baboon ran and the parrot flew.
4. The panda walked and the eagle flew.

C. What were they doing when the tiger ran by? Write the letter.
Students read each sentence and find the corresponding person in the picture. Then they write the person's letter in the space provided.

Check answers by having a volunteer read each sentence and the letter he/she wrote.

Answer Key
1. B   2. A

Practice Time, Page 46

Write the questions and answers.
Students look at each numbered spot in the large scene. Then, for each number, they use the target pattern to write the corresponding question and answer.

Check answers by saying *Number 1* and having a volunteer read the question and answer. Do the same for numbers 2–5.

Answer Key
1. What was she doing when the tiger ran by? She was buying groceries when the tiger ran by.
2. What was she doing when the moose walked by? She was doing laundry when the moose walked by.
3. What was he doing when the parrot flew by? He was taking out the garbage when the parrot flew by.
4. What were they doing when the kangaroo hopped by? They were reading a newspaper when the kangaroo hopped by.
5. What was he doing when the camel ran by? He was taking a nap when the camel ran by.

Reading Time, Page 47

A. Read and fill in the blanks.
Students read the informational sign and fill in the blanks.

Check answers by choosing a volunteer to read the first line of the sign. Do the same for each bulleted fact.

Answer Key
Welcome to the American Black Bear Home at the Lovetown Zoo!

Here are some facts about American black bears:
- When black bears are born, they weigh eight to sixteen ounces. Adults weigh 135 to 350 pounds.
- Black bears eat everything: vegetables, fruits, nuts, leaves, fish, and meat.
- Black bears hibernate for five to seven months in the winter.
- Black bears are not endangered. Around 750,000 black bears are alive today.

B. Read the question. Write the answer.
Students read and answer each question based on the reading in exercise A.

Check answers by reading each question and having a volunteer read his/her answer.

Answer Key
1. How much do adult black bears weigh? They weigh 135 to 350 pounds.
2. What do black bears eat? They eat everything: vegetables, fruits, nuts, leaves, fish, and meat.
3. Do black bears hibernate in the winter? Yes, they do.
4. How many black bears are alive today? Around 750,000 black bears are alive today.

C. Read and circle True or False.
For each number, students read the sentence and circle *True* if the sentence is true and *False* if it is not.

Check answers by having a volunteer read each sentence and say if he/she circled *True* or *False*.

Answer Key
1. False   2. True   3. False   4. False

Your Time, Page 48

A. What's your favorite animal? Draw and write.
Students draw a picture of their favorite animal. Then they write a few sentences about the animal.

Check answers by having students take turns standing up, showing their picture, and sharing the sentences they wrote.

Answer Key
Answers will vary.

B. Write questions and answers. Use each picture once.

For each number, students select one picture from each column in the chart and, using the target pattern, use the pictures they have chosen to write the question and answer.

Check answers by having several students pick their favorite sentence and read it to the class.

Answer Key
Answers will vary.

Unit 8

Conversation Time, Page 49

A. Circle the mistakes and write.

For each number, students read the line of conversation and circle the mistake(s). Then they rewrite the sentence with the correct word(s).

Check answers by saying *Number 1. Annie, please come to the chair.* Then have a volunteer say the word he/she circled and read the corrected line of conversation. Do the same for numbers 2–6.

Answer Key
1. Annie, please come to the <u>chair</u>.
   Annie, please come to the front.
2. <u>Wrote</u> the letter "d" on the board.
   Write the letter "d" on the board.
3. I don't know <u>why</u>. I'm <u>good</u>, Ms. Smart.
   I don't know how. I'm sorry, Ms. Smart.
4. That's okay. Let me <u>showed</u> you how. <u>It</u> easy.
   That's okay. Let me show you how. It's easy.
5. <u>Yes</u>, I can't. It's <u>not</u> hard.
   No, I can't. It's too hard.
6. Come <u>one</u>, Annie. <u>Please</u> give up.
   Come on, Annie. Don't give up.

B. Look at A. Read and write True or False.

Students read each sentence and write *True* if the sentence is true and *False* if it is not, based on the conversation in exercise A.

Check answers by saying *Number 1. It's easy for Annie to write the letter "d."* Then have a volunteer say if he/she wrote *True* or *False*. Do the same for numbers 2–4.

Answer Key
1. False   2. True   3. False   4. False

Word Time, Page 50

A. Look and write.

Students look at each picture and write the corresponding verb phrase.

Check answers by pointing to each picture and having a volunteer say the corresponding phrase.

Answer Key
1. blow a bubble   2. peel an orange
3. speak English   4. say the alphabet
5. build a sand castle   6. cut out a heart

B. What are they doing? Look and write.

For each number, students look at the small picture cue and find that person in the scene above. Then they write what that person is doing.

Check answers by saying *Number 1* and having a volunteer read the sentence. Do the same for numbers 2–4.

Answer Key
1. He's throwing a ball.   2. She's counting to ten.
3. He's catching a frog.   4. She's spelling a word.

Focus Time, Page 51

A. Fill in the blanks.

Quickly teach the word *tennis*. Students then fill in the blanks based on the information in the pictures.

Check answers by saying *Number 1* and having a volunteer read the first sentence. Then have another volunteer read the second sentence. Do the same for number 2.

Answer Key
1. He <u>can</u> play tennis. He <u>can't</u> play badminton.
2. He <u>could</u> throw a ball. He <u>couldn't</u> catch a ball.

B. Look and write. Use could and couldn't.

For each number, students write a sentence using *could* and a sentence using *couldn't*.

Check answers by saying *Number 1* and having a volunteer read the sentences he/she wrote. Do the same for number 2.

Answer Key
1. He could peel an orange. He couldn't blow a bubble.
2. She could build a sand castle. She couldn't cut out a heart.

C. Read and write. Use could or couldn't.

Students write *could* or *couldn't* to complete each sentence.

Check answers by saying *Number 1* and having a volunteer read the sentence. Do the same for number 2.

Answer Key
1. When Digger was little, he <u>could</u> catch a frog.
2. When Digger was little, he <u>couldn't</u> spell a word.

Practice Time, Page 52
A. Read and check True or False.
For each number, students look at the picture and read the sentence. They check *True* if the picture and sentence correspond and *False* if they do not.

Check answers by saying *Number 1*. Then choose a volunteer to read the sentence and say if it is true or false. Do the same for numbers 2–4.

Answer Key
1. False   2. True   3. False   4. True

B. Look and write.
Students look at each numbered thought bubble. Then, for each number, they use the target pattern to write the corresponding sentence.

Check answers by saying *Number 1* and having a volunteer read the sentence. Do the same for numbers 2–4.

Answer Key
1. When he was little, he could say the alphabet.
2. When he was little, he could throw a ball.
3. When he was little, he couldn't catch a frog.
4. When he was little, he couldn't spell a word.

Reading Time, Page 53
A. Read. Choose the correct words and fill in the blanks.
Students read the letter and choose the correct words to complete the sentences. Then they write the words on the blanks.

Check answers by choosing a volunteer to read the first sentence of the letter. Do the same for all the remaining sentences in the letter.

Answer Key
Dear Jill,

When you <u>moved</u> away, I was sad. I miss you very much. Do you <u>miss</u> me?
Last Monday, I went to Ms. Bird's house for dinner. She <u>showed me</u> old photos of our <u>kindergarten</u> class. She told some <u>funny</u> stories, too. She said when you were <u>little</u>, you could build enormous snowmen. Remember?
Do you like New York? Are you <u>making</u> a lot of <u>friends</u>? Please write <u>soon</u>!

Your friend,
Jack

B. Read the question. Write the answer.
Students read and answer each question based on the reading in exercise A.

Check answers by reading each question and having a volunteer read the answer.

Answer Key
1. What did Jack do last Monday? <u>He went to Ms. Bird's house for dinner.</u>
2. What did Ms. Bird show Jack? <u>She showed him old photos.</u>
3. Who does Jack miss? <u>Jack misses Jill.</u>
4. Who could build enormous snowmen? <u>Jill could build enormous snowmen.</u>
5. Where does Jill live? <u>She lives in New York.</u>

Your Time, Page 54
A. What could you do when you were little? Check.
Students read each phrase in the chart and check *Could* if they could do the activity when they were little and *Couldn't* if they couldn't.

Check answers by saying *When you were little, you could cut out a heart*. Have students raise their hands if they checked *Could*. Then say *When you were little, you couldn't cut out a heart*. Have students raise their hands if they checked *Couldn't*. Do the same for the remaining verb phrases in the chart.

Answer Key
Answers will vary.

B. What could you do when you were little? Write two sentences.
Students write two sentences about what they could do when they were little.

Check answers by asking *What could you do when you were little?* and having several students share their answers with the class.

Answer Key
Answers will vary.

C. What couldn't you do when you were little? Write two sentences.
Students write two sentences about what they couldn't do when they were little.

Check answers by asking *What couldn't you do when you were little?* and having several students share their answers with the class.

Answer Key
Answers will vary.

Unit 9

Conversation Time, Page 55

A. Read and number the sentences in the correct order.
Students look at the scenes and number the lines of conversation in the correct order.

Check answers by saying *Do you ever fly abroad?* and having a volunteer say the number he/she wrote. Do the same with the remaining lines of the conversation. Then have a volunteer read the entire conversation in the correct order.

Answer Key
3 Do you ever fly abroad?
7 Do you like being a pilot?
6 No. I always have a copilot.
4 Yes. I have an overseas flight once a month.
8 Yes, very much!
1 How many female pilots work for your airline?
5 Do you fly the plane by yourself?
2 I think one third of the pilots are female.

B. Look at A. Answer the questions.
Students answer the questions based on the conversation in exercise A.

Check answers by reading each question and having a volunteer read the answer.

Answer Key
1. Is the woman a chef? <u>No, she isn't. She's a pilot.</u>
2. Does she ever have a copilot? <u>Yes, she always has a copilot.</u>
3. How often does she fly abroad? <u>She has an overseas flight once a month.</u>

Word Time, Page 56

A. Write the names of the cities.
Students look at each city on the map. Then, for each number, they write the city's name below.

Check answers by saying *Number 1* and having a volunteer say and spell the name of the city he/she wrote. Do the same for numbers 2–10.

Answer Key
1. Tokyo
2. Honolulu
3. San Francisco
4. Rome
5. Paris
6. Taipei
7. London
8. Seoul
9. New York
10. Hong Kong

B. Write the questions and answers.
Following the example, students write a question and answer about each picture.

Check answers by saying *Number 1* and having a volunteer read the question and answer. Do the same for numbers 2–6.

Answer Key
1. Where is she from? She's from Paris.
2. Where is she from? She's from Rome.
3. Where is he from? He's from Honolulu.
4. Where is he from? He's from Taipei.
5. Where is she from? She's from London.
6. Where is he from? He's from Tokyo.

Focus Time, Page 57

A. Connect the months in order.
Students follow the maze from January to December, connecting the months in chronological order.

Check answers by having a volunteer say the name of the first month. A different volunteer then says the second month. Continue until all months have been said.

Answer Key

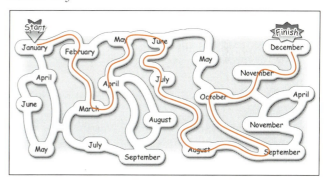

B. Read and write.
Students read each question and complete the answer based on the man and woman's schedule.

Check answers by having a volunteer read each question and answer.

Answer Key
1. When did they go to Paris? They went in <u>May</u>.
2. When did they go to Rome? They went in <u>November</u>.
3. When did they go to Seoul? They went in <u>September</u>.

C. Read and write.
Students complete each answer.

Check answers by having a volunteer read each question and answer.

Answer Key
1. When did she go to Paris? She went in <u>April</u>.
2. How long was she there? She was there for <u>four days</u>.

Practice Time, Page 58
A. Write the questions and answers.
Students look at each picture and use the target patterns to write the corresponding question and answer.

Check answers by saying *Number 1* and having a volunteer read the questions and answers. Do the same for numbers 2–3.

Answer Key
1. When did she go to San Francisco? She went in October.
   How long was she there? She was there for two weeks.
2. When did he go to Rome? He went in August.
   How long was he there? He was there for five days.
3. When did they go to Tokyo? They went in April.
   How long were they there? They were there for eight days.

B. Read the question. Write the answer.
Students read and answer each question about the letter.

Check answers by reading each question and having a volunteer read the answer.

Answer Key
1. How long was Tom in New York? <u>He was there for one month</u>.
2. When did Susie go to Taipei? <u>She went in June</u>.
3. How long was she there? <u>She was there for two weeks</u>.
4. When did Jack go to London? <u>He went in March</u>.

Reading Time, Page 59
A. Read.
Students read the travel brochure.

B. Read and match.
Students read each phrase in the left-hand column and match it to the phrase in the right-hand column that completes the sentence.

Check answers by saying *Number 1* and having a volunteer read the corresponding sentence. Do the same for numbers 2–4.

Answer Key
1. There are 100 thousand/hotel rooms in Orlando.
2. There are 82/parks in Orlando.
3. Over 35 million people/visit Orlando every year.
4. There are hundreds of/shops in Orlando.

C. Read and circle True or False.
Students read each sentence and circle *True* if the sentence is true and *False* if it is not, based on the reading in exercise A.

Check answers by saying *Number 1* and having a volunteer read the sentence and say if he/she circled *True* or *False*. Do the same for numbers 2–4.

Answer Key
1. True   2. False   3. True   4. False

Your Time, Page 60
A. Write the months in order. Write what you like to do in each month.
Students write the months in chronological order. Then they write what they like to do in each month.

Check answers by saying *Number 1* and having a volunteer read the month and the sentence he/she wrote. Do the same for numbers 2–12.

Answer Key
1. January   2. February
3. March   4. April
5. May   6. June
7. July   8. August
9. September   10. October
11. November   12. December

Sentences will vary.

B. What's your favorite month? Why? Draw and write.
Students pick their favorite month. They write about why they like that month and illustrate their writing.

Check answers by having students take turns standing up, showing their picture, and sharing their answer.

Answer Key
Answers will vary.

Unit 10

Conversation Time, Page 61

Unscramble and write.
Students unscramble and write each sentence.

Check answers by saying *Number 1* and having a volunteer read the sentence. Do the same for numbers 2–8.

Answer Key
1. Hi, Matt. Where were you yesterday afternoon?
2. At Annie's house. We were watching TV.
3. What was on?
4. A program about animals in Africa.
5. Aw, I missed it.
6. Did you watch the soccer game last night?
7. No, my mom was watching the news. Besides, I don't like watching soccer on TV.
8. Me, neither. It's not as fun as watching a real game.

Word Time, page 62

A. Use the code to write the words.
Students use the code to decipher each verb phrase.

Check answers by saying *Number 1* and having a volunteer read the corresponding phrase. Do the same for numbers 2–6.

Answer Key
1. go to bed late
2. fall off my chair
3. take off my jacket
4. get a good grade
5. turn off the fan
6. lose my favorite pencil

B. Match and write.
Students connect the words to make the target verb phrases. Then they write each verb phrase.

Check answers by saying *Number 1* and having a volunteer read the phrase. Do the same for numbers 2–4.

Answer Key
1. win a prize
2. forget my homework
3. make a mistake
4. skip lunch

Focus Time, Page 63

A. Number the pictures.
Students find the picture that corresponds to each word and write the number in the space provided.

Check answers by pointing to each picture and having a volunteer say the corresponding number and word.

Answer Key
3, 9, 6, 1, 2, 4, 5, 7, 10, 8

B. Read and match.
For each number, students match the first part of the sentence to the most logical ending.

Check answers by saying *Number 1* and having a volunteer read the sentence. Do the same for number 2.

Answer Key
1. If you go to bed late,/you'll be tired.
2. If she gets a good grade,/she'll be happy.

Practice Time, Page 64

A. Read and write.
Using the verb phrase and adjective combinations learned on the Student Book Practice Time page, students complete the sentences.

Check answers by saying *Number 1* and having a volunteer read the sentence. Do the same for numbers 2–5.

Answer Key
1. If you skip lunch, you'll <u>be hungry.</u>
2. If we win a prize, <u>we'll be proud.</u>
3. If you forget your homework, <u>you'll be nervous.</u>
4. If we make a mistake, <u>we'll be disappointed.</u>
5. It you lose your favorite pencil, <u>you'll be sad.</u>

B. Look and write.
Using the target pattern, students look at each picture and write the corresponding sentence.

Check answers by pointing to each picture and having a volunteer read the sentence.

Answer Key
1. If she gets a good grade, she'll be happy.
2. If he takes off his jacket, he'll be cold.
3. If they turn off the fan, they'll be hot.
4. If she falls off her chair, she'll be embarrassed.

Reading Time, Page 65

A. Read.
Students read the information on the web site.

B. Read the question. Write the answer.
Students read and answer each question based on the reading in exercise A.

Check answers by reading each question and having a volunteer read the answer.

Answer Key
1. What went on sale in 1981? <u>The first small computer for homes went on sale.</u>
2. What percent of American homes had a computer in 1984? <u>In 1984, 13 percent of American homes had a computer.</u>
3. How many web sites were there in 1995? <u>There were 100 thousand web sites.</u>
4. Where did the first computer store open? <u>The first computer store opened in California.</u>

C. Read and write.
Students complete each sentence based on the reading in exercise A.

Check answers by saying *Number 1* and having a volunteer read the sentence. Do the same for numbers 2–4.

Answer Key
1. In 1999, <u>40 percent of American homes</u> had a computer.
2. Nolan Bushnell <u>invented the first video game</u> in 1971.
3. 14 million <u>people used the Internet</u> in <u>1995.</u>
4. In 1940, <u>John Atanasoff and Clifford Berry</u> built <u>the first electric computer.</u>

Your Time, Page 66

A. Write sentences. Use the phrases in the boxes.
Students use the verb phrases in the boxes to write *If* sentences about themselves.

Check answers by saying a verb phrase and having several students read the sentence they wrote using that phrase. Do the same for each phrase.

Answer Key
Answers will vary.

B. Read the question. Write the answer.
Students read and answer each question based on their personal feelings.

Check answers by saying *Number 1. When do you feel proud?* Have several students share their answers. Do the same for numbers 2–3.

Answer Key
Answers will vary.

C. Write and draw.
Students answer both questions and then draw a picture to illustrate their answers.

Check answers by having students take turns standing up, sharing their answers, and showing their picture.

Answer Key
Answers will vary.

Review 2

Conversation Time, Page 67

A. Read the question. Write the answer.
Students read and answer each question. If they need help, they can look back at the Workbook Conversation Time pages.

Check answers by reading each question and having a volunteer read the answer.

Answer Key
1. What was Dan's emergency? <u>There was something in his backyard.</u>
2. Does the pilot ever fly the plane by herself? <u>No. She always has a copilot.</u>
3. What kind of TV program did Matt watch? <u>He watched a program about animals in Africa.</u>
4. Who showed Annie how to write the letter "d"? <u>Ms. Smart showed Annie how to write the letter "d."</u>
5. Who helped Annie move the bass? <u>Ted helped Annie move the bass.</u>
6. Why was Ted in the music room? <u>Because he was helping Mr. Tune clean up.</u>
7. What is Dan's address? <u>49 Maple Lane.</u>
8. How often does the pilot have an overseas flight? <u>The pilot has an overseas flight once a month.</u>

B. Read and match.
Students match each sentence in the left-hand column with the most logical response in the right-hand column.

Check answers by saying *Number 1* and having a volunteer read the corresponding sentences. Do the same for numbers 2–5.

Answer Key
1. Do you fly the plane by yourself?/No. I always have a copilot.
2. Do you want some help?/Sure. You can move the bass.
3. I don't like watching soccer on TV./Me, neither. It's not as fun as watching a real game.
4 911. What's the emergency?/Help! There's something in my backyard.
5. No, I can't. It's too hard./Come on, Annie. Don't give up.

Word Time, Page 68

A. What did the animals do? Look and write.
For each number, students look at the small picture cue and find that animal in the scene above. Then, following the example sentence, they write what the animal did and in which city.

Check answers by saying *Number 1* and pointing to the animal in the large scene. Then have a volunteer read the corresponding sentence. Do the same for numbers 2–6.

Answer Key
1. A baboon played the drums in New York.
2. A parrot blew a bubble in Paris.
3. A bear played the cymbals in Seoul.
4. A panda threw a ball in Tokyo.
5. A kangaroo peeled an orange in London.
6. A tiger played the harp in Taipei.

B. What are they doing? Look and write.
Students look at each picture and write what the people are doing.

> Check answers by saying *Number 1* and pointing to the picture. Then have a volunteer read the answer. Do the same for number 2.
>
> *Answer Key*
> 1. They're building a sand castle.
> 2. He's turning off the fan.

Focus Time, Page 69
A. Circle the odd word.
For each number, students look at the set of words and circle the word that does not belong in the same category as the other words.

> Check answers by saying *Number 1* and choosing a volunteer to say the word he/she circled. Do the same for numbers 2–6.
>
> *Answer Key*
> 1. happy   2. fly
> 3. badly   4. Monday
> 5. sadly   6. quietly

B. Look and write. Use can or could.
Students look at each numbered spot. Then, for each number, they write a sentence using *can* or *could*.

> Check answers by saying *Number 1* and having a volunteer read the sentence he/she wrote. Do the same for numbers 2–4.
>
> *Answer Key*
> 1. He can climb a tree.
> 2. She can build a snowman.
> 3. When he was little, he could blow a bubble. *or* He could blow a bubble.
> 4. When she was little, she could spell a word. *or* She could spell a word.

Practice Time, Page 70
A. Write the questions and answers.
For each number, students complete the question and write the corresponding answer.

> Check answers by saying *Number 1* and having a volunteer read the question. A different volunteer reads the answer. Do the same for number 2.
>
> *Answer Key*
> 1. How did he play <u>the tuba?</u> <u>He played the tuba loudly.</u>
> 2. What was she doing <u>when the parrot flew by?</u> <u>She was ironing a shirt when the parrot flew by.</u>

B. Look and write.
Students look at each picture and complete the sentences using the correct pattern.

> Check answers by saying *Number 1* and having a volunteer read the sentence. Do the same for number 2.
>
> *Answer Key*
> 1. When he was little, <u>he could throw a ball.</u>
> 2. If she <u>falls off her chair, she'll be embarrassed.</u>

C. Write the questions and answers.
Students use the word cues to write the questions and answers (following the Unit 9 target patterns).

> Check answers by saying *Number 1* and having a volunteer read the questions and answers. Do the same for number 2.
>
> *Answer Key*
> 1. When did she go to Rome?
>   She went in May.
>   How long was she there?
>   She was there for four days.
> 2. When did you go to London?
>   We went in June.
>   How long were you there?
>   We were there for one week.

Reading Time, Page 71
A. Read.
Students read the personal statements.

B. Answer the questions.
Based on the personal statements in exercise A, students answer each question for every person in the chart.

> Check answers by reading each question for every person in the chart and having a volunteer read the answer.
>
> *Answer Key*
> Laura: Jack's house/showed Jack old photos/write to Jill soon
> John: American Black Bear Home at the Lovetown Zoo/gave the bears some nuts and fruit/go to the zoo again
> Sandy: Orlando/gave a performance/be the soloist on the flute
> Tom: a computer store/bought the new computer/make a web site about the history of computers

Your Time, Page 72
A. Read and write.
Students complete each sentence about themselves.

> Check answers by saying *Number 1* and having several students read the sentence. Do the same for numbers 2–4.
>
> *Answer Key*
> Answers will vary.

B. Read and write.

Students complete each sentence about themselves.

Check answers by saying *Number 1* and having several students read the sentence they wrote. Do the same for numbers 2–4.

Answer Key
Answers will vary.

C. Write and draw.

Students complete the sentences about themselves and draw pictures to illustrate what they wrote.

Check answers by having students take turns standing up, sharing their answers, and showing their pictures.

Answer Key
Answers will vary.

Units 1–10 Reviews

Conversation Time Review, Page 73

Read and match.

Students match each sentence in the left-hand column with the most logical response in the right-hand column.

Check answers by saying *Number 1* and having a volunteer read the corresponding sentences. Do the same for numbers 2–10.

Answer Key
1. How many female pilots work for your airline?/I think one third of the pilots are female.
2. What kinds of pie do you have today?/We have lemon and peach.
3. What's today's special?/Spaghetti and meatballs.
4. Can you take a message?/Sure. Who's calling?
5. Do you think it's going to rain?/Maybe. It's getting cloudy.
6. What's going on in here?/We're cleaning up.
7. What is it?/I think…I think it's a wild animal!
8. I can't. It's too hard./Come on, Annie. Don't give up.
9. Did you watch the soccer game last night?/No, my mom was watching the news.
10. How much does it cost to get in?/It's three dollars for adults and two dollars for children.

Word Time Review, Page 74

A. Write the words in the correct category.

Students look at the picture and write each illustrated word in the correct category.

Check answers by saying *hotel* and having several volunteers say a word they wrote in that category. Do the same for all the categories.

Answer Key
hotel, bank, post office, barbershop
lemonade, coffee, garlic bread, apple pie
bear, moose, camel, leopard
cymbals, trumpet, flute, cello

B. What are they doing? Look and write.

Students look at each numbered spot. Then, for each number, they write a sentence about what that person is doing.

Check answers by saying *Number 1* and having a volunteer read the sentence. Do the same for numbers 2–6.

Answer Key
1. She's blowing a bubble.
2. She's getting a sunburn.
3. She's talking on the phone.
4. He's listening to pop music.
5. He's throwing a ball.
6. He's reading a newspaper.

Focus Time and Practice Time Review, Page 75

A. Write the questions. Then number the pictures.

For each number, students read the answer and write the corresponding question. Then they find the corresponding picture and write the number in the space provided.

Check answers by saying *Number 1* and having a volunteer read the question. A different volunteer reads the answer and points to the corresponding picture. Do the same for numbers 2–5.

Answer Key
1. <u>How often does she take a math test?</u> She takes a math test once a week.
2. <u>How much iced tea did they have?</u> *or* <u>How many glasses of iced tea did they have?</u> They had six glasses of iced tea.
3. <u>Do they ever sign autographs?</u> Yes, they sometimes sign autographs.
4. <u>What was she doing when the eagle flew by?</u> She was taking a nap when the eagle flew by.
5. <u>How did he play the trumpet?</u> He played the trumpet well.

The pictures are numbered: 2, 4, 1, 5, 3

B. Unscramble and write.

Students unscramble and write the sentences.

Check answers by saying *Number 1* and having a volunteer read the sentence. Do the same for number 2.

Answer Key
1. He walked to school by himself.
2. If I skip lunch, I'll be hungry.

Reading Time Review, Page 76

Read and write.

Students complete the sentences with the correct words. If students need help, they can look back at the Workbook Reading Time pages.

Check answers by saying *Number 1* and having a volunteer read the sentences. Do the same for numbers 2–10.

Answer Key
1. The first grade teachers wrote and performed a play. The teachers' orchestra performed music by Mozart and Chopin.
2. Peter bothers us. He takes our things without asking. Our teacher told us to be patient. It's not fair!
3. American black bears weigh 135 to 350 pounds. They hibernate for five to seven months in the winter.
4. In 1750, John Montagu invented the sandwich. Now there is a sandwich shop in every town.
5. Over 35 million people visit Orlando every year. It's one of the world's most exciting places.
6. Ms. Bird showed me old photos of our kindergarten class. She told some funny stories, too.
7. Big Mama's is a new Italian restaurant. Big Mama is the owner and the chef.
8. Today I visited Universal Studios, a movie studio. I watched the actors rehearse a scene. Then I talked to Michael Stiles (the movie star).
9. In 1995, there were 100 thousand web sites. In 1999, 40 percent of American homes had a computer.
10. Sally forgot the grocery list. She ran home and got the list. Then she ran back to the store and put the groceries in the cart.

Storybook Instructions and Answer Key

Digger and the Thief

Introduce the Storybook
Direct students' attention to the map of the museum at the beginning of the Storybook. Ask students to tell you what they can about the picture. For example: *This is a museum. Here's a gift shop.* Then ask students *Have you ever been to a museum? What can you do at a museum? Do you like going to museums?*

Read the Storybook
For each chapter, follow the steps below:

Introduce the Chapter
1. Students turn to the first two pages of the chapter, and take turns using complete sentences to name any items they recognize in the scenes. They then guess what the characters might be saying in each scene.

2. Students look at the text accompanying each scene. Encourage them to read the sentences and guess the meaning of any words they do not know. Then teach the new vocabulary items at the bottom of the page.

Read the Chapter
1. Hold up the Storybook so that students can see it. Read the text on the first two pages clearly, at natural speed, and dramatically, using a different voice for each character. Pause between scenes to indicate the change to the next scene. Students listen.

2. Read the text again in the same way. Students listen and follow along in their Storybooks.

3. Follow the same procedure as above for the rest of the chapter, starting with Step 1 of Introduce the Chapter.

Play the Recording
1. Play the recording of the chapter. Students listen and follow along in their Storybooks, pointing to each scene or the text for each scene. Play the recording as many times as necessary for students to be able to follow along with ease.

2. Play the recording again. Pause after each line and have students repeat.

3. Ask volunteers to try to read the text for each scene out loud. Prompt when necessary.

4. Divide the class into groups of three to four. Each group works together to read the text. Circulate among the groups, and prompt when necessary.

Check Comprehension
1. Ask comprehension questions to check students' understanding of the chapter. (For suggested questions, see pages 181–182.)

2. Do the chapter's review in class or assign it as homework. (See answer keys on pages 181–182.)

Activities for the Chapter
1. **Favorite Scenes.** Students take turns holding up their Storybooks, pointing to their favorite scenes in the chapter, and telling the class what is happening in that scene. They also say why it is their favorite.

2. **What Happened Next?** Students close their Storybooks and take turns saying, in chronological order, what happened in the story. Prompt as necessary, and write students' responses on the board. Then point to the responses and have a volunteer read them as the rest of the class looks at the corresponding scenes in their Storybooks.

3. **Act It Out.** Divide students into groups of the same number of students as there are characters in the chapter. Students in each group take on the roles of the characters. Play the recording and have students in each group act out the story as the recording plays.

4. **Role Play.** Bring same number of volunteers as there are characters in the chapter to the front of the classroom. Each volunteer takes on the role of one of the characters and says his/her lines of the story. Choose another volunteer to read the narration.

After Completing the Storybook
1. Play the recording of the entire Storybook. Students listen and follow in their books, reading along where they can.

2. Students draw a picture or design a poster of their favorite character or scene and show it to the class.

3. Students form groups and role-play their favorite scene(s) or chapter.

4. Students create their own version of the story and read or role-play it for the class.

Chapter 1: Pages 2–8

Students open their Storybooks to page 2. Proceed through the chapter as described on Teacher's Book page 180.

Comprehension Questions
Ask students the following questions.

Pages 2–3
Was it winter?
Where is Ms. Day going?
Where did Annie's class go?

Pages 4–5
What time did the museum open?
How much does it cost to get in?
What does Ms. Apple want the students to do?

Pages 6–7
What does Kim want?
What is Annie going to do?
Was Annie's mother in her office?

Answer Key
Review 1, Page 8
Cross out the mistakes. Write the correct words.
1. Look at those <u>elephant</u> bones!
   Look at those dinosaur bones!
2. That includes the <u>Director</u> Workshop at 10:00.
   That includes the Detective Workshop at 10:00.
3. There was a <u>library</u> beside the post office.
   There was a school beside the post office.
4. I'll have a <u>bowl</u> of Dinosaur Pop.
   I'll have a bottle of Dinosaur Pop.
5. How <u>many</u> does it cost to get in?
   How much does it cost to get in?
6. Maybe she's at the <u>Nature</u> Exhibit.
   Maybe she's at the Costumes Exhibit.

Chapter 2: Pages 9–15

Students open their Storybooks to page 9. Proceed through the chapter as described on Teacher's Book page 180.

Comprehension Questions
Ask students the following questions.

Pages 9–10
Did people drive cars in 1900?
Who wrote the book about cars?
What did the professor find in the car?

Pages 11–12
Who did Professor Walker tell about the dog?
What kinds of cookies does the Snack Bar have?
Is anybody reading a newspaper at the Costumes Exhibit?

Pages 13–14
What is the dog doing?
Why does the professor call Ms. Day?
Where is Ms. Day?

Answer Key
Review 2, Page 15
A. Read and circle True or False.
1. False 2. True 3. False
4. True 5. False 6. True

B. Match.
1. matches the fifth picture
2. matches the second picture
3. matches the fourth picture
4. matches the first picture
5. matches the sixth picture
6. matches the third picture

Chapter 3: Pages 16–21

Students open their Storybooks to page 16. Proceed through the chapter as described on Teacher's Book page 180.

Comprehension Questions
Ask students the following questions.

Pages 16–17
Did Ms. Day bring Digger to the museum?
Why is Detective Westwood at the museum?

Pages 18–19
What did the detective show the students how to do?
What did Detective Westwood find on the table?
Where did Digger go?

Answer Key
Review 3, pages 20–21
A. Fill in the blanks.
1. Professor Walker took Digger to the <u>Lecture Room</u>.
2. Annie was <u>surprised</u> to see Digger.
3. Detective Westwood put Digger on a <u>leash</u>.
4. Annie saw a man in a <u>blue</u> hat.
5. Digger wanted to see the <u>shiny gold</u> in the Gold Rush Exhibit.
6. There was a very loud noise. It was an <u>alarm</u>.

B. Read and answer the questions.
1. Who did Annie see in the hall? <u>Annie saw a man in a blue hat in the hall.</u>
2. What did Detective Westwood show the children? <u>He showed them a magnifying glass and a fingerprint kit.</u>
3. Whose footprint did Detective Westwood find? <u>Detective Westwood found Digger's footprint.</u>
4. Why did Digger jump? <u>Digger jumped because he wanted to see the shiny gold.</u>

C. Whose diary is it? Read and write the name.
1. Ms. Apple
2. Annie
3. Professor Walker
4. Ms. Day

Chapter 4: Pages 22–28

Students open their Storybooks to page 22. Proceed through the chapter as described on Teacher's Book page 180.

Comprehension Questions
Ask students the following questions.

Pages 22–23
Why is Emily scared?
What is Ms. Day going to do?
Who followed Professor Walker?

Pages 24–25
Why is Ms. Apple going to call 911?
What are the students going to do?

Pages 26–27
Why was Detective Westwood rubbing his head?
Why are the children going to use the detective's tools?
What did Digger find?

> ### Answer Key
> *Review 4, Page 28*
> **Which one happened first? Read and check.**
> 1. The man in the blue hat was in the Costumes Exhibit.
> 2. Emily said, "I'm scared."
> 3. Annie said, "Digger is gone!"
> 4. Detective Westwood said, "My head hurts."
> 5. Mike said, "Let's get Detective Westwood's tools!"
> 6. Annie said, "Digger has a good nose."
> 7. Ms. Day turned off the alarm.
> 8. Professor Walker said, "I'll go with you."

Chapter 5: Pages 29–35

Students open their Storybooks to page 29. Proceed through the chapter as described on Teacher's Book page 180.

Comprehension Questions
Ask students the following questions.

Pages 29–30
Why did the professor call Ms. Sweet?
What did Emily find?
Does Joe like being a detective?

Pages 31–32
What did Bill find?
What did Kim see near the footprint?

Pages 33–34
What was the man in the blue hat doing in Ms. Day's office?
What did Officer Tan do?

> ### Answer Key
> *Review 5, Page 35*
> **A. Read and circle True or False.**
> 1. True   2. False   3. True
> 4. True   5. True   6. False

B. Read and answer the questions.
1. What was Professor Walker doing when the children came back to the Gold Rush Exhibit? Professor Walker was talking on the phone when the children came back to the Gold Rush Exhibit.
2. Who found the fingerprint? Emily found the fingerprint.
3. Who found the man's footprint? Bill found the man's footprint.
4. Where were the children when the police officers arrived? They were in the entrance hall by the dinosaur bones when the police officers arrived.

Chapter 6: Pages 36–41

Students open their Storybooks to page 36. Proceed through the chapter as described on Teacher's Book page 180.

Comprehension Questions
Ask students the following questions.

Pages 36–37
Who caught the thief?
Who is Mr. Shade?
Who set off the alarm?

Pages 38–39
Who made a mistake?
Why did Detective Westwood put handcuffs on Mr. Shade?
Why was Detective Westwood embarrassed?

> ### Answer Key
> *Review 6, Pages 40–41*
> **A. Cross out the mistakes. Write the correct words.**
> 1. We saw the thief!
>   We caught the thief!
> 2. I think he ran into the Gold Rush Exhibit and turned off the alarm.
>   I think he ran into the Gold Rush Exhibit and set off the alarm.
> 3. I wanted to protect the alarm. I put it near the safe.
>   I wanted to protect the gold. I put it in the safe.
> 4. Yeah! We saw Digger's footprints by the door!
>   Yeah! We saw Digger's footprints by the display!
> 5. Then who set off the display?
>   Then who set off the alarm?
> 6. You made a mistake. I'm sorry, Mr. Shade.
>   We made a mistake. I'm sorry, Mr. Shade.
>
> **B. Number the sentences in the correct order. Then number the pictures.**
> 3 Digger escaped from the leash.
> 6 The police arrived.
> 1 Ted and Jan found Digger in the Nature Exhibit.
> 5 Mr. Shade took the gold out of the display.
> 4 The alarm went off.
> 2 Detective Westwood put Digger on a leash.
>
> The pictures are numbered: 6, 4, 3, 5, 2, 1

Worksheet Instructions and Answer Key

Unit 1

Worksheet 1: An Old Town

A. Read and write.
Students look at the picture. Then they answer the questions.

Answer Key
1. No, there wasn't.
2. Was there a hotel beside the theater? Yes, there was.
3. Was there a post office behind school?
   No, there wasn't.
4. Was there a hotel above the barbershop?
   Yes, there was.
5. Was there a library across from the theater?
   Yes, there was.
6. Was there a bridge behind the theater?
   Yes, there was.

B. Look at A. Read and answer the questions.
Students read the questions and answer them based on A.

1. It was across from the theater. It was beside the school. What was it? It was the library.
2. It was near the barbershop. It was in front of the bridge. What was it? It was the theater.

Worksheet 2: Ice Cream Sandwiches

A. Read.
Students read the personal statement.

B. Read and circle True or False.
Based on the reading, students circle *True* if the statement is true and *False* if it is not.

Answer Key
1. True   2. False   3. False   4. True

C. Read and match.
Students draw a line from each question to the corresponding picture and then from the picture to the corresponding answer.

Answer Key

2. (fourth picture) He bought it in 1995.
3. When did Steven buy his ice cream shop? (first picture) He bought it in 1999.
4. What does Steven sell? (third picture) He sells ice cream sandwiches.

Unit 2

Worksheet 3: How Many?/How Much?

A. Read and write.
Students look at each picture and write the corresponding question and answer.

Answer Key

2. How much ham did he have?
   He had three slices of ham.
3. How many glasses of iced tea did they have?
   They had two glasses of iced tea.
4. How much root beer did he have?
   He had one bottle of root beer.

B. Read and write.
Students look at the food items and their prices. Then they answer the questions based on the prices.

Answer Key

2. You have three dollars. How many cups of coffee can you buy? I can buy three cups of coffee.
3. You have five dollars. How much lemonade can you buy? I can buy five cans of lemonade.
4. You have ten dollars. How much apple pie and fruit salad can you buy? I can buy two pieces of apple pie and two bowls of fruit salad.

Worksheet 4: Annie's Diary

A. Read.
Students read Annie's diary entry.

B. What did Ted and Annie eat? Look at A and write.
Students look at the reading in exercise A and make lists of what Ted and Annie ate (including quantities).

Answer Key
Annie
a bowl of soup
spaghetti and meatballs
two cups of coffee

Ted

C. Your turn. Answer the questions.
Students answer each question about themselves.

Answer Key

Worksheet Instructions and Answer Key 183

Unit 3

Worksheet 5: Play a Game

Point to a number. Play the game with a partner.
Focus students' attention on the speech bubbles at the top of the page. Elicit the patterns. Then divide the class into pairs. Each student chooses an item to be a marker, such as a coin, a pen top, or an eraser, and places it on the *Start* square. Students take turns closing their eyes, pointing to a number at the top of the page, and moving their marker along the game board the corresponding number of squares. Students then look at the square on which they have landed and use the picture and word cue to make the appropriate positive and negative target sentences. For example: *I walked to school by myself. I didn't walk to school by myself.* If a student correctly says the sentences, he/she remains on that space. If he/she does not, he/she returns the marker to where it was at the beginning of that turn. The first student in each pair to reach the *Finish* square wins.

Worksheet 6: The Cashier's Tale

A. Read. Then put the paragraphs in order.
Students read a–e. They then read again and put the paragraphs in chronological order. Students write the numbers on the spaces provided.

Answer Key
a. 2
b. 4
c. 1
d. 5
e. 3

B. Look at A. Write the letter.
Students look at exercise A and match each paragraph to the corresponding picture.

Answer Key
e   c   d
 a   b

Unit 4

Worksheet 7: Do You Ever...?

A. Ask your classmates questions. Write their names and answers.
Students circulate around the classroom and ask their classmates *Do you ever (put on makeup)?* They record the answers they hear on the chart.

Answer Key
Answers will vary.

B. Look and write.
For each number, students write the target question and answer.

Answer Key
1. Do they ever sign autographs? Yes, they always sign autographs.
2. Does she ever drive a sports car? Yes, she usually drives a sports car.
3. Does he ever take a nap? Yes, he sometimes takes a nap.
4. Do they ever put on makeup? No, they hardly ever put on makeup.

Worksheet 8: Movie Stars

A. Read.
Students read the two letters.

B. Read and write True or False.
Based on the reading, students write *True* for the true sentences and *False* for the false sentences.

Answer Key
1. False
2. True
3. False
4. True
5. False
6. False
7. False
8. True

Unit 5

Worksheet 9: How Often?

Pairwork.
Divide the class into pairs. Students fold the page on the dotted line and look at their respective columns. Student 1 begins by looking at the first picture in the left-hand column and using the target pattern to ask Student 2 *How often do they visit a museum?* Student 2 looks at his/her first picture and answers *They visit a museum twice a week.* Student 1 then circles the correct answer. Students do the same for numbers 2–3. Student 2 then takes a turn, asking questions in the same way for numbers 4–6.

Answer Key
1. b
2. b
3. a
4. a
5. a
6. b

Worksheet 10: Am I a Pest?

A. Read.
Students read the personal statement.

B. Read the question. Write the answer.
Students answer each question based on the information provided in the reading.

Answer Key
1. How often does Ben take comic books from Billy? Ben takes comic books from Billy once a day.
2. Where did Ben follow Billy and John? Ben followed Billy and John into the basement.
3. What did Billy call Ben? Billy called Ben a pest.
4. Is Ben a pest? (Answers will vary.)

C. Read and match.
Students match each statement to the corresponding picture.

Answer Key
1. c
2. a
3. b

Unit 6

Worksheet 11: Instruments

Look. Then read and write.
Students look at the pictures and words. Then they write the answers and/or questions based on the information they see.

Answer Key
1. How did he play the electric keyboard? He played the electric keyboard quickly.
2. How did she play the trumpet? She played the trumpet well.
3. How did he play the tuba? He played the tuba quietly.
4. How did they play the flute? They played the flute sadly.

Worksheet 12: Spring Performance

A. Read.
Students read the letter.

B. Read the question. Write the answer.
Students answer each question based on the information provided in the reading.

Answer Key
1. How did the chorus sing? The chorus sang very loudly.
2. Why couldn't Kate hear her recorder? Because she was next to the cymbals.
3. Did Kate's grandpa see the performance? No, he didn't.

C. Look and match.
Students match each picture to the corresponding sentence.

Answer Key
1. Ben Jones played the violin happily.
2. The soloist, Kelly Green, sang well.
3. I couldn't hear my recorder.
4. We had a pizza party after the performance.

Unit 7

Worksheet 13: What Were You Doing?

Pairwork.
Divide the class into pairs. Students fold the page on the dotted line and look at their respective columns. Student 1 begins by looking at the first picture in the left-hand column and asking Student 2 *What was he doing when the tiger ran by?* Student 2 looks at his/her first picture and answers *He was chopping vegetables when the tiger ran by.* Student 1 then circles the correct answer. Students do the same for numbers 2–3. Student 2 then takes a turn, asking questions in the same way for numbers 4–6.

Answer Key
1. b
2. a
3. b
4. b
5. a
6. a

Worksheet 14: Animal Facts

A. Read.
Students read the facts about the animals.

B. Read and write.
Students complete the chart with information about each animal.

Answer Key
Leopards
60 to 300 pounds
meat
all four legs
Africa and Asia
yes

Tigers
200 to 500 pounds
meat
all four legs
Asia
yes

Baboons
30 to 90 pounds
fruit, plants, small animals
all four legs
Africa
no

Unit 8

Worksheet 15: When I Was Little

A. Pairwork.
Divide the class into pairs. Students fold the page on the dotted line and look at their respective columns. Student 1 begins by looking at the first set of pictures in the left-hand column and telling Student 2 about that person, saying *When he was little, he could say the alphabet. When he was little, he couldn't spell a word.* Student 2 looks at his/her pictures and writes a ✓ or ✗ for each picture based on what Student 1 said. Students do the same for number 2. Student 2 then takes a turn, saying sentences in the same way for numbers 3–4.

Answer Key
1. ✓
   ✗
2. ✗
   ✓
3. ✓
   ✗
4. ✗
   ✓

B. Choose two from A. Write the sentences.
Students look at exercise A and pick two numbers. They then write the corresponding target sentences.

Answer Key
Answers will vary.

Worksheet 16: New Friends

A. Read.
Students read the personal statement.

B. Read and match. Then write.
Students match each question to the corresponding answer. They then write the missing words to complete each answer.

Answer Key
1. When did Stan move to Washington?/He moved to Washington <u>last week.</u>
2. Does Stan like to go to the beach?/Yes, he likes to <u>go to the beach.</u>
3. Where was Stan's school?/It was near the <u>Sunnyville Zoo.</u>
4. Did Stan walk to school by himself in Sunnyville?/No, <u>he didn't.</u>

C. Your turn. Write about yourself.
Students fill in the blanks to create a story about themselves.

Answer Key
Answers will vary.

Unit 9

Worksheet 17: Cities of the World

Pairwork.
Divide the class into pairs. Students fold the page on the dotted line and look at their respective halves of the page. Student 1 begins by looking at his/her chart and using the target patterns to ask Student 2 questions about the missing information. For the *How long* questions, students can ask either *How long was (Sue) there?* or *How long was (Sue) in (San Francisco)?* If necessary, write these options on the board for students' reference. Student 2 answers based on the information in his/her chart. Student 1 then writes the answer in the appropriate space in the chart. Once Student 1 has filled in his/her chart completely, students change roles.

Answer Key

Name	City	When?	How Long?
Annie	Seoul	April	two weeks
Kim	Hong Kong	September	one year
Bill	Honolulu	August	nine days
Sue	San Francisco	October	five days
Ted	Rome	January	one month
Matt	Taipei	June	four weeks

Worksheet 18: Ted's Trip to London

A. Read.
Students read Ted's diary entry.

B. Put the sentences in order.
Students number the sentences in chronological order, based on the reading.

Answer Key
2
4
1
3

C. Read and match.
Students match each sentence to the corresponding picture.

Answer Key
1. b
2. c
3. a

Unit 10

Worksheet 19: If....

Look. Then read and write.
Students look at the pictures and words. Then they write the target statement about each person/pair of people based on the information they see.

Answer Key
1. If he skips lunch, he'll be hungry.
2. If they get a good grade, they'll be happy.
3. If she wins a prize, she'll be proud.
4. If they make a mistake, they'll be disappointed.

Worksheet 20: My Grandmother

A. Read.
Students read the personal statement.

B. Put the sentences in order.
Students number the sentences in chronological order, based on the reading.

Answer Key
4
3
1
2

C. Your turn. Answer the questions.
Students answer each question about themselves.

Answer Key
Answers will vary.

Worksheet Instructions and Answer Key

Unit 1, Worksheet 1: An Old Town

A. Read and write.

1. Was there a train station near the bridge? _____
2. Was there a hotel beside the theater? _____
3. Was there a post office behind the school? _____
4. Was there a _____ above the barbershop? Yes, _____
5. Was there a library across from the _____

   Yes, _____
6. Was there a _____ behind the theater? Yes, _____

B. Look at A. Read and answer the questions.

1. It was across from the theater. It was beside the school.

   What was it? _____
2. It was near the barbershop. It was in front of the bridge.

   What was it? _____
3. It was across from the school. It was above the barbershop.

   What was it? _____

Unit 1, Worksheet 2: Ice Cream Sandwiches

A. Read.

Hi! I'm Steven Conner. I own an ice cream sandwich shop. It's called Cold Sandwiches. In 1995, I bought my first ice cream churn. I made ice cream at home. Then, in 1999, I bought an ice cream shop. Across from my shop there was an ice cream shop called Snow Treats. Ice cream shops were on every block in my town. So I decided to sell just ice cream sandwiches at my shop. The delicious taste of ice cream between two cookies is my favorite. I use all kinds of ice cream, from chocolate and strawberry to banana. Come over to Cold Sandwiches and buy your favorite ice cream sandwich.

B. Read and circle True or False.

1. Steven uses banana ice cream to make ice cream sandwiches.   **True   False**
2. The taste of pasta between two cookies is Steven's favorite.   **True   False**
3. Steven owns a bakery.   **True   False**
4. You can buy ice cream sandwiches at Steven's shop.   **True   False**

C. Read and match.

1. Who is the owner of Cold Sandwiches?  He sells ice cream sandwiches.

2. When did Steven buy his first ice cream churn?  Steven Conner is the owner.

3. When did Steven buy his ice cream shop?  He bought it in 1995.

4. What does Steven sell?  He bought it in 1999.

Unit 2, Worksheet 3: How Many?/How Much?

A. Read and write.

1. How many _____ of _____ did she have?

   She had _____
   _____

2.  How much _____ did he have?

   _____
   _____

3.  _____ glasses of _____
   _____
   _____

4.  _____ much _____
   _____
   _____

B. Read and write.

1. You have six dollars. How many bowls of fruit salad can you buy?
   _____

2. You have three dollars. How many cups of coffee can you buy?
   _____

3. You have five dollars. How much lemonade can you buy?
   _____

4. You have ten dollars. How much apple pie and fruit salad can you buy?
   _____

Unit 2, Worksheet 4: Annie's Diary

A. Read.

Annie

Saturday, May 12

I had a nice day today. Ted and I went to Papa Joe's new Italian restaurant. Papa Joe is the chef. He made a great dinner. I had a bowl of soup, spaghetti and meatballs, and two cups of coffee. Ted had two loaves of garlic bread, three slices of pizza, and a can of lemonade. Ted loved the pizza, but he felt sick from all the garlic bread. After dinner, we met Mr. Minelli. He is the owner of the restaurant. I love Papa Joe's because their food is the best in town!

B. What did Ted and Annie eat? Look at A and write.

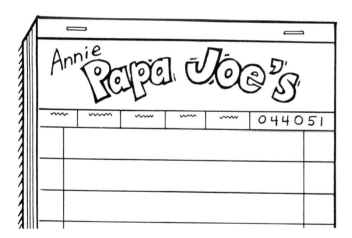
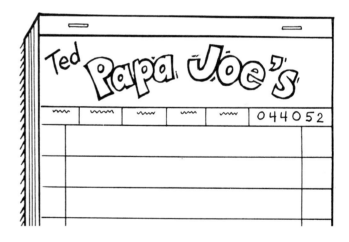

C. Your turn. Answer the questions.

1. What's your favorite restaurant?

_____

2. Does your favorite restaurant serve breakfast?

_____

3. Does your favorite restaurant have good prices?

_____

Unit 3, Worksheet 5: Play a Game

Point to a number. Play the game with a partner.

Unit 3, Worksheet 6: The Cashier's Tale

A. Read. Then put the paragraphs in order.

a. The boy ran back into the store. He had the list in his hand. He got a cart and put groceries in it. _____

b. Then he came back. He got in my checkout line again. He paid for the groceries and went home. He left his cart of groceries in the store. _____

c. I'm a cashier at the Sunnyville Supermarket. A 13-year-old boy ran into the store. He stopped and said, "Oh, no! I forgot the list!" He ran out. _____

d. Then a woman walked in with him. She shouted, "Where are my groceries?" I showed her the cart. She took it and walked out. She left the boy at the store. _____

e. He came to my checkout line. He said, "Oh, no! I forgot the money!" and ran back home. _____

B. Look at A. Write the letter.

Unit 4, Worksheet 7: Do You Ever...?

A. Ask your classmates questions. Write their names and answers.

	Name	How often?
wear a wig		
put on makeup		
get a sunburn		
take a nap		
sign autographs		
have an accident		
talk on the phone		
listen to pop music		
fall in love		
drive a sports car		

never

hardly ever

always

sometimes

usually

often

B. Look and write.

1.

Do they ever sign autographs?

2.

3.

4.

Unit 4, Worksheet 8: Movie Stars

A. Read.

Annie

Dear Miss Pillman,

My family and I visited your movie studio in California. We saw you rehearse a scene. It was cool. You are my favorite movie star. Do you ever sign autographs? I love your hair. Do you ever wear a wig? I can't wait for your next movie!

Your friend,

Annie Day

Debra Pillman

Dear Annie,

Thank you for your nice letter. I'm happy you like my movies. Yes, I often sign autographs. It's my favorite thing to do. I like my hair too, but I sometimes wear a wig. We're going to make my next movie at the train station in Sunnyville. You can come and watch.

Sincerely,

Debra Pillman

B. Read and write True or False.

1. Miss Pillman never signs autographs. _____
2. Miss Pillman is Annie's favorite movie star. _____
3. Annie and her family visited a movie studio in New York. _____
4. Annie and her family saw Miss Pillman rehearse a scene. _____
5. Annie doesn't love Miss Pillman's hair. _____
6. Miss Pillman is making her next movie at the bank in Sunnyville. _____
7. Miss Pillman never wears a wig. _____
8. Annie can't wait for Miss Pillman's next movie. _____

Unit 5, Worksheet 9: How Often?

Pairwork.

Student 1

Ask the question. Listen and circle.

1.
   a. once a week
   b. twice a week

2.
   a. four times a day
   b. twice a day

3.
   a. once a year
   b. three times a year

Answer the question.

4.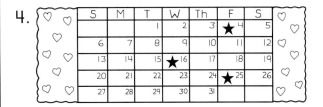

5.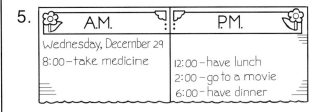

6.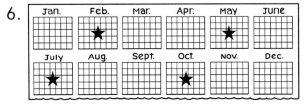

Student 2

Answer the question.

1.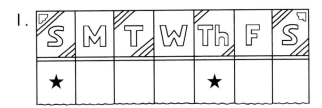

2.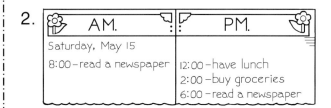

3.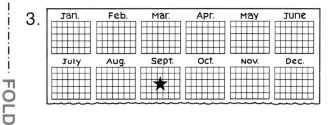

Ask the question. Listen and circle.

4.
   a. three times a month
   b. four times a month

5.
   a. once a day
   b. three times a day

6.
   a. twice a year
   b. four times a year

Unit 5, Worksheet 10: Am I a Pest?

A. Read.

Hi, I'm Ben. I follow my older brother Billy and his friends all the time. I go into Billy's room once a day and take his comic books. One day Billy invited his friend John over to play. When Billy and John went outside to play basketball, I went to Billy's room and took a comic book.

When I finished reading, I followed Billy and John into the basement to listen to pop music. Billy said, "You always bother me! You are a pest." I didn't know what a pest was. I found my mom and asked, "What's a pest?" My mom said, "A pest bothers people." Then I asked, "Am I a pest?"

B. Read the question. Write the answer.

1. How often does Ben take comic books from Billy?

2. Where did Ben follow Billy and John?

3. What did Billy call Ben?

4. Is Ben a pest?

C. Read and match.

1. He takes his brother's comic books.

2. He's Billy's friend.

3. He thinks his brother is a pest.

a.

b.

c.

Unit 6, Worksheet 11: Instruments

Look. Then read and write.

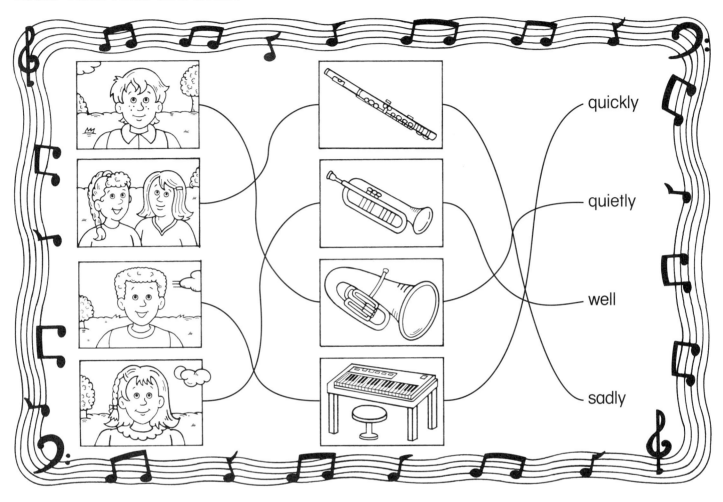

1.  How did he play the electric keyboard?
   _____

2.  How did she play the trumpet?
   _____

3. _____
   He _____ quietly.

4.  _____
   They _____ sadly.

Unit 6, Worksheet 12: Spring Performance

A. Read.

Dear Grandpa,

I'm sorry you missed our spring performance. It was a great show. The play was called *Wake Up! Spring Is Here!* The actors were good. The chorus sang a lot of songs. They sang very loudly. The soloist, Kelly Green, sang well.

I played the recorder in the orchestra. Because I was next to the cymbals, I couldn't hear my recorder! Ben Jones played the violin happily. My parents had a good time. We had a pizza party at Papa Joe's after the performance. It was fun. I'm sad the performance is finished, but we will perform again next fall. Please come!

Love,
Kate

B. Read the question. Write the answer.

1. How did the chorus sing? _____
2. Why couldn't Kate hear her recorder? _____
3. Did Kate's grandpa see the performance? _____

C. Look and match.

1.
2.
3.
4.

I couldn't hear my recorder.

Ben Jones played the violin happily.

We had a pizza party after the performance.

The soloist, Kelly Green, sang well.

Unit 7, Worksheet 13: What Were You Doing?

Pairwork.

Student 1

Ask the question. Listen and circle.

1.
   a. taking a nap
   b. chopping vegetables

2.
   a. putting on makeup
   b. climbing a tree

3.
   a. talking on the phone
   b. watching TV

Answer the question.

4.

5.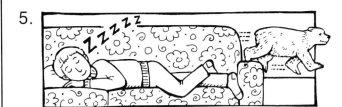

6.

Student 2

Answer the question.

1.

2.

3.

Ask the question. Listen and circle.

4.
   a. climbing a tree
   b. feeding the birds

5.
   a. taking a nap
   b. washing the car

6.
   a. climbing a tree
   b. taking out the garbage

Unit 7, Worksheet 14: Animal Facts

A. Read.

Leopards usually weigh 60 to 300 pounds.

Leopards eat meat.

Leopards walk and run on all four legs. They can climb trees.

Leopards live in Africa and Asia. They are endangered.

Tigers weigh 200 to 500 pounds.

Tigers eat meat. They eat ten pounds of meat every day.

Tigers walk and run on all four legs.

Tigers live in Asia. They are endangered.

Baboons weigh 30 to 90 pounds.

Baboons eat fruit, plants, and small animals.

Baboons walk and run on all four legs. They can stand on two legs.

Baboons live in Africa. They are not endangered.

B. Read and write.

	Leopards	Tigers	Baboons
How much do they weigh?			
What do they eat?			
On how many legs do they walk and run?			
Where do they live?			
Are they endangered?			

Unit 8, Worksheet 15: When I Was Little

A. Pairwork.

Student 1	Student 2

Say the sentences.

1.
2.

Listen and write ✓ and ✗.

1.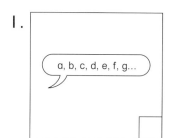
2.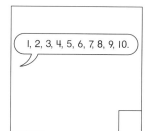

Listen and write ✓ and ✗.

3.
4.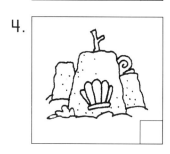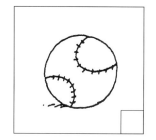

Say the sentences.

3.
4.

B. Choose two from A. Write the sentences.

1. _____

2. _____

Unit 8, Worksheet 16: New Friends

A. Read.

Hi, class! My name is Stan Harris. I'm from a small town called Sunnyville. I moved to Washington last week. I had a lot of friends in Sunnyville. I walked to school with my friends five times a week.

Our school was near the Sunnyville Zoo. We could see the pandas and the baboons. I love animals. My friend Annie has a dog named Digger. I want to get a dog, too. When we were little, we sometimes went to the beach with Digger. I could build enormous sand castles. I like going to the beach.

I miss my friends. We had fun together! But I think I'll make good friends in Washington, too. I'm going to have a party at my house. I want everyone to come!

B. Read and match. Then write.

1. When did Stan move to Washington?
2. Does Stan like to go to the beach?
3. Where was Stan's school?
4. Did Stan walk to school by himself in Sunnyville?

- It was near the _____
- No, _____
- He moved to Washington _____
- Yes, he likes to _____

C. Your turn. Write about yourself.

My name is _____. I live in _____. I like to _____. I don't like to _____. My house is near _____. I go to school by _____. When I was little I could _____. I couldn't _____.

Unit 9, Worksheet 17: Cities of the World

Pairwork.

Student 1

Ask the questions, listen, and write. Then answer your partner's questions.

Name	City	When?	How Long?
Annie	Seoul		two weeks
Kim	Hong Kong	September	one year
Bill	Honolulu		
Sue	San Francisco	October	
Ted	Rome	January	
Matt	Taipei		four weeks

------ FOLD ------

Student 2

Answer your partner's questions. Then ask the questions, listen, and write.

Name	City	When?	How Long?
Annie	Seoul	April	
Kim	Hong Kong		
Bill	Honolulu	August	nine days
Sue	San Francisco		five days
Ted	Rome		one month
Matt	Taipei	June	

Unit 9, Worksheet 18: Ted's Trip to London

A. Read.

August 10

There is so much to do in London! It's a big city. Millions of people live here. In the morning I went shopping at Harry's Department Store. Then I took a bus. When I got off the bus it was getting cloudy. I took a walk and looked at all the stores, restaurants, and museums. I ate lunch at a restaurant and sat outside. It started to rain. I ran into a museum. I went on a tour of the museum. I saw the bird exhibit. In the evening I had dinner at a restaurant called Neptune. After dinner I went to the theater and saw a play. I had a great day!

B. Put the sentences in order.

_____ Ted took a walk and looked at stores, restaurants, and museums.

_____ Ted saw a play.

_____ Ted went shopping at Harry's Department Store.

_____ It started to rain.

C. Read and match.

1. Ted ate lunch at a restaurant and sat outside. •

a.

2. Ted ran into a museum. •

b.

3. Ted had dinner at a restaurant called Neptune. •

c.

Unit 10, Worksheet 19: If....

Look. Then read and write.

1.  If he _____

2. If they _____

3. _____

4. _____

Unit 10, Worksheet 20: My Grandmother

A. Read.

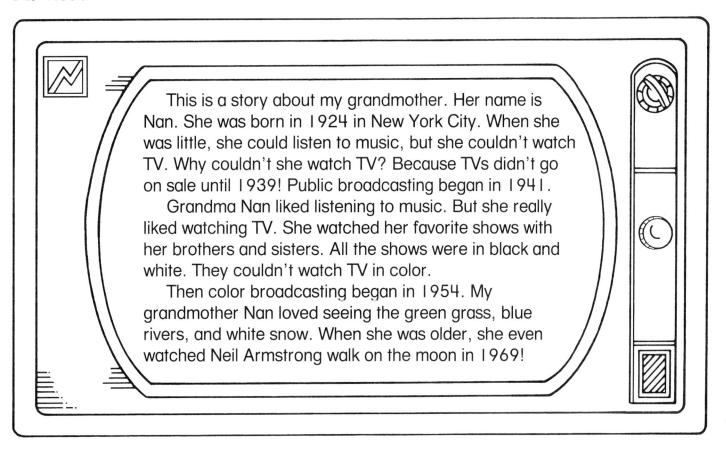

This is a story about my grandmother. Her name is Nan. She was born in 1924 in New York City. When she was little, she could listen to music, but she couldn't watch TV. Why couldn't she watch TV? Because TVs didn't go on sale until 1939! Public broadcasting began in 1941.

Grandma Nan liked listening to music. But she really liked watching TV. She watched her favorite shows with her brothers and sisters. All the shows were in black and white. They couldn't watch TV in color.

Then color broadcasting began in 1954. My grandmother Nan loved seeing the green grass, blue rivers, and white snow. When she was older, she even watched Neil Armstrong walk on the moon in 1969!

B. Put the sentences in order.

_____ Neil Armstrong walked on the moon.

_____ Color broadcasting began in the U.S.

_____ Nan was born.

_____ The first televisions went on sale.

C. Your turn. Answer the questions.

1. Are you a TV fan?

_____

2. Do you ever use a remote control?

_____

3. What's your favorite TV show?

_____

Test Instructions and Answer Key

For each listening exercise, read the script as many times as necessary for students to complete the task.

Unit 1 Test

A. Listen and match.
Read the script. For each number, students listen and match the question to the corresponding response.

Teacher:
A. Listen and match.
1. How much does it cost to get in?/It's three dollars for adults and two dollars for children.
2. What are your hours?/We're open from 9:00 to 6:00.
3. Are you open on Sundays?/Yes. We're open daily, except on holidays.

Answer Key
1. How much does it cost to get in?/It's three dollars for adults and two dollars for children.
2. What are your hours?/We're open from 9:00 to 6:00.
3. Are you open on Sundays?/Yes. We're open daily, except on holidays.

B. Listen and put the sentences in order.
Read the script. Students listen and number the sentences in chronological order.

Teacher:
B. Listen and put the sentences in order.
Ice cream has a long history in the United States. In 1843, Nancy Johnson invented the first ice cream churn. The first ice cream factory opened in Baltimore in 1851. The first ice cream shop opened in New York in 1876. Today there is an ice cream shop in every town. A man in St. Louis made the first ice cream cone in 1896. Ice cream is now one of America's favorite desserts.

Answer Key
2
4
1
3

C. Read and write.
Students look at the picture and write the missing words to complete the questions and answers.

Answer Key
1. Was there a <u>library</u> across from the bank?
   Yes, <u>there was.</u>
2. Was there a library near the school?
   <u>Yes, there was.</u>
3. Was there a hotel <u>beside</u> the bank?
   Yes, <u>there was.</u>
4. Was there a bank behind the library?
   <u>No, there wasn't.</u>
5. Was there a school above the hotel?
   <u>No, there wasn't.</u>
6. Was there a sidewalk in front of the bank?
   <u>Yes, there was.</u>

Unit 2 Test

A. Listen and write.
Read the script. Students listen and write the missing words to complete the conversation. If students need additional support, write the following on the board:
Thanks   have   today's   .   mood   Here   Spaghetti

Teacher:
A. Listen and write.
1. What's today's special?
2. Spaghetti and meatballs.
3. Good! I'm in the mood for spaghetti. I'll have that.
4. Here you are.
5. Thanks. It looks delicious.

Answer Key
1. What's <u>today's</u> special?
2. <u>Spaghetti</u> and meatballs.
3. Good! I'm in the <u>mood</u> for spaghetti. I'll <u>have</u> that.
4. <u>Here</u> you are.
5. <u>Thanks.</u> It looks delicious.

B. Listen and ✓ the sentences you hear.
Read the script. Students listen and write ✓ next to each sentence they hear.

Teacher:
B. Listen and ✓ the sentences you hear.
Papa Joe's is a new Italian restaurant in downtown Sunnyville. It opened on May 5th. Who is Papa Joe? Is it the owner, Mr. Minelli? No! The real Papa Joe is Mr. Minelli's father. Papa Joe is the chef at Papa Joe's Restaurant.

Answer Key
Numbers 1 and 3 are checked.

C. Read and write.
Students look at each picture and write the corresponding question and/or answer.

Answer Key
1. How <u>much</u> lemonade did she have? *or* How <u>many cans of</u> lemonade did she have? She <u>had two cans of lemonade.</u>
2. How many <u>pieces</u> of apple pie did he have? <u>He had one piece of apple pie.</u>
3. <u>How much ham did they have?</u> *or* <u>How many slices of ham did they have?</u>
   They had two slices of ham.
4. <u>How much coffee did they have?</u> *or* <u>How many cups of coffee did they have?</u>
   They had three cups of coffee.

Unit 3 Test

A. Listen and write ✓ or ✗.
Read the script. For each number, students look at the picture and listen to the line(s) of conversation. If the picture illustrates the line(s) of conversation, students write ✓ in the space provided. If it does not, students write ✗.

Teacher:
A. Listen and write ✓ or ✗.
1. Good morning. Can I help you?/Yes, please. What kinds of pie do you have today?
2. We have lemon, pineapple, and blueberry.
3. Do you have any cherry pies?

Answer Key
1. ✓
2. ✗
3. ✗

B. Listen and put the sentences in order.
Read the script. Students listen and number the sentences in chronological order.

Teacher:
B. Listen and put the sentences in order.
Bill arrived at the grocery store. "Oh, no!" Bill said. "I forgot the list!" He went home and got the list. Then he ran back to the store. Bill put the groceries in the cart. Then he went to the checkout line. "Oh, no!" he said. "I forgot the money!" He ran home, got the money, and ran back to the store. Then he paid for the groceries and went home. "Hi, Bill," said his mother. "Where are the groceries?" "Oh, no!" he said. "I left them at the store!"

Answer Key
1   4
2   3

C. Read and write.
Students look at each picture and complete the corresponding sentence.

Answer Key
1. He <u>washed his hair</u> by <u>himself.</u>
2. They <u>bought groceries by themselves.</u>
3. I didn't <u>iron a shirt by myself.</u>
4. She didn't <u>take a bus by herself.</u>

Unit 4 Test

A. Listen and circle.
Read the script. For each number, students listen to the question and circle the corresponding response.

Teacher:
A. Listen and circle.
1. Hello. May I speak to Robert, please?/He's not in right now.
2. What time will he be back?/I'm sorry. I don't know.
3. What's your number?/917-555-1839.

Answer Key
1. a
2. b
3. a

B. Listen and put the pictures in order.
Read the script. Students listen and number the pictures in chronological order.

Teacher:
B. Listen and put the pictures in order.
Hi, Emily!
I'm having a good time in California with my family. Yesterday we went to a movie studio. Today we visited Hollywood. It was fun! Tonight we're going to eat dinner at a nice restaurant. We're going to go to the beach tomorrow. I can't wait! See you on Monday!
Love, Annie

Answer Key
2   3   1

C. Look and write.
For each number, students write the target question and answer based on the picture cues and information from the chart.

Answer Key
1. Does he ever listen to pop music? Yes, he always listens to pop music.
2. Does he ever talk on the phone? Yes, he usually talks on the phone.
3. Does he ever sign autographs? No, he never signs autographs.
4. Does he ever drive a sports car? No, he hardly ever drives a sports car.

Unit 5 Test

A. Listen and match.
Read the script. For each number, students match the two parts of the conversation they hear.

Teacher:
A. Listen and match.
1. Hi, Mr. Day./Hello, Charlie. Have a seat.
2. Phew! It's hot today./That's right. It's 92 degrees!
3. Do you think it's going to rain?/Maybe. It's getting cloudy.
4. How's your family?/They're fine. But my sister has the flu.
5. Take care, Charlie./Bye, Mr. Day.

Answer Key
1. Hi, Mr. Day./Hello, Charlie. Have a seat.
2. Phew! It's hot today./That's right. It's 92 degrees!
3. Do you think it's going to rain?/Maybe. It's getting cloudy.
4. How's your family?/They're fine. But my sister has the flu.
5. Take care, Charlie./Bye, Mr. Day.

B. Listen and ✓ the words you hear.
Read the script. Students listen and write ✓ next to each word they hear.

Teacher:
B. Listen and ✓ the words you hear.
Dear Gabby,
I am thirteen years old and I have a big problem. My little brother is a pest! He follows me all the time and always bothers me and my friends. He goes into my room and takes my things without asking. My mom tells me to be patient because I am older. It's not fair! What can I do?
Going Crazy

Answer Key
Numbers 2, 3, 6, 7, and 8 are checked.

C. Read and write.
Students look at each picture and write the corresponding question and answer.

Answer Key
1. How often does she visit a museum? She <u>visits a museum twice a year.</u>
2. <u>How often does he</u> take the subway? <u>He takes the subway five times a week.</u>
3. <u>How often do they</u> go on a date? <u>They go on a date three times a month.</u>

Midterm Test

A. Listen and circle.
Read the script. For each number, students listen and circle the response they hear.

Teacher:
A. Listen and circle.
1. Phew! It's hot today./That's right. It's 92 degrees!
2. Does that include the special photo exhibit of old Sunnyville?/Yes, it does.
3. What time will he be back?/I'm sorry. I don't know.
4. How much are the peach pies?/They're five dollars each.
5. What's today's special?/Spaghetti and meatballs.
6. Can you take a message?/Sure. Who's calling?

Answer Key
1. b
2. a
3. b
4. b
5. a
6. b

B. Listen and number the pictures.
Read the script. For each number, students listen and find the picture that corresponds to those lines of conversation. They then write that number in the space provided.

Teacher:
B. Listen and number the pictures.
1. Hi! What are your hours?/We're open from 9:00 to 6:00.
2. Okay, I'll take one./Great! I'll get you a fresh pie.
3. Hello. Are you ready to order?/I think so. I'll have a steak.
4. Okay, I'll give him your message./Thanks./You're welcome.
5. Look! It's starting to rain./I'd better go home.

Answer Key
4   5   1
  2   3

C. Circle and write.
For each number, students circle and write the word to complete the sentence.

Answer Key
1. b
2. a
3. c
4. c
5. a
6. a

D. Read and write.
Students look at each picture and write the missing words to complete the corresponding sentences.

Answer Key
1. How many <u>cans of lemonade did he have?</u> He <u>had two cans of lemonade.</u>
2. Was there <u>a hotel across from the bank?</u> *or* Was there <u>a bank across from the hotel?</u> Yes, <u>there was.</u>
3. He <u>did laundry by</u> himself. He didn't <u>slice fruit by himself.</u>
4. She <u>washed her hair by herself.</u> She didn't <u>walk to school by herself.</u>

E. Read and match. Then write.
For each number, students match the question in the left-hand column to the corresponding picture. Then they write the answer to the question.

Answer Key
1. Does he ever take a nap? (fourth picture) No, <u>he hardly ever takes a nap.</u>
2. How often do they go on a date? (first picture) <u>They go on a date twice a week.</u>
3. Does she ever get a sunburn? (second picture) <u>Yes, she always gets a sunburn.</u>
4. How often does he feed the birds? (third picture) <u>He feeds the birds once a month.</u>

F. Read and write.
Students look at each picture and write the corresponding question and answer.

Answer Key
1. How many <u>bottles of root beer did she have?</u> She <u>had one bottle of root beer.</u>
2. How much <u>fruit salad did they have?</u> <u>They had two bowls of fruit salad.</u>

G. Write the question and the answer.
Students use the word cues to write the questions. Then they look at the picture and write the answers.

Answer Key
1. Was there a library beside the train station? Yes, there was.
2. Was there a bank above the theater? No, there wasn't.
3. Was there a post office behind the bank? No, there wasn't.

H. Write the questions.
Students look at the answers and write the question that corresponds with each answer.

Answer Key
1. <u>How many</u> slices of <u>ham did he have?</u> He had three slices of ham.
2. <u>Does she ever drive a sports car?</u> Yes, she usually drives a sports car.
3. <u>How often do you take a bus?</u> I take a bus once a day.
4. <u>Does he ever have an accident?</u> No, he never has an accident.
5. <u>How often do they visit a museum?</u> They visit a museum twice a year.

Unit 6 Test

A. Listen and match.
Read the script. For each number, students listen and match the question to the corresponding response.

Teacher:
A. Listen and match.
1. Do you want some help?/Sure. You can move the bass.
2. It's so heavy./Here. I'll take it.
3. What's going on in here?/We're cleaning up.

Answer Key
1. Do you want some help?/Sure. You can move the bass.
2. It's so heavy./Here. I'll take it.
3. What's going on in here?/We're cleaning up.

B. Listen and match.
Read the script. Students listen and match each picture to the corresponding words.

Teacher:
B. Listen and match.
The students at Sunnyville Elementary School gave their spring performance last night. Students in the first and second grades wrote and performed a play. The chorus sang a lot of songs. Kelly Green was the soloist. The orchestra performed music by Bach and Beethoven. Ben Jones was the soloist on the violin.

Answer Key
1. the orchestra
2. Kelly Green
3. the chorus

C. Look and write.
Students look at each picture and write the corresponding question and answer.

Answer Key
1. How did she play the cymbals? She played the cymbals loudly.
2. How did he play the harp? He played the harp happily.
3. How did he play the drums? He played the drums quickly.
4. How did she play the flute? She played the flute sadly.

Unit 7 Test

A. Listen and write ✓ or ✗.
Read the script. For each number, students look at the picture and listen to the conversation. If the picture illustrates the conversation, students write ✓ in the space provided. If it does not, students write ✗.

Teacher:
A. Listen and write ✓ or ✗.
1. Is this the wild animal?/Sorry, officer. I'll take him./ Oh, Digger!
2. What is it?/I think…I think it's a wild animal! I can see its eyes!
3. Look out! There's a box behind you!

Answer Key
1. ✓
2. ✗
3. ✗

B. Listen and write ✓ or ✗.
Read the script. Students listen. For each number, students write ✓ if the sentence is true and ✗ if it is false.

Teacher:
B. Listen and write ✓ or ✗.
Welcome to Sunnyville Zoo's Giant Panda Home! Bob and Lili are our giant pandas. Bob is 15 years old. Lili is 20 years old. When giant pandas are born, they weigh three to five ounces. Adults usually weigh 176 to 276 pounds. Giant pandas eat bamboo. They eat for 12 to 16 hours daily.

Answer Key
1. ✗
2. ✓
3. ✓
4. ✗

C. Read and match. Then write.
For each number, students read the question and match it to the corresponding picture. They then write the corresponding answer.

Answer Key
1. What were they doing when the moose ran by?
   (c) They were watching TV when the moose ran by.
2. What was she doing when the bear walked by?
   (d) She was talking on the phone when the bear walked by.
3. What was he doing when the kangaroo hopped by?
   (a) He was taking a nap when the kangaroo hopped by.
4. What were they doing when the eagle flew by?
   (b) They were climbing a tree when the eagle flew by.

Unit 8 Test

A. Listen and number the pictures.
Read the script. For each number, students listen and find the picture that corresponds to those lines of conversation. They then write that number in the space provided.

Teacher:
A. Listen and number the pictures.
1. Annie, please come to the front. Write the letter "d" on the board./I don't know how.
2. I'm sorry, Ms. Smart./That's okay. Let me show you how. It's easy.
3. Judy, please help me pass out the homework. Stan, erase the board, please.
4. What did you get?/I got a hundred!/Yay! So did I!

Answer Key
2   4
1   3

B. Listen and ✓ the words you hear.
Read the script. Students listen and write ✓ next to each word they hear.

Teacher:
B. Listen and ✓ the words you hear.
Dear Stan,
How are you? When you moved away, we were sad. We miss you very much. Do you miss us? Last Saturday, we saw Ms. Smart. She was our kindergarten teacher. Do you remember her? Annie and I went to her house for lunch. She said when you were little, you could build enormous sand castles. Do you like Washington? Please write soon.
Your friend,
Ted Lee

Answer Key
Numbers 2, 5, 6, 7, and 9 are checked.

C. Look and write.
Students look at each picture and write the words to complete the corresponding sentence.

Answer Key
1. When he was little, he couldn't say the alphabet.
2. When she was little, she could cut out a heart.
3. When they were little, they couldn't build a sand castle.

Unit 9 Test

A. Listen and match.
Read the script. For each number, students listen and match the question to the corresponding response.

Teacher:
A. Listen and match.
1. How many female pilots work for your airline?/I think one third of the pilots are female.
2. Do you ever fly abroad?/Yes. I have an overseas flight once a month.
3. Do you fly the plane by yourself?/No. I always have a copilot.
4. Do you like being a pilot?/Yes, very much!

Answer Key
1. How many female pilots work for your airline?/I think one third of the pilots are female.
2. Do you ever fly abroad?/Yes. I have an overseas flight once a month.
3. Do you fly the plane by yourself?/No. I always have a copilot.
4. Do you like being a pilot?/Yes, very much!

B. Listen and ✓ the sentences you hear.
Read the script. Students listen and write ✓ next to each sentence they hear.

Teacher:
B. Listen and ✓ the sentences you hear.
Over 30 million people visit New York City every year. Why? Because it's one of the world's most exciting places. There are 18 thousand restaurants, 10 thousand shops, and 150 museums. Basketball, opera, theater, jazz…New York City has it all! For information, call us at 1 (800) 555-2112.

Answer Key
Numbers 2 and 3 are checked.

C. Read and write.
Students look at each picture and write the corresponding question or answer.

Answer Key
1. When did she go to London? She went in October.
   How long was she there? She was there for five days.
2. When did they go to Tokyo? They went in February.
   How long were they there? They were there for one week.

Unit 10 Test

A. Listen and write. Then match.
Read the script. Students listen and write the missing words to complete the conversation. They then match each number to its corresponding picture. If students need additional support, write the following on the board:
on good house about cool ? were TV . it

Teacher:
A. Listen and write. Then match.
1. Where were you yesterday afternoon?/At Annie's house. We were watching TV.
2. What was on?/A program about animals in Africa.
3. Aw, I missed it. Was it good?/Yeah, it was. The gorillas were really cool.

Answer Key
1. Where were you yesterday afternoon?/At Annie's house. We were watching TV. (c)
2. What was on?/A program about animals in Africa. (a)
3. Aw, I missed it. Was it good?/Yeah, it was. The gorillas were really cool. (b)

B. Listen and put the sentences in order.
Read the script. Students listen and number the sentences in chronological order.

Teacher:
B. Listen and put the sentences in order.
1939 The first televisions go on sale.
1953 50 percent of American homes have a TV.
1954 Color broadcasting begins in the United States.
1956 The first televisions with remote control go on sale.
1969 720 million people watch Neil Armstrong walk on the moon.
1994 99 percent of American homes have a TV.

Answer Key
2   1
4   3

C. Read and write.
Students look at each picture and use the word cues to write the target statements.

Answer Key
1. If he turns off the fan, he'll be hot.
2. If she takes off her jacket, she'll be cold.
3. If they skip lunch, they'll be hungry.

Final Test

A. Listen and number the pictures.
Read the script. For each number, students listen and find the picture that corresponds to the lines of the conversation they hear. Then they write that number in the space provided.

Teacher:
A. Listen and number the pictures.
1. Good morning. Can I help you?/Yes, please. What kinds of pie do you have today?/We have lemon, peach, and blueberry.
2. Do you ever fly abroad?/Yes. I have an overseas flight once a month./Do you fly the plane by yourself?/No. I always have a copilot.
3. Is this the wild animal?/Sorry, officer. I'll take him./Oh, Digger!
4. Do you want some help?/Sure. You can move the bass. Put it over there, by the window./Ugh! I can't lift it by myself.
5. Hi, Mr. Day./Hello, Charlie. Have a seat./Thanks. Phew! It's hot today./That's right. It's 92 degrees!
6. What was on?/A program about animals in Africa./Aw, I missed it. Was it good?/Yeah, it was. The gorillas were really cool.

Answer Key
5   6   1
2   4   3

B. Listen and ✓ the sentences you hear.
Read the script. For each number, students write ✓ by the sentences they hear.

Teacher:
B. Listen and ✓ the sentences you hear.
1. Hello. Are you ready to order?/I think so. I'll have a steak./Rare, medium, or well done?/Medium, please. And a baked potato.
2. Hello. May I speak to Robert, please?/He's not in right now./What time will he be back?/I'm sorry. I don't know./Can you take a message?/Sure. Who's calling?
3. 911. What's the emergency?/Help! There's something in my backyard!/What is it?/I think…I think it's a wild animal! I can see its eyes!
4. I'm sorry, Ms. Smart./That's okay. Let me show you how. It's easy./No, I can't. It's too hard./Come on, Annie. Don't give up./Hey! I can do it!/Good work, Annie. Please sit down.

Answer Key
1. b
2. a
3. b
4. b

C. Listen and write ✓ or ✗.
Read the script. For each number, students listen and write ✓ if the sentence describes the picture, and ✗ if it does not.

Teacher:
C. Listen and write ✓ or ✗.
1. I didn't walk to school by myself.
2. When I was little, I could throw a ball.
3. If she gets a good grade, she'll be happy.
4. He had three bottles of root beer.
5. I never listen to pop music.
6. She was washing the car when the eagle flew by.

Answer Key
1. ✗
2. ✓
3. ✓
4. ✓
5. ✗
6. ✓

D. Look and write.
Students look at each picture and write the corresponding word(s).

Answer Key
1. bridge
2. cello
3. coffee
4. panda
5. San Francisco
6. baboon
7. recorder
8. Tokyo

E. Read and match.
For each number, students match the sentence in the left-hand column to the most logical response in the right-hand column.

Answer Key
1. What's going on in here?/We're cleaning up.
2. What did you get?/I got a hundred!
3. Could we ask you a few questions?/Sure. Go ahead.
4. How can I help you?/Hi! What are your hours?
5. Okay. I'll take one./Great! I'll get a fresh pie for you.
6. Do you want to come over?/I can't. My mom won't let me watch TV on a school night.
7. What should I do?/Stay calm.

F. Write and match.
For each number, students fill in the missing words to complete the question and answer. They then match them to the corresponding picture.

Answer Key
1. How did they play the violin? They played the violin badly. (c)
2. Was there a hotel near the bridge? Yes, there was. (b)
3. What was she doing when the tiger ran by? She was taking out the garbage when the tiger ran by. (d)
4. How much lemonade did he have? He had four cans of lemonade. (a)

G. Read and match. Then write.
For each number, students match the question in the left-hand column to the most logical response in the right-hand column. They then write the missing words to complete each sentence.

Answer Key
1. What were they doing when the moose walked by?/They were doing laundry when the moose walked by.
2. How long were they there?/They were there for one month.
3. Do they ever drive a sports car?/Yes, they always drive a sports car.
4. When did they go to Paris?/They went in December.
5. How did they play the drums?/They played the drums slowly.
6. Was there a library near the hotel?/No, there wasn't.

H. Look and write.
Students look at each picture and write the corresponding questions and answers.

Answer Key
1. When did she go to Rome? She went in September. How long was she there? She was there for five days.
2. When did they go to Paris? They went in July. How long were they there? They were there for one week.

I. Read and match.
For each number, students read the story and match it to the corresponding picture.

Answer Key
1. b
2. c
3. a

J. Unscramble and write.
Students unscramble and write each sentence.

Answer Key
1. Do you ever have an accident?
   No, I never have an accident.
2. How often do they take a math test?
   They take a math test two times a month.

K. Circle the mistakes and write. Then match.
Students circle the mistake(s) in each sentence. They then rewrite the sentence using the correct word(s) and match it to the corresponding picture.

Answer Key
1. She ironed a shirt to herself.
   She ironed a shirt by herself. (d)
2. For I was little, I couldn't speak English.
   When I was little, I couldn't speak English. (a)
3. If he go to bed late, he be tired.
   If he goes to bed late, he'll be tired. (f)
4. He went to the dentist with himself.
   He went to the dentist by himself. (c)
5. If she'll win a prize, she'll be happy.
   If she wins a prize, she'll be happy. (e)
6. When I want little, I could catch a frog.
   When I was little, I could catch a frog. (b)

Test Instructions and Answer Key

UNIT 1 TEST

A. Listen and match.

1. How much does it cost to get in? •
2. What are your hours? •
3. Are you open on Sundays? •

• Yes. We're open daily, except on holidays.
• We're open from 9:00 to 6:00.
• It's three dollars for adults and two dollars for children.

B. Listen and put the sentences in order.

_____ The first ice cream factory opened in Baltimore.
_____ A man in St. Louis made the first ice cream cone.
_____ Nancy Johnson invented the first ice cream churn.
_____ The first ice cream shop opened in New York.

C. Read and write.

1. Was there a _____ across from the bank?
   Yes, _____

2. Was there a library near the school?
   _____

3. Was there a hotel _____ the bank?
   Yes, _____

4. Was there a bank behind the library?
   _____

5. Was there a school above the hotel?
   _____

6. Was there a sidewalk in front of the bank?
   _____

UNIT 2 TEST

A. Listen and write.

1. What's _____ special?
2. _____ and meatballs.
3. Good! I'm in the _____ for spaghetti. I'll _____ that.
4. _____ you are.
5. _____ It looks delicious.

B. Listen and ✓ the sentences you hear.

1. Papa Joe's is a new Italian restaurant in downtown Sunnyville. _____
2. Who is Mama Joe? Is she a woman? Yes! _____
3. Papa Joe is the chef at Papa Joe's Restaurant. _____

C. Read and write.

1.

   How _____ lemonade did she have?
   She _____

2.

   How many _____ of apple pie did he have?
   _____

3.

   _____
   They had two slices of ham.

4.

   _____
   They had three cups of coffee.

UNIT 3 TEST

A. Listen and write ✓ or ✗.

1.
2.
3.

B. Listen and put the sentences in order.

_____ Bill forgot the grocery list.　　　_____ Bill forgot the groceries.

_____ Bill went home and got the list.　　_____ Bill forgot the money.

C. Read and write.

1.

He _____ by _____

2.

They _____

3.

I didn't _____

4.

She didn't _____

UNIT 4 TEST

A. Listen and circle.

1. Hello. May I speak to Robert, please?
   a. He's not in right now.
   b. I'm sorry. I don't know.
2. What time will he be back?
   a. I'll see him at one o'clock.
   b. I'm sorry. I don't know.
3. What's your number?
   a. 917-555-1839.
   b. 917-555-1855.

B. Listen and put the pictures in order.

C. Look and write.

1. Does he ever _____
   Yes, _____

2. _____

3. _____

4. _____

UNIT 5 TEST

A. Listen and match.

1. Hi, Mr. Day. •
2. Phew! It's hot today. •
3. Do you think it's going to rain? •
4. How's your family? •
5. Take care, Charlie. •

• That's right. It's 92 degrees!
• They're fine. But my sister has the flu.
• Hello, Charlie. Have a seat.
• Maybe. It's getting cloudy.
• Bye, Mr. Day.

B. Listen and ✓ the words you hear.

1. _____ twelve
2. _____ brother
3. _____ pest
4. _____ helps
5. _____ sometimes
6. _____ friends
7. _____ room
8. _____ patient
9. _____ talk

C. Read and write.

1.

How often does she visit a museum?
She _____
_____

2.

_____ take the subway?
_____
_____

3.

_____ go on a date?
_____
_____

MIDTERM TEST

A. **Listen and circle.**

1. Phew! It's hot today.
   a. They're fine. But my sister has the flu.
   b. That's right. It's 92 degrees!

2. Does that include the special photo exhibit of old Sunnyville?
   a. Yes, it does.
   b. You're welcome.

3. What time will he be back?
   a. He's not in right now.
   b. I'm sorry. I don't know.

4. How much are the peach pies?
   a. Oh, that's too expensive.
   b. They're five dollars each.

5. What's today's special?
   a. Spaghetti and meatballs.
   b. How about a salad?

6. Can you take a message?
   a. I'm sorry, I can't.
   b. Sure. Who's calling?

B. **Listen and number the pictures.**

MIDTERM TEST

C. Circle and write.

1. She had two _____ of coffee.
   a. plates
   b. cups
   c. slices

2. We walked to school by _____.
   a. ourselves
   b. yourselves
   c. themselves

3. They had three _____ of apple pie.
   a. loaves
   b. glasses
   c. pieces

4. He didn't drive a sports car by _____.
   a. myself
   b. herself
   c. himself

5. I had one _____ of ham.
   a. slice
   b. bottle
   c. bowl

6. I sliced fruit by _____.
   a. myself
   b. herself
   c. himself

D. Read and write.

1.

How many _____
_____
He _____
_____

2.

Was there _____
_____
Yes, _____
_____

3.

He _____
_____ himself.
He didn't _____
_____

4.

She _____
_____
She _____
_____

MIDTERM TEST

E. Read and match. Then write.

1. Does he ever take a nap? •

_____
_____
_____

2. How often do they go on a date? •

_____
_____
_____

3. Does she ever get a sunburn? •

_____
_____
_____

4. How often does he feed the birds? •

No, _____
_____
_____

F. Read and write.

1.

How many _____
She _____

2.

How much _____
_____

MIDTERM TEST

G. Write the question and the answer.

1. library / beside / train station

2. bank / above / theater

3. post office / behind / bank

H. Write the questions.

1. _____ slices of _____

   He had three slices of ham.

2. _____

   Yes, she usually drives a sports car.

3. _____

   I take a bus once a day.

4. _____

   No, he never has an accident.

5. _____

   They visit a museum twice a year.

UNIT 6 TEST

A. Listen and match.

1. Do you want some help? •
2. It's so heavy. •
3. What's going on in here? •

• Here. I'll take it.
• We're cleaning up.
• Sure. You can move the bass.

B. Listen and match.

1.
2.
3.

Kelly Green   the chorus   the orchestra

C. Look and write.

1.

   How did she play _____
   She _____

2.

3.

4.

UNIT 7 TEST

A. 🎧 **Listen and write ✓ or ✗.**

1.
2.
3.

B. 🎧 **Listen and write ✓ or ✗.**

1. Bob is 15 years old. Lili is 22 years old. _____
2. When giant pandas are born, they weigh three to five ounces. _____
3. Adults usually weigh 176 to 276 pounds. _____
4. They eat for 24 hours daily. _____

C. Read and match. Then write.

1. What were they doing when the moose ran by?

   a.

2. What was she doing when the bear walked by?

   b.

3. What was he doing when the kangaroo hopped by?

   c.

   They were _____

4. What were they doing when the eagle flew by?

   d.

UNIT 8 TEST

A. Listen and number the pictures.

B. Listen and ✓ the words you hear.

1. _____ hello
2. _____ moved away
3. _____ happy
4. _____ tired
5. _____ miss
6. _____ kindergarten
7. _____ lunch
8. _____ listen
9. _____ little

C. Look and write.

1.  When _____ little, he _____
_____

2.  _____ little, she _____
_____

3.  _____
_____

UNIT 9 TEST

A. Listen and match.

1. How many female pilots work for your airline?
2. Do you ever fly abroad?
3. Do you fly the plane by yourself?
4. Do you like being a pilot?

- Yes, very much!
- No. I always have a copilot.
- Yes. I have an overseas flight once a month.
- I think one third of the pilots are female.

B. Listen and ✓ the sentences you hear.

1. Over 30 billion people visit San Francisco every year. _____
2. Because it's one of the world's most exciting places. _____
3. There are 18 thousand restaurants, 10 thousand shops, and 150 museums. _____
4. Basketball, opera, theater, jazz…San Francisco has it! _____

C. Read and write.

1.

When did she go to London?

_____

How long was she there?

_____

2.

_____

They went in February.

_____

They were there for one week.

UNIT 10 TEST

A. Listen and write. Then match.

1. Where _____ you yesterday afternoon?
   At Annie's _____
   We were watching _____

2. What was _____
   A program _____ animals in Africa.

3. Aw, I missed _____
   Was it _____
   Yeah, it was. The gorillas were really _____

a.
b.
c.

B. Listen and put the sentences in order.

_____ Color broadcasting begins in the U.S.   _____ The first televisions go on sale.
_____ 99 percent of American homes have a TV.   _____ Neil Armstrong walks on the moon.

C. Read and write.

1.  he / turn off the fan / hot

2.  she / take off her jacket / cold

3.  they / skip lunch / hungry

FINAL TEST

A. Listen and number the pictures.

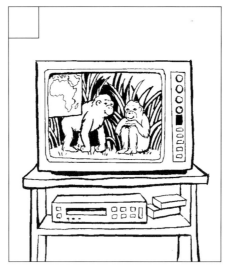

B. Listen and ✓ the sentences you hear.

1. a. How about a salad?
   Sounds good. _____

   b. Rare, medium, or well done?
   Medium, please. _____

2. a. Can you take a message?
   Sure. _____

   b. Got it! What's your number?
   917-555-1859. _____

3. a. Are your parents home?
   No. They went to a movie. _____

   b. I think…I think it's a wild animal! _____

4. a. That's okay.
   Let him show you how. It's hard. _____

   b. Hey! I can do it!
   Good work, Annie. _____

230   Tests   © Oxford University Press. Permission granted to reproduce for instructional use.

FINAL TEST

C. Listen and write ✓ or ✗.

1.
2.
3.
4.
5.
6.

D. Look and write.

1.
2.
3.
4.
5.
6.
7.
8.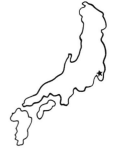

FINAL TEST

E. Read and match.

1. What's going on in here? •
2. What did you get? •
3. Could we ask you a few questions? •
4. How can I help you? •
5. Okay. I'll take one. •
6. Do you want to come over? •
7. What should I do? •

• I can't. My mom won't let me watch TV on a school night.
• We're cleaning up.
• Stay calm.
• Sure. Go ahead.
• I got a hundred!
• Hi! What are your hours?
• Great! I'll get a fresh pie for you.

F. Write and match.

1. How did they _____
   They _____ the violin badly.

2. _____ a hotel near _____ bridge?
   Yes, _____

3. What was she _____
   _____
   _____ taking out the garbage
   _____ tiger ran _____

4. How much _____
   _____
   He _____ four _____ of lemonade.

FINAL TEST

G. Read and match. Then write.

1. What were they doing when the moose walked by?

2. How long were they there?

3. Do they ever drive a sports car?

4. When did they go to Paris?

5. How did they play the drums?

6. Was there a library near the hotel?

• _____ in December.

• They played _____ slowly.

• They _____ for one month.

• _____ always drive a sports car.

• _____ there wasn't.

• They were doing laundry when the moose _____.

H. Look and write.

1.

When did _____

How long _____

2.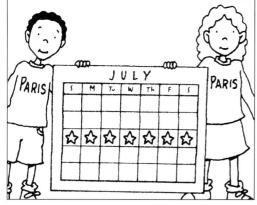

_____
_____
_____
_____

FINAL TEST

I. Read and match.

1. Last Saturday, Kelly Jones and her friend DeeDee Smith had lunch at Papa Joe's. "Their pizza is the best pizza in town," Kelly said. DeeDee said, "I'm going to bring my children here. Kids under five eat free!"

2. The students at Sunnyville Elementary School gave their spring performance last night. The chorus and orchestra were very good. After the performance, the school had a pizza party at Papa Joe's for the students, their families, and the teachers.

3. Last night Annie and Ted ate dinner with their kindergarten teacher. They ate at a deli that serves the best sandwiches in town. Ted ate a vegetable sandwich, and Annie had a cheese sandwich.

a.

b.

c.

J. Unscramble and write.

1. | accident | Do | ? | you | have | ever | an |

_____

| never | . | I | an | have | accident | No | , |

_____

2. | test | do | often | a | How | they | ? | take | math |

_____

| a | take | They | math | two | month | a | test | times | . |

_____

234   Tests   © Oxford University Press. Permission granted to reproduce for instructional use.

FINAL TEST

K. Circle the mistakes and write. Then match.

1. She ironed a shirt to herself.

   _____ •

   a.

2. For I was little, I couldn't speak English.

   _____ •

   b.

3. If he go to bed late, he be tired.

   _____ •

   c.

4. He went to the dentist with himself.

   _____ •

   d.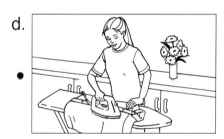

5. If she'll win a prize, she'll be happy.

   _____ •

   e.

6. When I want little, I could catch a frog.

   _____ •

   f.

Card List

Unit 1: Pages 1–4
school
library
barbershop
bank
hotel
train station
post office
sidewalk
bridge
theater
beside
behind
across from
in front of
near
above

Unit 2: Pages 5–8
root beer
lemonade
roast beef
ham
chicken soup
fruit salad
iced tea
coffee
apple pie
garlic bread
a bottle of root beer
a can of lemonade
a slice of ham
a piece of apple pie
a bowl of chicken soup
a glass of iced tea
a cup of coffee
a loaf of garlic bread

Unit 3: Pages 9–12
walk to school
go to the dentist
do laundry
chop vegetables
iron a shirt
slice fruit
take a bus
wash my hair
stay home
buy groceries
by myself
by himself
by herself
by yourself
by yourselves
by themselves
by ourselves

Unit 4: Pages 13–16
wear a wig
drive a sports car
put on makeup
fall in love
get a sunburn
listen to pop music
take a nap
talk on the phone
sign autographs
have an accident
always
usually
often
sometimes
hardly ever
never

Unit 5: Pages 17–20
feed the birds
read a newspaper
take medicine
go on a date
visit a museum
take the subway
give a speech
take a math test
bake bread
get a haircut
once a day
twice a week
three times a month
four times a year

Unit 6: Pages 21–24
tuba
flute
cymbals
drums
xylophone
electric keyboard
harp
cello
recorder
trumpet
well
badly
quietly
loudly
quickly
slowly
happily
sadly

Unit 7: Pages 25–28

tiger
eagle
panda
bear
kangaroo
parrot
moose
camel
baboon
leopard
run → ran
walk → walked
fly → flew
hop → hopped

Unit 8: Pages 29–32

say the alphabet
throw a ball
blow a bubble
count to ten
build a sand castle
spell a word
catch a frog
cut out a heart
peel an orange
speak English
Annie **is** tall.
Annie **was** short.
Ted **can** play basketball.
Ted **could** play basketball.

Unit 9: Pages 33–38

Rome
Taipei
Tokyo
London
Seoul
New York City
Paris
Honolulu
San Francisco
Hong Kong
January
February
March
April
May
June
July
August
September
October
November
December

Unit 10: Pages 39–42

skip lunch
forget my homework
go to bed late
fall off my chair
get a good grade
lose my favorite pencil
make a mistake
take off my jacket
win a prize
turn off the fan
hungry
nervous
tired
embarrassed
happy
sad
disappointed
cold
hot
proud

Grammar Cards: Pages 43–59

Word List

The numbers to the right of the entries indicate the page on which the word is introduced.

A

a lot of	5
about	47
above	3
abroad	55
accident	20
across from	3
actor	23
adults	1
adventure	23
after	41
airline	55
alive	47
alphabet	50
always	21
A.M.	11
apple pie	8
April	57
around	47
arrive	17
assignment	viii
attention	29
August	57
autographs	20
available	59

B

baboon	44
backyard	43
badly	39
bake bread	26
baked potato	7
bamboo	47
bank	2
barbershop	2
baseball	65
bass	37
bear	44
begin	65
behind	3
being	55
bell	61
beside	3
besides	61
best	11
better	25
blow a bubble	50
blueberry	13
board	49
born	47
bother	29
bottle	9
bowl	9
bridge	2
broadcasting	65
bubble	50
build a sand castle	50
buy groceries	14

C

calling	19
calm	43
camel	44
can	9
captain	55
cart	17
catch a frog	50
CD player	viii
cello	38
Celsius	25
checkout line	17
chef	11
cherry	13
chicken soup	8
children	1
chop vegetables	14
chopped	15
chopping	45
chorus	41
churn	5
climbing	45
cloudy	25
coffee	8
cold	63
come on	49
come over	61
concert	37
cone	5
copilot	55
cost	1
could	51
couldn't	51
count to ten	50
crazy	29
cup	9
cut out a heart	50
cymbals	38

D

daily	1
date	26
December	57
degrees	25
dentist	14
disappointed	63
do laundry	14
downtown	11
drive a sports car	20
drives	21
drums	38
due	viii

E

eagle	44
electric keyboard	38
embarrassed	63
emergency	43
endangered	47
enormous	53
erase	49
ever	21
every	5
except	1
exhibit	1
expensive	13

F

fact	47
factory	5
Fahrenheit	25
fair	29
fall in love	20
fall off my chair	62
falls	21
family	23
fan	62, 65
February	57
feed the birds	26
feeding	45
female	55
few	55
field trip	viii
find out	65
first	5
flavors	5
flew	45
flight	55
flu	25
flute	38
forget my homework	62
forgot	17
free	1
fresh	13
frog	50
front	49
fruit salad	8
funny	53

238

G

garlic bread	8
get a good grade	62
get a haircut	26
get a sunburn	20
get in	1
gets	21
giant	47
give	19
give a speech	26
give up	49
glass	9
go ahead	55
go home	17
go on a date	26
go on sale	65
go to bed late	62
go to the dentist	14
good work	49
gorilla	61
got	17
grade	62
grams	47
grocery list	17
grow up	29

H

ham	8
happily	39
happy	63
hardly ever	21
harp	38
have a good time	23
have a seat	25
have an accident	20
hear	25
heart	50
help	1
helping	37
herself	15
hibernate	47
himself	15
history	5
hit	41
holidays	1
Hong Kong	56
Honolulu	56
hop	45
hopped	45
hot	63
hotel	2
hours	1
hundred	49
hungry	63

I

iced tea	8
if	63
in front of	3
include	1
information	59
interview	55
invent	5
iron a shirt	14
ironed	15
Italian	11

J

January	57
jazz	59
July	57
June	57

K

kangaroo	44
kilograms	47
kindergarten	53
kinds	13
know how	49

L

last	41
laundry	14
left	17
lemonade	8
leopard	44
letter	49
library	2
lift	37
listen to pop music	20
loaf	9
loaves	10
London	56
long	57
look out	37
lose my favorite pencil	62
loud	39
loudly	39

M

make a mistake	62
make friends	53
March	57
math test	26
May	57
meatballs	7
medium	7
message	19
million	59
miss	53
mistake	62
month	27
mood	7
moose	44
most exciting	59
move	37
move away	53
movie star	23
movie studio	23
myself	15

N

near	3
neither	61
nervous	63
never	21
new	11
New York City	56
news	61
newspaper	26
November	57
number	viii

O

October	57
often	21
once	27
one third	55
open	1
opera	59
orchestra	41
order	7
ounces	47
ourselves	15
overseas	55
owner	11

P

paid	17
panda	44
parents	viii
Paris	56
parrot	44
pass out	49
patient	29
peel an orange	50
percent	65
perform	41
performance	41
permission form	viii
pest	29
phew	25
photo	1
piece	9
pilot	55
play	41
pleasure	55
P.M.	11
pop music	20
post office	2
pound	47
price	11
program	61
projects	viii
proud	63
public	65
put on makeup	20
puts	21
putting	45

Q

questions	55
quickly	39
quietly	39

Word List **239**

R

ran	45
rare	7
read a newspaper	26
ready	7
real	11
recess	53
recorder	38
rehearse	23
remote control	65
rent	59
roast beef	8
Rome	56
root beer	8

S

sad	63
sadly	39
San Francisco	56
sand castle	50
say the alphabet	50
school	2
second	41
sending	43
Seoul	56
September	57
serious	25
serve	11
should	43
show	53
sidewalk	2
sign autographs	20
signs	21
sit down	49
skip lunch	62
skips	63
slice	9
slice fruit	14
sliced	15
slowly	39
soloist	41
something	43
sometimes	21
soon	53
speak English	50
special	1
speech	26
spell a word	50
spelling test	viii
spend time	29
sports car	20
starting	25
stay home	14
stayed	15
steak	7
sunburn	20
supermarket	17

T

Taipei	56
take a bus	14
take a math test	26
take a nap	20
take care	25
take medicine	26
take off my jacket	62
take the subway	26
takes	21
talk on the phone	20
talks	21
television	65
tell	29
theater	2
themselves	15
thousand	59
throw a ball	50
tiger	44
times	27
tired	63
today	23
today's	7
Tokyo	56
tonight	23
tour	1
track	viii
train station	2
trumpet	38
tuba	38
turn off the fan	62
turn on	viii
twice	27

U

usually	21

V

vanilla	5
visit a museum	26

W

walk to school	14
walked	15
wash my hair	14
washing	45
wear a wig	20
wears	21
web site	65
week	27
weekend	viii
weigh	47
well	39
well done	7
what's going on	37
wig	20
wild	43
win a prize	62
without	29
word	50
work	55
world	59

X

xylophone	38

Y

year	27
yesterday	23
yourself	15
yourselves	15